MznLnx

Missing Links Exam Preps

Exam Prep for

Marketing: The Core

Kerin, Hartley, & Rudelius, 2nd Edition

The MznLnx Exam Prep is your link from the texbook and lecture to your exams.
The MznLnx Exam Preps are unauthorized and comprehensive reviews of your textbooks.

All material provided by MznLnx and Rico Publications (c) 2010
Textbook publishers and textbook authors do not particpate in or contribute to these reviews.

MznLnx

Rico
Publications

Exam Prep for Marketing: The Core
2nd Edition
Kerin, Hartley, & Rudelius

Publisher: Raymond Houge
Assistant Editor: Michael Rouger
Text and Cover Designer: Lisa Buckner
Marketing Manager: Sara Swagger
Project Manager, Editorial Production: Jerry Emerson
Art Director: Vernon Lowerui

Product Manager: Dave Mason
Editorial Assitant: Rachel Guzmanji
Pedagogy: Debra Long
Cover Image: Jim Reed/Getty Images
Text and Cover Printer: City Printing, Inc.
Compositor: Media Mix, Inc.

(c) 2010 Rico Publications

ALL RIGHTS RESERVED. No part of this work covered by the copyright may be reproduced or used in any form or by an means--graphic, electronic, or mechanical, including photocopying, recording, taping, Web distribution, information storage, and retrieval systems, or in any other manner--without the written permission of the publisher.

Printed in the United States
ISBN:

For more information about our products, contact us at:
Dave.Mason@RicoPublications.com

For permission to use material from this text or product, submit a request online to:
Dave.Mason@RicoPublications.com

Contents

CHAPTER 1
Creating Customer Relationships and Value through Marketing — 1

CHAPTER 2
Developing Successful Marketing and Corporate Strategies — 7

CHAPTER 3
Scanning the Marketing Environment — 15

CHAPTER 4
Ethics and Social Responsibility in Marketing — 33

CHAPTER 5
Consumer Behavior — 43

CHAPTER 6
Organizational Markets and Buyer Behavior — 52

CHAPTER 7
Reaching Global Markets — 57

CHAPTER 8
Marketing Research: From Information to Action — 69

CHAPTER 9
Identifying Market Segments and Targets — 77

CHAPTER 10
Developing New Products and Services — 84

CHAPTER 11
Managing Products, Services, and Brands — 92

CHAPTER 12
Pricing Products and Services — 103

CHAPTER 13
Managing Marketing Channels and Supply Chains — 114

CHAPTER 14
Retailing and Wholesaling — 122

CHAPTER 15
Integrated Marketing Communications and Direct Marketing — 134

CHAPTER 16
Advertising, Sales Promotion, and Public Relations — 146

CHAPTER 17
Personal Selling and Sales Management — 156

CHAPTER 18
Implementing Interactive and Multichannel Marketing — 162

ANSWER KEY — 176

TO THE STUDENT

COMPREHENSIVE

The *MznLnx* Exam Prep series is designed to help you pass your exams. Editors at MznLnx review your textbooks and then prepare these practice exams to help you master the textbook material. Unlike study guides, workbooks, and practice tests provided by the texbook publisher and textbook authors, *MznLnx* gives you **all** of the material in each chapter in exam form, not just samples, so you can be sure to nail your exam.

MECHANICAL

The MznLnx Exam Prep series creates exams that will help you learn the subject matter as well as test you on your understanding. Each question is designed to help you master the concept. Just working through the exams, you gain an understanding of the subject--its a simple mechanical process that produces success.

INTEGRATED STUDY GUIDE AND REVIEW

MznLnx is not just a set of exams designed to test you, its also a comprehensive review of the subject content. Each exam question is also a review of the concept, making sure that you will get the answer correct without having to go to other sources of material. You learn as you go! Its the easiest way to pass an exam.

HUMOR

Studying can be tedious and dry. MznLnx's instructional design includes moderate humor within the exam questions on occassion, to break the tedium and revitalize the brain

Chapter 1. Creating Customer Relationships and Value through Marketing

1. _____ is defined by the American _____ Association as the activity, set of institutions, and processes for creating, communicating, delivering, and exchanging offerings that have value for customers, clients, partners, and society at large. The term developed from the original meaning which referred literally to going to market, as in shopping, or going to a market to sell goods or services.

   _____ practice tends to be seen as a creative industry, which includes advertising, distribution and selling.

   a. Marketing
   b. Product naming
   c. Customer acquisition management
   d. Marketing myopia

2. The _____ is a professional association for marketers. As of 2008 it had approximately 40,000 members. There are collegiate chapters on 250 campuses.
   a. American Marketing Association
   b. ACNielsen
   c. AMAX
   d. ADTECH

3. _____ - an information and communication based electronic exchange environment - is a relatively new concept in marketing. Since physical boundaries no longer interfere with buy/sell decisions, the world has grown into several industry specific _____s which are integration of marketplaces through sophisticated computer and telecommunication technologies. The term _____ was introduced by Rayport and Sviokla in 1994 (see Rayport, Jeffrey F.
   a. Kano model
   b. Market segment
   c. Marketspace
   d. Value chain

4. _____ is the practice of individuals including commercial businesses, governments and institutions, facilitating the sale of their products or services to other companies or organizations that in turn resell them, use them as components in products or services they offer _____ is also called business-to-_____ for short. (Note that while marketing to government entities shares some of the same dynamics of organizational marketing, B2G Marketing is meaningfully different.)
   a. Business marketing
   b. Law of disruption
   c. Mass marketing
   d. Disruptive technology

5. A _____ is a written document that details the necessary actions to achieve one or more marketing objectives. It can be for a product or service, a brand, or a product line. _____s cover between one and five years.
   a. Marketing strategy
   b. Marketing plan
   c. Prosumer
   d. Disruptive technology

6. _____ is a broad label that refers to any individuals or households that use goods and services generated within the economy. The concept of a _____ is used in different contexts, so that the usage and significance of the term may vary.

   A _____ is a person who uses any product or service.

   a. Consumer
   b. 6-3-5 Brainwriting
   c. 180SearchAssistant
   d. Power III

Chapter 1. Creating Customer Relationships and Value through Marketing

7. _____ is a form of government regulation which protects the interests of consumers. For example, a government may require businesses to disclose detailed information about products--particularly in areas where safety or public health is an issue, such as food. _____ is linked to the idea of consumer rights (that consumers have various rights as consumers), and to the formation of consumer organizations which help consumers make better choices in the marketplace.

   a. Trademark dilution   b. Sound trademark
   c. Federal Bureau of Investigation   d. Consumer protection

8. The _____ is generally accepted as the use and specification of the four p's describing the strategic position of a product in the marketplace. One version of the origins of the _____ starts in 1948 when James Culliton said that a marketing decision should be a result of something similar to a recipe. This version continued in 1953 when Neil Borden, in his American Marketing Association presidential address, took the recipe idea one step further and coined the term 'Marketing-Mix'.

   a. Marketing mix   b. Power III
   c. 6-3-5 Brainwriting   d. 180SearchAssistant

9. _____ in economics and business is the result of an exchange and from that trade we assign a numerical monetary value to a good, service or asset. If I trade 4 apples for an orange, the _____ of an orange is 4 - apples. Inversely, the _____ of an apple is 1/4 oranges.

   a. Contribution margin-based pricing   b. Discounts and allowances
   c. Pricing   d. Price

10. _____ involves disseminating information about a product, product line, brand, or company. It is one of the four key aspects of the marketing mix. (The other three elements are product marketing, pricing, and distribution). P>_____ is generally sub-divided into two parts:

- Above the line _____: Promotion in the media (e.g. TV, radio, newspapers, Internet and Mobile Phones) in which the advertiser pays an advertising agency to place the ad
- Below the line _____: All other _____. Much of this is intended to be subtle enough for the consumer to be unaware that _____ is taking place. E.g. sponsorship, product placement, endorsements, sales _____, merchandising, direct mail, personal selling, public relations, trade shows

   a. Cashmere Agency   b. Bottling lines
   c. Promotion   d. Davie Brown Index

11. _____ is a form of marketing developed from direct response marketing campaigns conducted in the 1970's and 1980's which emphasizes customer retention and satisfaction, rather than a dominant focus on 'point of sale' transactions.

_____ differs from other forms of marketing in that it recognizes the long term value to the firm of keeping customers, as opposed to direct or 'Intrusion' marketing, which focuses upon acquisition of new clients by targeting majority demographics based upon prospective client lists.

_____ refers to long-term and mutually beneficial arrangement wherein both buyer and seller focus on value enhancement through the certain of more satisfying exchange. This approach attempts to transcend the simple purchase exchange process with customer to make more meaningful and richer contact by providing a more holistic, personalized purchase, and use orn consumption experience to create stronger ties.

a. Global marketing
b. Guerrilla Marketing
c. Relationship marketing
d. Diversity marketing

12. A personal and cultural _____ is a relative ethic _____, an assumption upon which implementation can be extrapolated. A _____ system is a set of consistent _____s and measures that is soo not true. A principle _____ is a foundation upon which other _____s and measures of integrity are based.

a. Package-on-Package
b. Supreme Court of the United States
c. Perceptual maps
d. Value

13. _____ is a rivalry between individuals, groups, nations for territory, a niche, or allocation of resources. It arises whenever two or more parties strive for a goal which cannot be shared. _____ occurs naturally between living organisms which co-exist in the same environment.

a. Competition
b. Non-price competition
c. Price fixing
d. Price competition

14. A _____ is a process that can allow an organization to concentrate its limited resources on the greatest opportunities to increase sales and achieve a sustainable competitive advantage. A _____ should be centered around the key concept that customer satisfaction is the main goal.

A _____ is most effective when it is an integral component of corporate strategy, defining how the organization will successfully engage customers, prospects, and competitors in the market arena.

a. Societal marketing
b. Marketing strategy
c. Cyberdoc
d. Psychographic

15. In psychology, philosophy, and the cognitive sciences, _____ is the process of attaining awareness or understanding of sensory information. It is a task far more complex than was imagined in the 1950s and 1960s, when it was predicted that building perceiving machines would take about a decade, a goal which is still very far from fruition. The word _____ comes from the Latin words _____, percepio, meaning 'receiving, collecting, action of taking possession, apprehension with the mind or senses.'

_____ is one of the oldest fields in psychology.

a. Groupthink
b. Perception
c. 180SearchAssistant
d. Power III

16. A _____ is a plan of action designed to achieve a particular goal.

_____ is different from tactics. In military terms, tactics is concerned with the conduct of an engagement while _____ is concerned with how different engagements are linked.

a. 180SearchAssistant
b. Power III
c. 6-3-5 Brainwriting
d. Strategy

17. _____, also referred to as i-marketing, web marketing, online marketing is the marketing of products or services over the Internet.

The Internet has brought many unique benefits to marketing, one of which being lower costs for the distribution of information and media to a global audience. The interactive nature of _____, both in terms of providing instant response and eliciting responses, is a unique quality of the medium.

a. ACNielsen
b. ADTECH
c. AMAX
d. Internet marketing

18. _____ can be regarded as an outcome of mental processes (cognitive process) leading to the selection of a course of action among several alternatives. Every _____ process produces a final choice. The output can be an action or an opinion of choice.

a. Decision making
b. Power III
c. 6-3-5 Brainwriting
d. 180SearchAssistant

19. There are many important decisions about product and service development and marketing. In the process of product development and marketing we should focus on strategic decisions about product attributes, product branding, product packaging, product labeling and product support services. But product strategy also calls for building a _____.

a. Technology acceptance model
b. Macromarketing
c. Product line
d. Pinstorm

20. A _____ is the use of an established product's brand name for a new item in the same product category. _____s occur when a company introduces additional items in the same product category under the same brand name such as new flavors, forms, colors, added ingredients, package sizes.

a. Comparison-Shopping agent
b. Pearson's chi-square
c. Retail floor planning
d. Product line extension

21. A product _____ is the use of an established product's brand name for a new item in the same product category. _____s occur when a company introduces additional items in the same product category under the same brand name such as new flavors, forms, colors, added ingredients, package sizes. Examples includei) Zen LXI, Zen VXIii) Surf, Surf Excel, Surf Excel Blueiii) Splendour, Splendour Plusiv) Coke, Diet Coke, Vanilla Cokev) Clinic All Clear, Clinic Plus

- brand
- brand management
- marketing
- product management
- Product lining

a. Perishability
b. Targeted advertising
c. Brand Development Index
d. Line extension

22. _____ is systematic determination of merit, worth, and significance of something or someone using criteria against a set of standards. _____ often is used to characterize and appraise subjects of interest in a wide range of human enterprises, including the arts, criminal justice, foundations and non-profit organizations, government, health care, and other human services.

Depending on the topic of interest, there are professional groups which look to the quality and rigor of the _____ process.

a. Evaluation
b. AMAX
c. ACNielsen
d. ADTECH

23. _____ is a branch of philosophy which seeks to address questions about morality, such as how a moral outcome can be achieved in a specific situation (applied _____), how moral values should be determined (normative _____), what moral values people actually abide by (descriptive _____), what the fundamental semantic, ontological, and epistemic nature of _____ or morality is (meta-_____), and how moral capacity or moral agency develops and what its nature is (moral psychology.)

Socrates was one of the first Greek philosophers to encourage both scholars and the common citizen to turn their attention from the outside world to the condition of man. In this view, Knowledge having a bearing on human life was placed highest, all other knowledge being secondary.

a. ACNielsen
b. AMAX
c. ADTECH
d. Ethics

24. The _____ concept is an enlightened marketing concept that holds that a company should make good marketing decisions by considering consumers' wants, the company's requirements, and society's long-term interests. It is closely linked with the principles of corporate social responsibility and of sustainable development.

The concept has an emphasis on social responsibility and suggests that for a company to only focus on exchange relationship with customers might not be suitable in order to sustain long term success.

a. Societal marketing
b. Business-to-business
c. Customer franchise
d. Marketing

25. _____ is a cohort which consists of those people born after the Generation X cohort. Its name is controversial and is synonymous with several alternative names including The Net Generation, Millennials, Echo Boomers, and iGeneration. _____ consists primarily of the offspring of the Generation Jones and Baby Boomers cohorts.

a. Generation X
b. Greatest Generation
c. Generation Y
d. AStore

26. _____ is an advertisement in which a particular product specifically mentions a competitor by name for the express purpose of showing why the competitor is inferior to the product naming it.

This should not be confused with parody advertisements, where a fictional product is being advertised for the purpose of poking fun at the particular advertisement, nor should it be confused with the use of a coined brand name for the purpose of comparing the product without actually naming an actual competitor. ('Wikipedia tastes better and is less filling than the Encyclopedia Galactica.')

In the 1980s, during what has been referred to as the cola wars, soft-drink manufacturer Pepsi ran a series of advertisements where people, caught on hidden camera, in a blind taste test, chose Pepsi over rival Coca-Cola.

a. Heavy-up
c. Comparative advertising
b. Cost per conversion
d. GL-70

27. In economics, _____ is a measure of the relative satisfaction from consumption of various goods and services. Given this measure, one may speak meaningfully of increasing or decreasing _____, and thereby explain economic behavior in terms of attempts to increase one's _____. For illustrative purposes, changes in _____ are sometimes expressed in units called utils.

a. AMAX
c. ACNielsen
b. Utility
d. ADTECH

Chapter 2. Developing Successful Marketing and Corporate Strategies

1. _____s is the social science that studies the production, distribution, and consumption of goods and services. The term _____s comes from the Ancient Greek oá¼°κονομῖα from oá¼¶κος (oikos, 'house') + vÏŒμος (nomos, 'custom' or 'law'), hence 'rules of the house(hold)'. Current _____ models developed out of the broader field of political economy in the late 19th century, owing to a desire to use an empirical approach more akin to the physical sciences.

   a. Industrial organization   b. ACNielsen
   c. ADTECH   d. Economic

2. _____ is defined by the American _____ Association as the activity, set of institutions, and processes for creating, communicating, delivering, and exchanging offerings that have value for customers, clients, partners, and society at large. The term developed from the original meaning which referred literally to going to market, as in shopping, or going to a market to sell goods or services.

_____ practice tends to be seen as a creative industry, which includes advertising, distribution and selling.

   a. Marketing   b. Marketing myopia
   c. Product naming   d. Customer acquisition management

3. A _____ is a process that can allow an organization to concentrate its limited resources on the greatest opportunities to increase sales and achieve a sustainable competitive advantage. A _____ should be centered around the key concept that customer satisfaction is the main goal.

A _____ is most effective when it is an integral component of corporate strategy, defining how the organization will successfully engage customers, prospects, and competitors in the market arena.

   a. Psychographic   b. Cyberdoc
   c. Societal marketing   d. Marketing strategy

4. A _____ is a plan of action designed to achieve a particular goal.

_____ is different from tactics. In military terms, tactics is concerned with the conduct of an engagement while _____ is concerned with how different engagements are linked.

   a. Power III   b. Strategy
   c. 6-3-5 Brainwriting   d. 180SearchAssistant

5. _____ is a measure of the strength of a brand, product, service relative to competitive offerings. There is often a geographic element to the competitive landscape. In defining _____, you must see to what extent a product, brand, or firm controls a product category in a given geographic area.

   a. Market system   b. Discretionary spending
   c. Market dominance   d. Productivity

6. _____ is the practice of individuals including commercial businesses, governments and institutions, facilitating the sale of their products or services to other companies or organizations that in turn resell them, use them as components in products or services they offer _____ is also called business-to-_____ for short. (Note that while marketing to government entities shares some of the same dynamics of organizational marketing, B2G Marketing is meaningfully different.)

Chapter 2. Developing Successful Marketing and Corporate Strategies

a. Mass marketing
b. Law of disruption
c. Business marketing
d. Disruptive technology

7. A _____ is a written document that details the necessary actions to achieve one or more marketing objectives. It can be for a product or service, a brand, or a product line. _____s cover between one and five years.

a. Disruptive technology
b. Marketing strategy
c. Prosumer
d. Marketing plan

8. A _____ is a brief statement of the purpose of a company, organization. It is ideally used to guide the actions of the organization.

_____s often contain the following:

- Purpose of the organization
- The organization's primary stakeholders: clients, stockholders, etc.
- Responsibilities of the organization towards these stockholders
- Products and services offered

Generally shorter _____s are more effective than longer ones.

In developing a _____:

- Encourage input as feasible from employees, volunteers, and other stakeholders
- Publicize it broadly

The _____ can be used to resolve differences between business stakeholders. Stakeholders include: employees including managers and executives, stockholders, board of directors, customers, suppliers, distributors, creditors, governments (local, state, federal, etc.), unions, competitors, NGO's, and the general public.

a. 180SearchAssistant
b. 6-3-5 Brainwriting
c. Power III
d. Mission statement

9. _____ is understood as a business unit within the overall corporate identity which is distinguishable from other business because it serves a defined external market where management can conduct strategic planning in relation to products and markets. When companies become really large, they are best thought of as being composed of a number of businesses (or _____s.)

In the broader domain of strategic management, the phrase '_____' came into use in the 1960s, largely as a result of General Electric's many units.

a. Business strategy
b. Cost leadership
c. Corporate strategy
d. Strategic business unit

Chapter 2. Developing Successful Marketing and Corporate Strategies

10. _____ is an idea in the field of Organizational studies and management which describes the psychology, attitudes, experiences, beliefs and Values (personal and cultural values)of an organization. It has been defined as 'the specific collection of values and norms that are shared by people and groups in an organization and that control the way they interact with each other and with stakeholders outside the organization.'

This definition continues to explain organizational values also known as 'beliefs and ideas about what kinds of goals members of an organization should pursue and ideas about the appropriate kinds or standards of behavior organizational members should use to achieve these goals. From organizational values develop organizational norms, guidelines or expectations that prescribe appropriate kinds of behavior by employees in particular situations and control the behavior of organizational members towards one another.'

_____ is not the same as corporate culture.

a. ACNielsen
b. ADTECH
c. Organizational structure
d. Organizational culture

11. _____ is difficult to define. For example, in 1952, Alfred Kroeber and Clyde Kluckhohn compiled a list of 164 definitions of '_____' in _____: A Critical Review of Concepts and Definitions. However, the word '_____' is most commonly used in three basic senses:

- excellence of taste in the fine arts and humanities
- an integrated pattern of human knowledge, belief, and behavior that depends upon the capacity for symbolic thought and social learning
- the set of shared attitudes, values, goals, and practices that characterizes an institution, organization or group.

When the concept first emerged in eighteenth- and nineteenth-century Europe, it connoted a process of cultivation or improvement, as in agriculture or horticulture. In the nineteenth century, it came to refer first to the betterment or refinement of the individual, especially through education, and then to the fulfillment of national aspirations or ideals.

a. AStore
b. African Americans
c. Albert Einstein
d. Culture

12. _____, a business term, is a measure of how products and services supplied by a company meet or surpass customer expectation. It is seen as a key performance indicator within business and is part of the four perspectives of a Balanced Scorecard.

In a competitive marketplace where businesses compete for customers, _____ is seen as a key differentiator and increasingly has become a key element of business strategy.

a. Customer satisfaction
b. Customer base
c. Supplier diversity
d. Psychological pricing

Chapter 2. Developing Successful Marketing and Corporate Strategies

13. _____, in strategic management and marketing, is the percentage or proportion of the total available market or market segment that is being serviced by a company. It can be expressed as a company's sales revenue (from that market) divided by the total sales revenue available in that market. It can also be expressed as a company's unit sales volume (in a market) divided by the total volume of units sold in that market.

   a. Customer relationship management
   b. Cyberdoc
   c. Demand generation
   d. Market share

14. Competitiveness is a comparative concept of the ability and performance of a firm, sub-sector or country to sell and supply goods and/or services in a given market. Although widely used in economics and business management, the usefulness of the concept, particularly in the context of national competitiveness, is vigorously disputed by economists, such as Paul Krugman .

The term may also be applied to markets, where it is used to refer to the extent to which the market structure may be regarded as perfectly _____.

   a. Customs union
   b. Geographical pricing
   c. Free trade zone
   d. Competitive

15. _____ is, in very basic words, a position a firm occupies against its competitors.

According to Michael Porter, the three methods for creating a sustainable _____ are through:

1. Cost leadership - Cost advantage occurs when a firm delivers the same services as its competitors but at a lower cost;

2.

   a. Competitive advantage
   b. 6-3-5 Brainwriting
   c. Power III
   d. 180SearchAssistant

16. _____ in marketing and strategic management is an assessment of the strengths and weaknesses of current and potential competitors. This analysis provides both an offensive and defensive strategic context through which to identify opportunities and threats. Competitor profiling coalesces all of the relevant sources of _____ into one framework in the support of efficient and effective strategy formulation, implementation, monitoring and adjustment.

   a. 6-3-5 Brainwriting
   b. 180SearchAssistant
   c. Power III
   d. Competitor analysis

17. In business, a _____ is a product or a business unit that generates unusually high profit margins: so high that it is responsible for a large amount of a company's operating profit. This profit far exceeds the amount necessary to maintain the _____ business, and the excess is used by the business for other purposes.

A firm is said to be acting as a _____ when its earnings per share (EPS) is equal to its dividends per share (DPS), or in other words, when a firm pays out 100% of its free cash flow (FCF) to its shareholders as dividends at the end of each accounting term.

Chapter 2. Developing Successful Marketing and Corporate Strategies

a. Cash cow
b. Corporate transparency
c. Goal setting
d. Crisis management

18. _____ is one of the four growth strategies of the Product-Market Growth Matrix defined by Ansoff. _____ occurs when a company enters/penetrates a market with current products. The best way to achieve this is by gaining competitors' customers (part of their market share.)

a. Horizontal market
b. Market penetration
c. Pasar pagi
d. Marketization

19. A _____ strategy targets non-buying customers in currently targeted segments. It also targets new customers in new segments. (Winer)

A marketing manager has to think about the following questions before implementing a _____ strategy: Is it profitable? Will it require the introduction of new or modified products? Is the customer and channel well enough researched and understood?

The marketing manager uses these four groups to give more focus to the market segment decision: existing customers, competitor customers, non-buying in current segments, new segments.

a. Commercial planning
b. Market development
c. Kano model
d. Perceptual mapping

20. In business and engineering, new _____ is the term used to describe the complete process of bringing a new product or service to market. There are two parallel paths involved in the Nproduct development process: one involves the idea generation, product design, and detail engineering; the other involves market research and marketing analysis. Companies typically see new _____ as the first stage in generating and commercializing new products within the overall strategic process of product life cycle management used to maintain or grow their market share.

a. New product screening
b. New product development
c. Specification tree
d. Product development

21. _____ in organizations and public policy is both the organizational process of creating and maintaining a plan; and the psychological process of thinking about the activities required to create a desired goal on some scale. As such, it is a fundamental property of intelligent behavior. This thought process is essential to the creation and refinement of a plan, or integration of it with other plans, that is, it combines forecasting of developments with the preparation of scenarios of how to react to them.

a. Planning
b. Power III
c. 6-3-5 Brainwriting
d. 180SearchAssistant

22. _____ is a strategic planning method used to evaluate the Strengths, Weaknesses, Opportunities, and Threats involved in a project or in a business venture. It involves specifying the objective of the business venture or project and identifying the internal and external factors that are favorable and unfavorable to achieving that objective. The technique is credited to Albert Humphrey, who led a research project at Stanford University in the 1960s and 1970s using data from Fortune 500 companies.

a. Product differentiation
b. Market environment
c. Lead scoring
d. SWOT analysis

Chapter 2. Developing Successful Marketing and Corporate Strategies

23. _____ is a marketing term, and involves evaluating the situation and trends in a particular company's market. _____ is often called the 'three c's', which refers to the three major elements that must be studied:

- Customers
- Costs
- Competition

The number of 'c's' is sometimes extended to four, five, or even six, with 'Collaboration', 'Company', and 'Competitive advantage'.

- Marketing mix
- SWOT analysis

a. Situation analysis
b. 180SearchAssistant
c. Power III
d. 6-3-5 Brainwriting

24. _____ involves establishing specific, measurable and time targeted objectives. Work on the theory of goal-setting suggests that it's an effective tool for making progress by ensuring that participants in a group with a common goal are clearly aware of what is expected from them if an objective is to be achieved. On a personal level, setting goals is a process that allows people to specify then work towards their own objectives - most commonly with financial or career-based goals.

a. Voice of the customer
b. Product marketing
c. Corporate transparency
d. Goal setting

25. A _____ is a subgroup of people or organizations sharing one or more characteristics that cause them to have similar product and/or service needs. A true _____ meets all of the following criteria: it is distinct from other segments (different segments have different needs), it is homogeneous within the segment (exhibits common needs); it responds similarly to a market stimulus, and it can be reached by a market intervention. The term is also used when consumers with identical product and/or service needs are divided up into groups so they can be charged different amounts.

a. Commercial planning
b. Customer insight
c. Production orientation
d. Market segment

26. The _____ is generally accepted as the use and specification of the four p's describing the strategic position of a product in the marketplace. One version of the origins of the _____ starts in 1948 when James Culliton said that a marketing decision should be a result of something similar to a recipe. This version continued in 1953 when Neil Borden, in his American Marketing Association presidential address, took the recipe idea one step further and coined the term 'Marketing-Mix'.

a. 180SearchAssistant
b. Power III
c. 6-3-5 Brainwriting
d. Marketing mix

27. In marketing, _____ has come to mean the process by which marketers try to create an image or identity in the minds of their target market for its product, brand, or organization. It is the 'relative competitive comparison' their product occupies in a given market as perceived by the target market.

Re-_____ involves changing the identity of a product, relative to the identity of competing products, in the collective minds of the target market.

Chapter 2. Developing Successful Marketing and Corporate Strategies 13

a. Containerization
b. Positioning
c. Moratorium
d. GE matrix

28. _____ is one of the four elements of marketing mix. An organization or set of organizations (go-betweens) involved in the process of making a product or service available for use or consumption by a consumer or business user.

The other three parts of the marketing mix are product, pricing, and promotion.

a. Comparison-Shopping agent
b. Better Living Through Chemistry
c. Japan Advertising Photographers' Association
d. Distribution

29. _____ is the realization of an application idea, model, design, specification, standard, algorithm an _____ is a realization of a technical specification or algorithm as a program, software component, or other computer system. Many _____s may exist for a given specification or standard.

a. ADTECH
b. AMAX
c. ACNielsen
d. Implementation

30. Human beings are also considered to be _____ because they have the ability to change raw materials into valuable _____. The term Human _____ can also be defined as the skills, energies, talents, abilities and knowledge that are used for the production of goods or the rendering of services. While taking into account human beings as _____, the following things have to be kept in mind:

- The size of the population
- The capabilities of the individuals in that population

Many _____ cannot be consumed in their original form. They have to be processed in order to change them into more usable commodities.

a. 180SearchAssistant
b. Power III
c. 6-3-5 Brainwriting
d. Resources

31. Consumer market research is a form of applied sociology that concentrates on understanding the behaviours, whims and preferences, of consumers in a market-based economy, and aims to understand the effects and comparative success of marketing campaigns. The field of consumer _____ as a statistical science was pioneered by Arthur Nielsen with the founding of the ACNielsen Company in 1923.

Thus _____ is the systematic and objective identification, collection, analysis, and dissemination of information for the purpose of assisting management in decision making related to the identification and solution of problems and opportunities in marketing.

a. Marketing research
b. Logit analysis
c. Marketing research process
d. Focus group

32. A _____ is a formal statement of a set of business goals, the reasons why they are believed attainable, and the plan for reaching those goals. It may also contain background information about the organization or team attempting to reach those goals.

The business goals may be defined for for-profit or for non-profit organizations.

a. Logistics management
b. Product marketing
c. Digital strategy
d. Business plan

33. An _____ is the manufacturing of a good or service within a category. Although _____ is a broad term for any kind of economic production, in economics and urban planning _____ is a synonym for the secondary sector, which is a type of economic activity involved in the manufacturing of raw materials into goods and products.

There are four key industrial economic sectors: the primary sector, largely raw material extraction industries such as mining and farming; the secondary sector, involving refining, construction, and manufacturing; the tertiary sector, which deals with services (such as law and medicine) and distribution of manufactured goods; and the quaternary sector, a relatively new type of knowledge _____ focusing on technological research, design and development such as computer programming, and biochemistry.

a. ADTECH
b. ACNielsen
c. AMAX
d. Industry

Chapter 3. Scanning the Marketing Environment

1. An _____ is the manufacturing of a good or service within a category. Although _____ is a broad term for any kind of economic production, in economics and urban planning _____ is a synonym for the secondary sector, which is a type of economic activity involved in the manufacturing of raw materials into goods and products.

   There are four key industrial economic sectors: the primary sector, largely raw material extraction industries such as mining and farming; the secondary sector, involving refining, construction, and manufacturing; the tertiary sector, which deals with services (such as law and medicine) and distribution of manufactured goods; and the quaternary sector, a relatively new type of knowledge _____ focusing on technological research, design and development such as computer programming, and biochemistry.

   a. ACNielsen
   b. Industry
   c. ADTECH
   d. AMAX

2. _____ is defined by the American _____ Association as the activity, set of institutions, and processes for creating, communicating, delivering, and exchanging offerings that have value for customers, clients, partners, and society at large. The term developed from the original meaning which referred literally to going to market, as in shopping, or going to a market to sell goods or services.

   _____ practice tends to be seen as a creative industry, which includes advertising, distribution and selling.

   a. Customer acquisition management
   b. Product naming
   c. Marketing myopia
   d. Marketing

3. The _____ is a marketing term and refers to all of the forces outside of marketing that affect marketing management's ability to build and maintain successful relationships with target customers. The _____ consists of both the macroenvironment and the microenvironment.

   The microenvironment refers to the forces that are close to the company and affect its ability to serve its customers.

   a. Market environment
   b. Business-to-consumer
   c. Psychographic
   d. Customer franchise

4. _____ is a process of gathering, analyzing, and dispensing information for tactical or strategic purposes. The _____ process entails obtaining both factual and subjective information on the business environments in which a company is operating or considering entering.

   There are three ways of scanning the business environment:

   - Ad-hoc scanning - Short term, infrequent examinations usually initiated by a crisis
   - Regular scanning - Studies done on a regular schedule (say, once a year)
   - Continuous scanning(also called continuous learning) - continuous structured data collection and processing on a broad range of environmental factors

   Most commentators feel that in today's turbulent business environment the best scanning method available is continuous scanning.This allows the firm to :

Chapter 3. Scanning the Marketing Environment

-act quickly-take advantage of opportunities before competitors do-respond to environmental threats before significant damage is done

The Macro Environment

_____ usually refers just to the macro environment, but it can also include:-industry -competitor analysis -marketing research(consumer analysis) -New Product Development(product innovations)- the company's internal environment

Macro _____ involves analysing:

- The Economy

GDP per capitaeconomic growthunemployment]] rateinflation]] rateconsumer and investor confidenceinventory levelscurrency exchange ratesmerchandise trade balancefinancial and political health of trading partnersbalance of paymentsfuture trends

- Government

political climate - amount of government activitypolitical stability and riskgovernment debtbudget deficit or surpluscorporate and personal tax ratespayroll taxesimport tariffs and quotasexport restrictionsrestrictions on international financial flows

- Legal

minimum wage lawsenvironmental protection lawsworker safety lawsunion lawscopyright and patent lawsanti- monopoly lawsSunday closing lawsmunicipal licenceslaws that favour business investment

- Technology

efficiency of infrastructure, including: roads, ports, airports, rolling stock, hospitals, education, healthcare, communication, etc.industrial productivitynew manufacturing processesnew products and services of competitorsnew products and services of supply chain partnersany new technology that could impact the companycost and accessibility of electrical power

- Ecology
    - ecological concerns that affect the firms production processes
    - ecological concerns that affect customers' buying habits
    - ecological concerns that affect customers' perception of the company or product
- Socio-Cultural
    - demographic factors such as:
        - population size and distribution
        - age distribution
        - education levels
        - income levels
        - ethnic origins
        - religious affiliations
    - attitudes towards:
        - materialism, capitalism, free enterprise
        - individualism, role of family, role of government, collectivism
        - role of church and religion
        - consumerism
        - environmentalism
        - importance of work, pride of accomplishment
    - cultural structures including:
        - diet and nutrition
        - housing conditions
- Potential Suppliers
    - Labour supply
        - quantity of labour available
        - quality of labour available
        - stability of labour supply
        - wage expectations
        - employee turn-over rate
        - strikes and labour relations
        - educational facilities
    - Material suppliers
        - quality, quantity, price, and stability of material inputs
        - delivery delays
        - proximity of bulky or heavy material inputs
        - level of competition among suppliers
    - Service Providers
        - quantity, quality, price, and stability of service facilitators
        - special requirements
- Stakeholders
    - Lobbyists
    - Shareholders
    - Employees
    - Partners

18   *Chapter 3. Scanning the Marketing Environment*

Scanning these macro environmental variables for threats and opportunities requires that each issue be rated on two dimensions. It must be rated on its potential impact on the company, and rated on its likeliness of occurrence.

    a. ADTECH
    b. ACNielsen
    c. AMAX
    d. Environmental scanning

5. A _____ is the space, actual or metaphorical, in which a market operates. The term is also used in a trademark law context to denote the actual consumer environment, ie. the 'real world' in which products and services are provided and consumed.
    a. 6-3-5 Brainwriting
    b. 180SearchAssistant
    c. Power III
    d. Marketplace

6. A personal and cultural _____ is a relative ethic _____, an assumption upon which implementation can be extrapolated. A _____ system is a set of consistent _____s and measures that is soo not true. A principle _____ is a foundation upon which other _____s and measures of integrity are based.
    a. Supreme Court of the United States
    b. Value
    c. Perceptual maps
    d. Package-on-Package

7. The United States _____ is the government agency that is responsible for the United States Census. It also gathers other national demographic and economic data.
    a. 180SearchAssistant
    b. Power III
    c. Census Bureau
    d. 6-3-5 Brainwriting

8. Competitiveness is a comparative concept of the ability and performance of a firm, sub-sector or country to sell and supply goods and/or services in a given market. Although widely used in economics and business management, the usefulness of the concept, particularly in the context of national competitiveness, is vigorously disputed by economists, such as Paul Krugman .

The term may also be applied to markets, where it is used to refer to the extent to which the market structure may be regarded as perfectly _____.

    a. Geographical pricing
    b. Competitive
    c. Free trade zone
    d. Customs union

9. _____ or _____ data refers to selected population characteristics as used in government, marketing or opinion research, or the _____ profiles used in such research. Note the distinction from the term 'demography' Commonly-used _____ include race, age, income, disabilities, mobility (in terms of travel time to work or number of vehicles available), educational attainment, home ownership, employment status, and even location.
    a. Demographic
    b. African Americans
    c. Albert Einstein
    d. AStore

10. The _____ , a nonprofit organization, informs people around the world about population, health, and the environment, and seeks to help them use that information. _____ is located in Washington, DC. It was founded in 1929 by Guy Irving Burch, with support of Raymond Pearl.

a. Merchandise Mart
b. John F. Kennedy International Airport
c. BSI Group
d. Population Reference Bureau

11. _____ is a condition where an organism's numbers exceed the carrying capacity of its habitat. In common parlance, the term usually refers to the relationship between the human population and its environment, the Earth.

_____ is not a function of the size or density of the population.

a. Albert Einstein
b. African Americans
c. AStore
d. Overpopulation

12. Regulation refers to 'controlling human or societal behaviour by rules or restrictions.' Regulation can take many forms: legal restrictions promulgated by a government authority, self-regulation, social regulation (e.g. norms), co-regulation and market regulation. One can consider regulation as actions of conduct imposing sanctions (such as a fine.) This action of administrative law, or implementing _____ law, may be contrasted with statutory or case law.

a. Regulatory
b. Right to Financial Privacy Act
c. Robinson-Patman Act
d. Privacy law

13. The _____ is an international organization whose stated aims are to facilitate cooperation in international law, international security, economic development, social progress, human rights and achieving world peace. The _____ was founded in 1945 after World War II to replace the League of Nations, to stop wars between countries and to provide a platform for dialogue.

There are currently 192 member states, including nearly every recognized independent state in the world.

a. AMAX
b. United Nations
c. ACNielsen
d. ADTECH

14. The _____ is the government agency that is responsible for the United States Census. It also gathers other national demographic and economic data.

a. ACNielsen
b. AMAX
c. ADTECH
d. United States Census Bureau

15. The _____ is the total number of living humans on Earth at a given time. As of March 2009, the world's population is estimated to be about 6.76 billion. The _____ has been growing continuously since the end of the Black Death around 1400.

a. African Americans
b. Albert Einstein
c. AStore
d. World population

16. _____ is a term used to describe a person who was born during the demographic Post-World War II baby boom. Many analysts now believe that two distinct cultural generations were born during this baby boom; the older generation is often called the Baby Boom Generation and the younger generation is often called Generation Jones. The term '_____' is sometimes used in a cultural context, and sometimes used to describe someone who was born during the post-WWII baby boom.

a. Greatest Generation
b. Generation X
c. AStore
d. Baby boomer

17. _____ is a term used to identify people born after the post-World War II increase in birth rates (the baby boom) The term has been used in demography, the social sciences, and marketing, though it is most often used in popular culture.

In the U.S. _____ was originally referred to as the 'baby bust' generation because of the drop in the birth rate following the baby boom.

In the UK the term was first used in a 1964 study of British youth by Jane Deverson.

a. Generation X
b. Generation Y
c. AStore
d. Greatest Generation

18. A _____ is the subset of the market on which a specific product is focusing on; Therefore the market niche defines the specific product features aimed at satisfy specific market needs, as well as the price range, production quality and the demographics that is intending to impact.

Every single product that is on sale can be defined by its _____. As of special note, the products aimed at a wide demographics audience, with the resulting low price (due to Price elasticity of demand), are said to belong to the Mainstream niche, in practice referred only as Mainstream or of high demand.

a. Commodity chain
b. Niche market
c. Local purchasing
d. Soft currency

19. _____ is a form of communication that typically attempts to persuade potential customers to purchase or to consume more of a particular brand of product or service. 'While now central to the contemporary global economy and the reproduction of global production networks, it is only quite recently that _____ has been more than a marginal influence on patterns of sales and production. The formation of modern _____ was intimately bound up with the emergence of new forms of monopoly capitalism around the end of the 19th and beginning of the 20th century as one element in corporate strategies to create, organize and where possible control markets, especially for mass produced consumer goods.
a. ACNielsen
b. AMAX
c. Advertising
d. ADTECH

20. _____ is a broad label that refers to any individuals or households that use goods and services generated within the economy. The concept of a _____ is used in different contexts, so that the usage and significance of the term may vary.

A _____ is a person who uses any product or service.

a. Power III
b. 6-3-5 Brainwriting
c. 180SearchAssistant
d. Consumer

21. _____ is a cohort which consists of those people born after the Generation X cohort. Its name is controversial and is synonymous with several alternative names including The Net Generation, Millennials, Echo Boomers, and iGeneration. _____ consists primarily of the offspring of the Generation Jones and Baby Boomers cohorts.

Chapter 3. Scanning the Marketing Environment   21

a. Greatest Generation
b. AStore
c. Generation Y
d. Generation X

22. If specified criteria are met, adjacent metropolitan and micropolitan statistical areas, in various combinations, may become the components of a new set of areas called _____s (Combined statistical areas.) Using Census Bureau data the OMB compiles lists of _____s. The areas that combine retain their own designations as metropolitan or micropolitan statistical areas within the larger _____.
   a. Metropolitan statistical area
   b. Power III
   c. 180SearchAssistant
   d. Combined statistical area

23. In the United States, the Office of Management and Budget (OMB) has produced a formal definition of metropolitan areas. These are referred to as '_____s' (_____s) and 'Combined Statistical Areas.' An earlier version of the _____ was the 'Standard _____' (SMetropolitan statistical area.) _____s are composed of counties and for some county equivalents.
   a. Power III
   b. Race and ethnicity in the United States Census
   c. 180SearchAssistant
   d. Metropolitan statistical area

24. _____ is difficult to define. For example, in 1952, Alfred Kroeber and Clyde Kluckhohn compiled a list of 164 definitions of '_____' in _____: A Critical Review of Concepts and Definitions. However, the word '_____' is most commonly used in three basic senses:

   - excellence of taste in the fine arts and humanities
   - an integrated pattern of human knowledge, belief, and behavior that depends upon the capacity for symbolic thought and social learning
   - the set of shared attitudes, values, goals, and practices that characterizes an institution, organization or group.

When the concept first emerged in eighteenth- and nineteenth-century Europe, it connoted a process of cultivation or improvement, as in agriculture or horticulture. In the nineteenth century, it came to refer first to the betterment or refinement of the individual, especially through education, and then to the fulfillment of national aspirations or ideals.

   a. African Americans
   b. AStore
   c. Albert Einstein
   d. Culture

25. _____s is the social science that studies the production, distribution, and consumption of goods and services. The term _____s comes from the Ancient Greek oá¼°κονομῖα from oá¼¶κος (oikos, 'house') + vÏŒμος (nomos, 'custom' or 'law'), hence 'rules of the house(hold)'. Current _____ models developed out of the broader field of political economy in the late 19th century, owing to a desire to use an empirical approach more akin to the physical sciences.
   a. Economic
   b. Industrial organization
   c. ADTECH
   d. ACNielsen

26. In economics, _____ is a rise in the general level of prices of goods and services in an economy over a period of time. The term '_____' once referred to increases in the money supply (monetary _____); however, economic debates about the relationship between money supply and price levels have led to its primary use today in describing price _____. Inflation can also be described as a decline in the real value of money--a loss of purchasing power in the medium of exchange which is also the monetary unit of account.

Chapter 3. Scanning the Marketing Environment

    a. ADTECH
    b. Industrial organization
    c. Inflation
    d. ACNielsen

27. The _____ is generally accepted as the use and specification of the four p's describing the strategic position of a product in the marketplace. One version of the origins of the _____ starts in 1948 when James Culliton said that a marketing decision should be a result of something similar to a recipe. This version continued in 1953 when Neil Borden, in his American Marketing Association presidential address, took the recipe idea one step further and coined the term 'Marketing-Mix'.

    a. 180SearchAssistant
    b. Power III
    c. 6-3-5 Brainwriting
    d. Marketing mix

28. In economics, the term _____ describes the reduction of a country's gross domestic product (GDP) for at least two quarters. The usual dictionary definition is 'a period of reduced economic activity', a business cycle contraction.

The United States-based National Bureau of Economic Research (NBER) defines economic _____ as: 'a significant decline in [the] economic activity spread across the country, lasting more than a few months, normally visible in real GDP growth, real personal income, employment (non-farm payrolls), industrial production, and wholesale-retail sales.' The NBER's Business Cycle Dating Committee is generally seen as the authority for dating US _____s.

    a. Leading indicator
    b. Law of demand
    c. Macroeconomics
    d. Recession

29. _____ is income after subtracting taxes and normal expenses (such as rent or mortgage and food) to maintain a certain standard of living. It is the amount of an individual's income available for spending after the essentials (such as food, clothing, and shelter) have been taken care of:

    _____ = Gross income - taxes - necessities

Despite the formal definitions above, disposable income is commonly used to denote _____. The meaning should therefore be interpreted from context.

    a. 180SearchAssistant
    b. Power III
    c. 6-3-5 Brainwriting
    d. Discretionary income

30. _____ is gross income minus income tax on that income.

Discretionary income is income after subtracting taxes and normal expenses (such as rent or mortgage and food) to maintain a certain standard of living. It is the amount of an individual's income available for spending after the essentials (such as food, clothing, and shelter) have been taken care of:

    Discretionary income = Gross income - taxes - necessities

Despite the formal definitions above, _____ is commonly used to denote Discretionary income.

a. Power III
b. 180SearchAssistant
c. 6-3-5 Brainwriting
d. Disposable income

31. _____ is commonly defined as the amount of a company's or a person's income before all deductions or any taxpayer's income, except that which is specifically excluded by the Internal Revenue Code, before taking deductions or taxes into account. For a business, this amount is pre-tax net sales less cost of sales. Section 61 of the Internal Revenue Code (Code) defines '_____' as 'all income from whatever source derived.' Section 61(a) of the Code lists fifteen examples of items included in _____; however, the list is not exhaustive.

a. 180SearchAssistant
b. 6-3-5 Brainwriting
c. Power III
d. Gross income

32. In economics, _____ is how a nation's total economy is distributed among its population. . _____ has always been a central concern of economic theory and economic policy. Classical economists such as Adam Smith, Thomas Malthus and David Ricardo were mainly concerned with factor _____, that is, the distribution of income between the main factors of production, land, labour and capital.

a. Internality
b. ACNielsen
c. Income distribution
d. Inflation rate

33. In economics, _____ is the desire to own something and the ability to pay for it. The term _____ signifies the ability or the willingness to buy a particular commodity at a given point of time .

a. Discretionary spending
b. Market dominance
c. Market system
d. Demand

34. _____ is one of the four elements of marketing mix. An organization or set of organizations (go-betweens) involved in the process of making a product or service available for use or consumption by a consumer or business user.

The other three parts of the marketing mix are product, pricing, and promotion.

a. Comparison-Shopping agent
b. Distribution
c. Japan Advertising Photographers' Association
d. Better Living Through Chemistry

35. The _____, a unit of the United States Department of Labor, is the principal fact-finding agency for the U.S. government in the broad field of labor economics and statistics. The BLS is an independent national statistical agency that collects, processes, analyzes, and disseminates essential statistical data to the American public, the U.S. Congress, other Federal agencies, State and local governments, business, and labor representatives. The BLS also serves as a statistical resource to the Department of Labor.

a. Gross national product
b. Power III
c. Consumer Expenditure Survey
d. Bureau of Labor Statistics

36. The _____ is a national account conducted by the Bureau of Labor Statistics (BLS) of the United States Department of Labor and administered by the Census Bureau. The program consists of two surveys -- the Interview and the Diary survey -- which provides information on the buying habits of American consumers. These surveys collect data on expenditures, income, and consumer unit demographic characteristics.

Chapter 3. Scanning the Marketing Environment

a. Bureau of Labor Statistics
b. Power III
c. Gross national product
d. Consumer Expenditure Survey

37. _____ is a mathematical science pertaining to the collection, analysis, interpretation or explanation, and presentation of data. It also provides tools for prediction and forecasting based on data. It is applicable to a wide variety of academic disciplines, from the natural and social sciences to the humanities, government and business.
a. Null hypothesis
b. Type I error
c. Median
d. Statistics

38. _____ is an advertisement in which a particular product specifically mentions a competitor by name for the express purpose of showing why the competitor is inferior to the product naming it.

This should not be confused with parody advertisements, where a fictional product is being advertised for the purpose of poking fun at the particular advertisement, nor should it be confused with the use of a coined brand name for the purpose of comparing the product without actually naming an actual competitor. ('Wikipedia tastes better and is less filling than the Encyclopedia Galactica.')

In the 1980s, during what has been referred to as the cola wars, soft-drink manufacturer Pepsi ran a series of advertisements where people, caught on hidden camera, in a blind taste test, chose Pepsi over rival Coca-Cola.

a. Heavy-up
b. GL-70
c. Cost per conversion
d. Comparative advertising

39. Electronic commerce, commonly known as _____ or eCommerce, consists of the buying and selling of products or services over electronic systems such as the Internet and other computer networks. The amount of trade conducted electronically has grown extraordinarily with wide-spread Internet usage. A wide variety of commerce is conducted in this way, spurring and drawing on innovations in electronic funds transfer, supply chain management, Internet marketing, online transaction processing, electronic data interchange (EDI), inventory management systems, and automated data collection systems.
a. ACNielsen
b. ADTECH
c. AMAX
d. E-commerce

40. _____ is exchange of capital, goods, and services across international borders or territories. In most countries, it represents a significant share of gross domestic product (GDP.) While _____ has been present throughout much of history, its economic, social, and political importance has been on the rise in recent centuries.
a. Incoterms
b. ADTECH
c. International trade
d. ACNielsen

41. _____ - an information and communication based electronic exchange environment - is a relatively new concept in marketing. Since physical boundaries no longer interfere with buy/sell decisions, the world has grown into several industry specific _____ s which are integration of marketplaces through sophisticated computer and telecommunication technologies. The term _____ was introduced by Rayport and Sviokla in 1994 (see Rayport, Jeffrey F.
a. Value chain
b. Kano model
c. Market segment
d. Marketspace

Chapter 3. Scanning the Marketing Environment

42. _____ is a rivalry between individuals, groups, nations for territory, a niche, or allocation of resources. It arises whenever two or more parties strive for a goal which cannot be shared. _____ occurs naturally between living organisms which co-exist in the same environment.
   a. Price competition
   b. Non-price competition
   c. Price fixing
   d. Competition

43. An _____ is a private network that uses Internet protocols, network connectivity, and possibly the public telecommunication system to securely share part of an organization's information or operations with suppliers, vendors, partners, customers or other businesses. An _____ can be viewed as part of a company's intranet that is extended to users outside the company (e.g.: normally over the Internet.) It has also been described as a 'state of mind' in which the Internet is perceived as a way to do business with a preapproved set of other companies business-to-business (B2B), in isolation from all other Internet users.
   a. AMAX
   b. ADTECH
   c. ACNielsen
   d. Extranet

44. _____ is a common market form. Many markets can be considered monopolistically competitive, often including the markets for restaurants, cereal, clothing, shoes and service industries in large cities. Short-run equilibrium of the firm under _____

Monopolistically competitive markets have the following characteristics:

- There are many producers and many consumers in a given market, and no business has total control over the market price.
- Consumers perceive that there are non-price differences among the competitors' products.
- There are few barriers to entry and exit.
- Producers have a degree of control over price.

Long-run equilibrium of the firm under _____

The characteristics of a monopolistically competitive market are almost the same as in perfect competition, with the exception of heterogeneous products, and that _____ involves a great deal of non-price competition (based on subtle product differentiation.) A firm making profits in the short run will break even in the long run because demand will decrease and average total cost will increase.

   a. Macroeconomics
   b. Recession
   c. Gross domestic product
   d. Monopolistic competition

45. An _____ is a market form in which a market or industry is dominated by a small number of sellers (oligopolists.) Because there are few participants in this type of market, each oligopolist is aware of the actions of the others. The decisions of one firm influence, and are influenced by, the decisions of other firms.
   a. Oligopoly
   b. AMAX
   c. ADTECH
   d. ACNielsen

46. _____ is the transfer of information over a distance without the use of electrical conductors or 'wires'. The distances involved may be short (a few meters as in television remote control) or long (thousands or millions of kilometers for radio communications.) When the context is clear, the term is often shortened to 'wireless'.

a. Wireless communication
c. 180SearchAssistant
b. 6-3-5 Brainwriting
d. Power III

47. _____, known in the United States as antitrust law, has three main elements:

- prohibiting agreements or practices that restrict free trading and competition between business entities. This includes in particular the repression of cartels.
- banning abusive behaviour by a firm dominating a market, or anti-competitive practices that tend to lead to such a dominant position. Practices controlled in this way may include predatory pricing, tying, price gouging, refusal to deal, and many others.
- supervising the mergers and acquisitions of large corporations, including some joint ventures. Transactions that are considered to threaten the competitive process can be prohibited altogether, or approved subject to 'remedies' such as an obligation to divest part of the merged business or to offer licences or access to facilities to enable other businesses to continue competing.

The substance and practice of _____ varies from jurisdiction to jurisdiction. Protecting the interests of consumers (consumer welfare) and ensuring that entrepreneurs have an opportunity to compete in the market economy are often treated as important objectives. _____ is closely connected with law on deregulation of access to markets, state aids and subsidies, the privatisation of state owned assets and the establishment of independent sector regulators. In recent decades, _____ has been viewed as a way to provide better public services.

a. Right to Financial Privacy Act
c. Competition law
b. Denominazione di origine controllata
d. Covenant not to compete

48. The _____ is an economic and political union of 27 member states, located primarily in Europe. It was established by the Treaty of Maastricht on 1 November 1993 upon the foundations of the pre-existing European Economic Community. With almost 500 million citizens, the _____ combined generates an estimated 30% share (US$16.8 trillion in 2007) of the nominal gross world product.

a. ACNielsen
c. Eurozone
b. European Union
d. ADTECH

49. The _____ or gross domestic income (GDI) is one of the measures of national income and output for a given country's economy. It is the total value of all final goods and services produced in a particular economy; the dollar value of all goods and services produced within a country's borders in a given year. _____ can be defined in three ways, all of which are conceptually identical.

a. Macroeconomics
c. Microeconomics
b. Gross Domestic Product
d. Leading indicator

50. In economics, a _____ exists when a specific individual or enterprise has sufficient control over a particular product or service to determine significantly the terms on which other individuals shall have access to it. Monopolies are thus characterized by a lack of economic competition for the good or service that they provide and a lack of viable substitute goods. The verb 'monopolize' refers to the process by which a firm gains persistently greater market share than what is expected under perfect competition.

Chapter 3. Scanning the Marketing Environment

a. Power III
b. 180SearchAssistant
c. 6-3-5 Brainwriting
d. Monopoly

51. _____ refers to 'controlling human or societal behaviour by rules or restrictions.' _____ can take many forms: legal restrictions promulgated by a government authority, self-_____, social _____, co-_____ and market _____. One can consider _____ as actions of conduct imposing sanctions (such as a fine.) This action of administrative law, or implementing regulatory law, may be contrasted with statutory or case law.
   a. Non-conventional trademark
   b. CAN-SPAM
   c. Rule of four
   d. Regulation

52. The _____ of 1936 (or Anti-Price Discrimination Act, 15 U.S.C. Â§ 13) is a United States federal law that prohibits what were considered, at the time of passage, to be anticompetitive practices by producers, specifically price discrimination. It grew out of practices in which chain stores were allowed to purchase goods at lower prices than other retailers.
   a. Registered trademark symbol
   b. Trademark infringement
   c. Fair Debt Collection Practices Act
   d. Robinson-Patman Act

53. The _____ requires the Federal government to investigate and pursue trusts, companies and organizations suspected of violating the Act. It was the first United States Federal statute to limit cartels and monopolies, and today still forms the basis for most antitrust litigation by the federal government.
   a. Power III
   b. 180SearchAssistant
   c. 6-3-5 Brainwriting
   d. Sherman Antitrust Act

54. A _____ is a business that is independently owned and operated, with a small number of employees and relatively low volume of sales. The legal definition of 'small' often varies by country and industry, but is generally under 100 employees in the United States and under 50 employees in the European Union. In comparison, the definition of mid-sized business by the number of employees is generally under 500 in the U.S. and 250 for the European Union.
   a. Product support
   b. Time to market
   c. Customer centricity
   d. Small business

55. The _____ was enacted in 1972 by the United States Congress. It established the United States Consumer Product Safety Commission as an independent agency of the United States federal government and defined its basic authority. The act gives CPSC the power to develop safety standards and pursue recalls for products that present unreasonable or substantial risks of injury or death to consumers.
   a. Power III
   b. Consumer Product Safety Act
   c. 6-3-5 Brainwriting
   d. 180SearchAssistant

56. The United States _____ is an independent agency of the United States government created in 1972 through the Consumer Product Safety Act to protect 'against unreasonable risks of injuries associated with consumer products.' As of 2006 its acting chairman is Nancy Nord, a Republican. The other commissioner is Thomas Hill Moore, a Democrat. Normally the board has three commissioners.
   a. 6-3-5 Brainwriting
   b. 180SearchAssistant
   c. Consumer Product Safety Commission
   d. Power III

57. _____ is a form of government regulation which protects the interests of consumers. For example, a government may require businesses to disclose detailed information about products--particularly in areas where safety or public health is an issue, such as food. _____ is linked to the idea of consumer rights (that consumers have various rights as consumers), and to the formation of consumer organizations which help consumers make better choices in the marketplace.

a. Trademark dilution
b. Sound trademark
c. Federal Bureau of Investigation
d. Consumer protection

58. _____ is the equation of personal happiness with consumption and the purchase of material possessions.

The term is often associated with criticisms of consumption starting with Thorstein Veblen.

Veblen's subject of examination, the newly emergent middle class arising at the turn of the twentieth century, comes to full fruition by the end of the twentieth century through the process of globalization.

In economics, _____ refers to economic policies placing emphasis on consumption.

a. Power III
b. 6-3-5 Brainwriting
c. 180SearchAssistant
d. Consumerism

59. _____ is a form of intellectual property which gives the creator of an original work exclusive rights for a certain time period in relation to that work, including its publication, distribution and adaptation; after which time the work is said to enter the public domain. _____ applies to any expressible form of an idea or information that is substantive and discrete. Some jurisdictions also recognize 'moral rights' of the creator of a work, such as the right to be credited for the work.

a. Copyright
b. Reasonable person standard
c. Celler-Kefauver Act
d. Collective mark

60. The _____ is a United States copyright law that implements two 1996 treaties of the World Intellectual Property Organization (WIPO.) It criminalizes production and dissemination of technology, devices whether or not there is actual infringement of copyright itself. In addition, the _____ heightens the penalties for copyright infringement on the Internet.

a. Copyright infringement
b. Priority right
c. Regulatory
d. Digital Millennium Copyright Act

61. The _____ is a US law that applies to labels on many consumer products. It requires the label to state:

- The identity of the product;
- The name and place of business of the manufacturer, packer, or distributor; and
- The net quantity of contents.

The contents statement must include both metric and U.S. customary units.

Passed under Lyndon B. Johnson in 1966, the law first took effect on July 1, 1967. The metric labeling requirement was added in 1992 and took effect on February 14, 1994.

a. Power III
b. 180SearchAssistant
c. 6-3-5 Brainwriting
d. Fair Packaging and Labeling Act

Chapter 3. Scanning the Marketing Environment

62. _____ is the practice of individuals including commercial businesses, governments and institutions, facilitating the sale of their products or services to other companies or organizations that in turn resell them, use them as components in products or services they offer _____ is also called business-to-_____ for short. (Note that while marketing to government entities shares some of the same dynamics of organizational marketing, B2G Marketing is meaningfully different.)
   a. Mass marketing
   b. Law of disruption
   c. Disruptive technology
   d. Business marketing

63. A _____ is a set of exclusive rights granted by a State to an inventor or his assignee for a limited period of time in exchange for a disclosure of an invention.

The procedure for granting _____s, the requirements placed on the _____ee and the extent of the exclusive rights vary widely between countries according to national laws and international agreements. Typically, however, a _____ application must include one or more claims defining the invention which must be new, inventive, and useful or industrially applicable.

   a. Product liability
   b. Foreign Corrupt Practices Act
   c. Reasonable person standard
   d. Patent

64. _____ in economics and business is the result of an exchange and from that trade we assign a numerical monetary value to a good, service or asset. If I trade 4 apples for an orange, the _____ of an orange is 4 - apples. Inversely, the _____ of an apple is 1/4 oranges.
   a. Pricing
   b. Price
   c. Discounts and allowances
   d. Contribution margin-based pricing

65. _____ exists when sales of identical goods or services are transacted at different prices from the same provider. In a theoretical market with perfect information, no transaction costs or prohibition on secondary exchange (or re-selling) to prevent arbitrage, _____ can only be a feature of monopoly and oligopoly markets, where market power can be exercised. Otherwise, the moment the seller tries to sell the same good at different prices, the buyer at the lower price can arbitrage by selling to the consumer buying at the higher price but with a tiny discount.
   a. Price
   b. Resale price maintenance
   c. Price discrimination
   d. Penetration pricing

66. A _____ or trade mark, identified by the symbols ™ (not yet registered) and ® (registered) business organization or other legal entity to identify that the products and/or services to consumers with which the _____ appears originate from a unique source of origin, and to distinguish its products or services from those of other entities. A _____ is a type of intellectual property, and typically a name, word, phrase, logo, symbol, design, image, or a combination of these elements. There is also a range of non-conventional _____s comprising marks which do not fall into these standard categories.
   a. Risk management
   b. Trademark
   c. Power III
   d. 180SearchAssistant

67. The _____, also conveniently known as the Madrid system or simply Madrid, is the primary international system for facilitating the registration of trademarks in multiple jurisdictions around the world.

Chapter 3. Scanning the Marketing Environment

The Madrid system provides a centrally administered system of obtaining a bundle of trademark registrations in separate jurisdictions. Registration through the Madrid system does not create an 'international' registration, as in the case of the European CTM system, rather it creates a bundle of national rights, able to be administered centrally.

- a. Developed country
- b. Sexism,
- c. Japan Advertising Photographers' Association
- d. Madrid system for the international registration of marks

68. _____ is an agreement between business competitors to sell the same product or service at the same price. In general, it is an agreement intended to ultimately push the price of a product as high as possible, leading to profits for all the sellers. _____ can also involve any agreement to fix, peg, discount or stabilize prices.
- a. Non-price competition
- b. Price fixing
- c. Direct competition
- d. Price competition

69. _____ is one of the four Ps of the marketing mix. The other three aspects are product, promotion, and place. It is also a key variable in microeconomic price allocation theory.
- a. Price
- b. Relationship based pricing
- c. Competitor indexing
- d. Pricing

70. A _____ or logistics network is the system of organizations, people, technology, activities, information and resources involved in moving a product or service from supplier to customer. _____ activities transform natural resources, raw materials and components into a finished product that is delivered to the end customer. In sophisticated _____ systems, used products may re-enter the _____ at any point where residual value is recyclable.
- a. Supply chain network
- b. Demand chain management
- c. Supply chain
- d. Purchasing

71. Once trademark rights are established in a particular jurisdiction, these rights are generally only enforceable in that jurisdiction, a quality which is sometimes known as territoriality. However, there is a range of international _____ and systems which facilitate the protection of trademarks in more than one jurisdiction

To avoid conflicts with earlier trademark rights, it is highly recommended to conduct trademark searches before the trademarks office (or 'trademarks registry') of a particular jurisdiction--e.g. US Patent and Trademark Office.

- a. Self branding
- b. Supreme Court of the United States
- c. Sigg bottles
- d. Trademark laws

72. In economics, '_____' can refer to any kind of predatory pricing. However, the word is now generally used only in the context of international trade law, where _____ is defined as the act of a manufacturer in one country exporting a product to another country at a price which is either below the price it charges in its home market or is below its costs of production. The term has a negative connotation, but advocates of free markets see '_____' as beneficial for consumers and believe that protectionism to prevent it would have net negative consequences.
- a. Dumping
- b. Gold Key Matching Service
- c. Sample sales
- d. Hawkers

Chapter 3. Scanning the Marketing Environment

73. _____ refers to the laws and rules defining the ways in which products can be advertised in a particular region. Rules can define a wide number of different aspects, such as placement, timing, and content. In the United States, false advertising and health-related ads are regulated the most.
   a. ADTECH
   b. Advertising regulation
   c. ACNielsen
   d. AMAX

74. A _____ is an order or request to halt an activity, or else face legal action. The recipient of the cease-and-desist may be an individual or an organization.
   a. Power III
   b. Cease and desist
   c. Leading question
   d. Contract price

75. False advertising or _____ is the use of false or misleading statements in advertising. As advertising has the potential to persuade people into commercial transactions that they might otherwise avoid, many governments around the world use regulations to control false, deceptive or misleading advertising. Truth in labeling refers to essentially the same concept, that customers have the right to know what they are buying, and that all necessary information should be on the label.
   a. Power III
   b. Fine print
   c. Misleading advertising
   d. Deceptive advertising

76. The _____ is an independent agency of the United States government, established in 1914 by the _____ Act. Its principal mission is the promotion of 'consumer protection' and the elimination and prevention of what regulators perceive to be harmfully 'anti-competitive' business practices, such as coercive monopoly.

The _____ Act was one of President Wilson's major acts against trusts.

   a. 6-3-5 Brainwriting
   b. 180SearchAssistant
   c. Power III
   d. Federal Trade Commission

77. The _____ of 1914 (15 U.S.C §§ 41-58, as amended) established the Federal Trade Commission (FTC), a bipartisan body of five members appointed by the President of the United States for seven year terms. This Commission was authorized to issue Cease and Desist orders to large corporations to curb unfair trade practices. This Act also gave more flexibility to the US congress for judicial matters.
   a. Federal Trade Commission Act
   b. Product liability
   c. Comparative negligence
   d. Gripe site

78. _____ is the ability of an individual or group to seclude themselves or information about themselves and thereby reveal themselves selectively. The boundaries and content of what is considered private differ among cultures and individuals, but share basic common themes. _____ is sometimes related to anonymity, the wish to remain unnoticed or unidentified in the public realm.
   a. 180SearchAssistant
   b. Power III
   c. Privacy
   d. 6-3-5 Brainwriting

79. _____ is a method of direct marketing in which a salesperson solicits to prospective customers to buy products or services, either over the phone or through a subsequent face to face or Web conferencing appointment scheduled during the call.

Chapter 3. Scanning the Marketing Environment

_____ can also include recorded sales pitches programmed to be played over the phone via automatic dialing. _____ has come under fire in recent years, being viewed as an annoyance by many.

a. Directory Harvest Attack
b. Phishing
c. Joe job
d. Telemarketing

80. In the United States consumer sales promotions known as _____ or simply sweeps (both single and plural) have become associated with marketing promotions targeted toward both generating enthusiasm and providing incentive reactions among customers by enticing consumers to submit free entries into drawings of chance (and not skill) that are tied to product or service awareness wherein the featured prizes are given away by sponsoring companies. Prizes can vary in value from less than one dollar to more than one million U.S. dollars and can be in the form of cash, cars, homes, electronics, etc.

_____ frequently have eligibility limited by international, national, state, local, or other geographical factors.

a. Claritas Prizm
b. Sweepstakes
c. Market segment
d. Commercial planning

81. _____, also referred to as i-marketing, web marketing, online marketing is the marketing of products or services over the Internet.

The Internet has brought many unique benefits to marketing, one of which being lower costs for the distribution of information and media to a global audience. The interactive nature of _____, both in terms of providing instant response and eliciting responses, is a unique quality of the medium.

a. ADTECH
b. ACNielsen
c. AMAX
d. Internet marketing

Chapter 4. Ethics and Social Responsibility in Marketing

1. _____ is a branch of philosophy which seeks to address questions about morality, such as how a moral outcome can be achieved in a specific situation (applied _____), how moral values should be determined (normative _____), what moral values people actually abide by (descriptive _____), what the fundamental semantic, ontological, and epistemic nature of _____ or morality is (meta-_____), and how moral capacity or moral agency develops and what its nature is (moral psychology.)

Socrates was one of the first Greek philosophers to encourage both scholars and the common citizen to turn their attention from the outside world to the condition of man. In this view, Knowledge having a bearing on human life was placed highest, all other knowledge being secondary.

   a. ADTECH
   b. ACNielsen
   c. AMAX
   d. Ethics

2. _____ - an information and communication based electronic exchange environment - is a relatively new concept in marketing. Since physical boundaries no longer interfere with buy/sell decisions, the world has grown into several industry specific _____s which are integration of marketplaces through sophisticated computer and telecommunication technologies. The term _____ was introduced by Rayport and Sviokla in 1994 (see Rayport, Jeffrey F.
   a. Value chain
   b. Market segment
   c. Kano model
   d. Marketspace

3. _____ is the practice of individuals including commercial businesses, governments and institutions, facilitating the sale of their products or services to other companies or organizations that in turn resell them, use them as components in products or services they offer _____ is also called business-to-_____ for short. (Note that while marketing to government entities shares some of the same dynamics of organizational marketing, B2G Marketing is meaningfully different.)
   a. Business marketing
   b. Law of disruption
   c. Mass marketing
   d. Disruptive technology

4. _____ in economics and business is the result of an exchange and from that trade we assign a numerical monetary value to a good, service or asset. If I trade 4 apples for an orange, the _____ of an orange is 4 - apples. Inversely, the _____ of an apple is 1/4 oranges.
   a. Contribution margin-based pricing
   b. Pricing
   c. Discounts and allowances
   d. Price

5. The _____ requires the Federal government to investigate and pursue trusts, companies and organizations suspected of violating the Act. It was the first United States Federal statute to limit cartels and monopolies, and today still forms the basis for most antitrust litigation by the federal government.
   a. 180SearchAssistant
   b. 6-3-5 Brainwriting
   c. Power III
   d. Sherman Antitrust Act

Chapter 4. Ethics and Social Responsibility in Marketing

6. _____ is difficult to define. For example, in 1952, Alfred Kroeber and Clyde Kluckhohn compiled a list of 164 definitions of '_____' in _____: A Critical Review of Concepts and Definitions. However, the word '_____' is most commonly used in three basic senses:

- excellence of taste in the fine arts and humanities
- an integrated pattern of human knowledge, belief, and behavior that depends upon the capacity for symbolic thought and social learning
- the set of shared attitudes, values, goals, and practices that characterizes an institution, organization or group.

When the concept first emerged in eighteenth- and nineteenth-century Europe, it connoted a process of cultivation or improvement, as in agriculture or horticulture. In the nineteenth century, it came to refer first to the betterment or refinement of the individual, especially through education, and then to the fulfillment of national aspirations or ideals.

a. African Americans
c. Albert Einstein
b. AStore
d. Culture

7. _____ is defined by the American _____ Association as the activity, set of institutions, and processes for creating, communicating, delivering, and exchanging offerings that have value for customers, clients, partners, and society at large. The term developed from the original meaning which referred literally to going to market, as in shopping, or going to a market to sell goods or services.

_____ practice tends to be seen as a creative industry, which includes advertising, distribution and selling.

a. Marketing myopia
c. Customer acquisition management
b. Product naming
d. Marketing

8. A _____ is a written document that details the necessary actions to achieve one or more marketing objectives. It can be for a product or service, a brand, or a product line. _____s cover between one and five years.

a. Disruptive technology
c. Marketing plan
b. Prosumer
d. Marketing strategy

9. In psychology, philosophy, and the cognitive sciences, _____ is the process of attaining awareness or understanding of sensory information. It is a task far more complex than was imagined in the 1950s and 1960s, when it was predicted that building perceiving machines would take about a decade, a goal which is still very far from fruition. The word _____ comes from the Latin words _____, percepio, meaning 'receiving, collecting, action of taking possession, apprehension with the mind or senses.'

_____ is one of the oldest fields in psychology.

a. Perception
c. 180SearchAssistant
b. Groupthink
d. Power III

Chapter 4. Ethics and Social Responsibility in Marketing

10. _____ are legal property rights over creations of the mind, both artistic and commercial, and the corresponding fields of law. Under _____ law, owners are granted certain exclusive rights to a variety of intangible assets, such as musical, literary, and artistic works; ideas, discoveries and inventions; and words, phrases, symbols, and designs. Common types of _____ include copyrights, trademarks, patents, industrial design rights and trade secrets.
   a. ACNielsen
   b. Intellectual property
   c. Opinion leadership
   d. Elasticity

11. In sociology, anthropology and cultural studies, a _____ is a group of people with a culture (whether distinct or hidden) which differentiates them from the larger culture to which they belong. If a particular _____ is characterized by a systematic opposition to the dominant culture, it may be described as a counterculture. As Ken Gelder notes, _____s are social, with their own shared conventions, values and rituals, but they can also seem 'immersed' or self-absorbed--another feature that distinguishes them from countercultures.
   a. Power III
   b. 180SearchAssistant
   c. 6-3-5 Brainwriting
   d. Subculture

12. An _____ is the manufacturing of a good or service within a category. Although _____ is a broad term for any kind of economic production, in economics and urban planning _____ is a synonym for the secondary sector, which is a type of economic activity involved in the manufacturing of raw materials into goods and products.

There are four key industrial economic sectors: the primary sector, largely raw material extraction industries such as mining and farming; the secondary sector, involving refining, construction, and manufacturing; the tertiary sector, which deals with services (such as law and medicine) and distribution of manufactured goods; and the quaternary sector, a relatively new type of knowledge _____ focusing on technological research, design and development such as computer programming, and biochemistry.

   a. ACNielsen
   b. ADTECH
   c. Industry
   d. AMAX

13. _____ is a form of communication that typically attempts to persuade potential customers to purchase or to consume more of a particular brand of product or service. 'While now central to the contemporary global economy and the reproduction of global production networks, it is only quite recently that _____ has been more than a marginal influence on patterns of sales and production. The formation of modern _____ was intimately bound up with the emergence of new forms of monopoly capitalism around the end of the 19th and beginning of the 20th century as one element in corporate strategies to create, organize and where possible control markets, especially for mass produced consumer goods.
   a. ACNielsen
   b. AMAX
   c. Advertising
   d. ADTECH

14. _____ is a broad label that refers to any individuals or households that use goods and services generated within the economy. The concept of a _____ is used in different contexts, so that the usage and significance of the term may vary.

A _____ is a person who uses any product or service.

   a. 6-3-5 Brainwriting
   b. 180SearchAssistant
   c. Power III
   d. Consumer

35

15. In 1962, President John F. Kennedy presented a speech to the United States Congress in which he extolled four basic consumer rights, later called The _____.

While later expanded, the original six basic beliefs of consumer protection are the most widely recognized.

In 1985, the concept of consumer rights was endorsed by the United Nations and expanded to included eight basic rights.

   a. 6-3-5 Brainwriting
   b. Power III
   c. 180SearchAssistant
   d. Consumer Bill of Rights

16. The United States _____ is an independent agency of the United States government created in 1972 through the Consumer Product Safety Act to protect 'against unreasonable risks of injuries associated with consumer products.' As of 2006 its acting chairman is Nancy Nord, a Republican. The other commissioner is Thomas Hill Moore, a Democrat. Normally the board has three commissioners.
   a. Power III
   b. Consumer Product Safety Commission
   c. 180SearchAssistant
   d. 6-3-5 Brainwriting

17. _____ is a form of government regulation which protects the interests of consumers. For example, a government may require businesses to disclose detailed information about products--particularly in areas where safety or public health is an issue, such as food. _____ is linked to the idea of consumer rights (that consumers have various rights as consumers), and to the formation of consumer organizations which help consumers make better choices in the marketplace.
   a. Sound trademark
   b. Trademark dilution
   c. Consumer Protection
   d. Federal Bureau of Investigation

18. The _____ is an independent agency of the United States government, established in 1914 by the _____ Act. Its principal mission is the promotion of 'consumer protection' and the elimination and prevention of what regulators perceive to be harmfully 'anti-competitive' business practices, such as coercive monopoly.

The _____ Act was one of President Wilson's major acts against trusts.

   a. Power III
   b. Federal Trade Commission
   c. 180SearchAssistant
   d. 6-3-5 Brainwriting

19. _____ is the ability of an individual or group to seclude themselves or information about themselves and thereby reveal themselves selectively. The boundaries and content of what is considered private differ among cultures and individuals, but share basic common themes. _____ is sometimes related to anonymity, the wish to remain unnoticed or unidentified in the public realm.
   a. Privacy
   b. 180SearchAssistant
   c. Power III
   d. 6-3-5 Brainwriting

20. Regulation refers to 'controlling human or societal behaviour by rules or restrictions.' Regulation can take many forms: legal restrictions promulgated by a government authority, self-regulation, social regulation (e.g. norms), co-regulation and market regulation. One can consider regulation as actions of conduct imposing sanctions (such as a fine.) This action of administrative law, or implementing _____ law, may be contrasted with statutory or case law.

Chapter 4. Ethics and Social Responsibility in Marketing

a. Robinson-Patman Act
b. Regulatory
c. Right to Financial Privacy Act
d. Privacy law

21. _____ is a method of direct marketing in which a salesperson solicits to prospective customers to buy products or services, either over the phone or through a subsequent face to face or Web conferencing appointment scheduled during the call.

_____ can also include recorded sales pitches programmed to be played over the phone via automatic dialing. _____ has come under fire in recent years, being viewed as an annoyance by many.

a. Telemarketing
b. Joe job
c. Directory Harvest Attack
d. Phishing

22. _____ refer to a collection of facts usually collected as the result of experience, observation or experiment or a set of premises. This may consist of numbers, words particularly as measurements or observations of a set of variables. _____ are often viewed as a lowest level of abstraction from which information and knowledge are derived.

a. Mean
b. Pearson product-moment correlation coefficient
c. Sample size
d. Data

23. _____ refers to 'controlling human or societal behaviour by rules or restrictions.' _____ can take many forms: legal restrictions promulgated by a government authority, self-_____, social _____, co-_____ and market _____. One can consider _____ as actions of conduct imposing sanctions (such as a fine.) This action of administrative law, or implementing regulatory law, may be contrasted with statutory or case law.

a. Rule of four
b. CAN-SPAM
c. Non-conventional trademark
d. Regulation

24. _____ is a rivalry between individuals, groups, nations for territory, a niche, or allocation of resources. It arises whenever two or more parties strive for a goal which cannot be shared. _____ occurs naturally between living organisms which co-exist in the same environment.

a. Competition
b. Price fixing
c. Non-price competition
d. Price competition

25. Organizational culture is not the same as _____. It is wider and deeper concepts, something that an organization 'is' rather than what it 'has' (according to Buchanan and Huczynski.)

_____ is the total sum of the values, customs, traditions and meanings that make a company unique.

a. Power III
b. Cross-functional team
c. 180SearchAssistant
d. Corporate culture

26. _____s is the social science that studies the production, distribution, and consumption of goods and services. The term _____s comes from the Ancient Greek οἰκονομία from οἶκος (oikos, 'house') + νόμος (nomos, 'custom' or 'law'), hence 'rules of the house(hold)'. Current _____ models developed out of the broader field of political economy in the late 19th century, owing to a desire to use an empirical approach more akin to the physical sciences.

a. Economic
b. Industrial organization
c. ACNielsen
d. ADTECH

27. The _____ of 1996 (18 U.S.C. § 1831-1839) makes the theft or misappropriation of a trade secret a federal crime. Unlike Espionage, which is governed by Title 18 U.S. Code Sections 792 - 799, the offense involves commercial information, not classified or national defense information.
    a. Express warranty
    b. Office action
    c. Imperial Group v. Philip Morris
    d. Economic Espionage Act

28. The _____ of 1977 (15 U.S.C. §§ 78dd-1, et seq.) is a United States federal law known primarily for two of its main provisions, one that addresses accounting transparency requirements under the Securities Exchange Act of 1934 and another concerning bribery of foreign officials.
    a. Tenth Amendment
    b. Copyright
    c. Trademark dilution
    d. Foreign Corrupt Practices Act

29. _____ is the use of governmental powers by government officials for illegitimate private gain. Misuse of government power for other purposes, such as repression of political opponents and general police brutality, is not considered _____. Neither are illegal acts by private persons or corporations not directly involved with the government.
    a. Political corruption
    b. AStore
    c. Albert Einstein
    d. African Americans

30. A _____ is a formula, practice, process, design, instrument, pattern by which a business can obtain an economic advantage over competitors or customers. In some jurisdictions, such secrets are referred to as 'confidential information' or 'classified information'.

    The precise language by which a _____ is defined varies by jurisdiction (as do the particular types of information that are subject to _____ protection.)

    a. Trade secret
    b. Priority right
    c. Federal Bureau of Investigation
    d. CAN-SPAM

31. The _____ is a professional association for marketers. As of 2008 it had approximately 40,000 members. There are collegiate chapters on 250 campuses.
    a. ADTECH
    b. American Marketing Association
    c. ACNielsen
    d. AMAX

32. _____ is a contract between two parties, one being the employer and the other being the employee. An employee may be defined as: 'A person in the service of another under any contract of hire, express or implied, oral or written, where the employer has the power or right to control and direct the employee in the material details of how the work is to be performed.' Black's Law Dictionary page 471 (5th ed. 1979.)
    a. Employment
    b. ADTECH
    c. AMAX
    d. ACNielsen

Chapter 4. Ethics and Social Responsibility in Marketing

33. A _____, in the field of business and marketing, is a geographic region or demographic group used to gauge the viability of a product or service in the mass market prior to a wide scale roll-out. The criteria used to judge the acceptability of a _____ region or group include:

1. a population that is demographically similar to the proposed target market; and
2. relative isolation from densely populated media markets so that advertising to the test audience can be efficient and economical.

The _____ ideally aims to duplicate 'everything' - promotion and distribution as well as `product' - on a smaller scale. The technique replicates, typically in one area, what is planned to occur in a national launch; and the results are very carefully monitored, so that they can be extrapolated to projected national results. The `area' may be any one of the following:

- Television area
- Test town
- Residential neighborhood
- Test site

A number of decisions have to be taken about any _____:

- Which _____?
- What is to be tested?
- How long a test?
- What are the success criteria?

The simple go or no-go decision, together with the related reduction of risk, is normally the main justification for the expense of _____s. At the same time, however, such _____s can be used to test specific elements of a new product's marketing mix; possibly the version of the product itself, the promotional message and media spend, the distribution channels and the price.

a. 180SearchAssistant
b. Power III
c. Test market
d. Preadolescence

34. _____ or _____ data refers to selected population characteristics as used in government, marketing or opinion research, or the _____ profiles used in such research. Note the distinction from the term 'demography' Commonly-used _____ include race, age, income, disabilities, mobility (in terms of travel time to work or number of vehicles available), educational attainment, home ownership, employment status, and even location.

a. Demographic
b. AStore
c. African Americans
d. Albert Einstein

Chapter 4. Ethics and Social Responsibility in Marketing

35. The U.S. _____ is an agency of the United States Department of Health and Human Services and is responsible for regulating and supervising the safety of foods, dietary supplements, drugs, vaccines, biological medical products, blood products, medical devices, radiation-emitting devices, veterinary products, and cosmetics. The FDA also enforces section 361 of the Public Health Service Act and the associated regulations, including sanitation requirements on interstate travel as well as specific rules for control of disease on products ranging from pet turtles to semen donations for assisted reproductive medicine techniques.

The FDA is an agency within the United States Department of Health and Human Services responsible for protecting and promoting the nation's public health.

   a. 6-3-5 Brainwriting
   b. 180SearchAssistant
   c. Power III
   d. Food and Drug Administration

36. _____ is the idea that the moral worth of an action is determined solely by its contribution to overall utility: that is, its contribution to happiness or pleasure as summed among all persons. It is thus a form of consequentialism, meaning that the moral worth of an action is determined by its outcome: put simply, the ends justify the means. Utility, the good to be maximized, has been defined by various thinkers as happiness or pleasure (versus suffering or pain), although preference utilitarians like Peter Singer define it as the satisfaction of preferences.
   a. Albert Einstein
   b. Utilitarianism
   c. AStore
   d. African Americans

37. _____ is the study of when, why, how, where and what people do or do not buy products. It blends elements from psychology, sociology, social psychology, anthropology and economics. It attempts to understand the buyer decision making process, both individually and in groups. It studies characteristics of individual consumers such as demographics and behavioural variables in an attempt to understand people's wants. It also tries to assess influences on the consumer from groups such as family, friends, reference groups, and society in general.
   a. Multidimensional scaling
   b. Communal marketing
   c. Consumer confidence
   d. Consumer behavior

38. _____ or cause-related marketing refers to a type of marketing involving the cooperative efforts of a 'for profit' business and a non-profit organization for mutual benefit. The term is sometimes used more broadly and generally to refer to any type of marketing effort for social and other charitable causes, including in-house marketing efforts by non-profit organizations. _____ differs from corporate giving (philanthropy) as the latter generally involves a specific donation that is tax deductible, while _____ is a marketing relationship generally not based on a donation.
   a. Digital marketing
   b. Cause marketing
   c. Cause-related Marketing
   d. Global marketing

39. According to the American Marketing Association, _____ is the marketing of products that are presumed to be environmentally safe. Thus _____ incorporates a broad range of activities, including product modification, changes to the production process, packaging changes, as well as modifying advertising. Yet defining _____ is not a simple task where several meanings intersect and contradict each other; an example of this will be the existence of varying social, environmental and retail definitions attached to this term.
   a. Customer Interaction Tracker
   b. Value proposition
   c. Commercialization
   d. Green marketing

Chapter 4. Ethics and Social Responsibility in Marketing

40. An alternative phenomenon is the creation of external _____ by groups or individuals independent of the accountable organisation and typically without its encouragement. External _____ thus also attempt to blur the boundaries between organisations and society and to establish social accounting as a fluid two-way communication process. Companies are sought to be held accountable regardless of their approval.

   a. Power III
   b. Social audits
   c. 6-3-5 Brainwriting
   d. 180SearchAssistant

41. The general definition of an _____ is an evaluation of a person, organization, system, process, project or product. _____s are performed to ascertain the validity and reliability of information; also to provide an assessment of a system's internal control. The goal of an _____ is to express an opinion on the person/organization/system (etc) in question, under evaluation based on work done on a test basis.

   a. ACNielsen
   b. AMAX
   c. ADTECH
   d. Audit

42. The Oxford University Press defines _____ as 'marketing on a worldwide scale reconciling or taking commercial advantage of global operational differences, similarities and opportunities in order to meet global objectives.' Oxford University Press' Glossary of Marketing Terms.

Here are three reasons for the shift from domestic to _____ as given by the authors of the textbook, _____ Management--3rd Edition by Masaaki Kotabe and Kristiaan Helsen, 2004.

One of the product categories in which global competition has been easy to track is in U.S. automotive sales.

   a. Global marketing
   b. Guerrilla Marketing
   c. Digital marketing
   d. Diversity marketing

43. _____ is a pattern of resource use that aims to meet human needs while preserving the environment so that these needs can be met not only in the present, but in the indefinite future. The term was used by the Brundtland Commission which coined what has become the most often-quoted definition of _____ as development that 'meets the needs of the present without compromising the ability of future generations to meet their own needs.'

_____ is the way in which developing nations undergoing the process of industrialisation will avoid becoming like current industralised carbon intensive nations with high level of emissions.

_____ ties together concern for the carrying capacity of natural systems with the social challenges facing humanity.

   a. Sustainable development
   b. Power III
   c. Sustainable packaging
   d. Simple living

44. In finance, the _____s between two currencies specifies how much one currency is worth in terms of the other. It is the value of a foreign nation's currency in terms of the home nation's currency. For example an _____ of 102 Japanese yen to the United States dollar means that JPY 102 is worth the same as USD 1.

   a. ACNielsen
   b. ADTECH
   c. AMAX
   d. Exchange rate

45. The _____ is the primary unit in the United States Department of Justice, serving as both a federal criminal investigative body and a domestic intelligence agency. The FBI has investigative jurisdiction over violations of more than 200 categories of federal crime. Its motto is 'Fidelity, Bravery, Integrity,' corresponding to the 'FBI' initialism.
   a. Service mark
   b. Trademark dilution
   c. Federal Bureau of Investigation
   d. Foreign Corrupt Practices Act

46. _____ is a cohort which consists of those people born after the Generation X cohort. Its name is controversial and is synonymous with several alternative names including The Net Generation, Millennials, Echo Boomers, and iGeneration. _____ consists primarily of the offspring of the Generation Jones and Baby Boomers cohorts.
   a. Greatest Generation
   b. AStore
   c. Generation Y
   d. Generation X

Chapter 5. Consumer Behavior

1. _____ is a broad label that refers to any individuals or households that use goods and services generated within the economy. The concept of a _____ is used in different contexts, so that the usage and significance of the term may vary.

A _____ is a person who uses any product or service.

   a. Power III
   b. 180SearchAssistant
   c. 6-3-5 Brainwriting
   d. Consumer

2. _____ is the study of when, why, how, where and what people do or do not buy products. It blends elements from psychology, sociology, social psychology, anthropology and economics. It attempts to understand the buyer decision making process, both individually and in groups. It studies characteristics of individual consumers such as demographics and behavioural variables in an attempt to understand people's wants. It also tries to assess influences on the consumer from groups such as family, friends, reference groups, and society in general.

   a. Consumer confidence
   b. Multidimensional scaling
   c. Communal marketing
   d. Consumer behavior

3. An _____ is the manufacturing of a good or service within a category. Although _____ is a broad term for any kind of economic production, in economics and urban planning _____ is a synonym for the secondary sector, which is a type of economic activity involved in the manufacturing of raw materials into goods and products.

There are four key industrial economic sectors: the primary sector, largely raw material extraction industries such as mining and farming; the secondary sector, involving refining, construction, and manufacturing; the tertiary sector, which deals with services (such as law and medicine) and distribution of manufactured goods; and the quaternary sector, a relatively new type of knowledge _____ focusing on technological research, design and development such as computer programming, and biochemistry.

   a. ACNielsen
   b. AMAX
   c. ADTECH
   d. Industry

4. _____ is defined by the American _____ Association as the activity, set of institutions, and processes for creating, communicating, delivering, and exchanging offerings that have value for customers, clients, partners, and society at large. The term developed from the original meaning which referred literally to going to market, as in shopping, or going to a market to sell goods or services.

_____ practice tends to be seen as a creative industry, which includes advertising, distribution and selling.

   a. Marketing
   b. Marketing myopia
   c. Customer acquisition management
   d. Product naming

5. _____ is an American magazine published monthly by Consumers Union. It publishes reviews and comparisons of consumer products and services based on reporting and results from its in-house testing laboratory. It also publishes cleaning and general buying guides.

   a. Magalog
   b. Power III
   c. Crossing the Chasm
   d. Consumer Reports

Chapter 5. Consumer Behavior

6. A personal and cultural _____ is a relative ethic _____, an assumption upon which implementation can be extrapolated. A _____ system is a set of consistent _____s and measures that is soo not true. A principle _____ is a foundation upon which other _____s and measures of integrity are based.
   - a. Supreme Court of the United States
   - b. Package-on-Package
   - c. Perceptual maps
   - d. Value

7. In psychology, philosophy, and the cognitive sciences, _____ is the process of attaining awareness or understanding of sensory information. It is a task far more complex than was imagined in the 1950s and 1960s, when it was predicted that building perceiving machines would take about a decade, a goal which is still very far from fruition. The word _____ comes from the Latin words _____, percepio, meaning 'receiving, collecting, action of taking possession, apprehension with the mind or senses.'

   _____ is one of the oldest fields in psychology.

   - a. 180SearchAssistant
   - b. Power III
   - c. Groupthink
   - d. Perception

8. _____ in organizations and public policy is both the organizational process of creating and maintaining a plan; and the psychological process of thinking about the activities required to create a desired goal on some scale. As such, it is a fundamental property of intelligent behavior. This thought process is essential to the creation and refinement of a plan, or integration of it with other plans, that is, it combines forecasting of developments with the preparation of scenarios of how to react to them.
   - a. Power III
   - b. 180SearchAssistant
   - c. Planning
   - d. 6-3-5 Brainwriting

9. A _____ is a collection of symbols, experiences and associations connected with a product, a service, a person or any other artifact or entity.

   _____s have become increasingly important components of culture and the economy, now being described as 'cultural accessories and personal philosophies'.

   Some people distinguish the psychological aspect of a _____ from the experiential aspect.

   - a. Brand
   - b. Brand equity
   - c. Store brand
   - d. Brandable software

10. In economics, an externality or spillover of an economic transaction is an impact on a party that is not directly involved in the transaction. In such a case, prices do not reflect the full costs or benefits in production or consumption of a product or service. A positive impact is called an _____ benefit, while a negative impact is called an _____ cost.
    - a. ADTECH
    - b. AMAX
    - c. ACNielsen
    - d. External

11. _____ is a form of communication that typically attempts to persuade potential customers to purchase or to consume more of a particular brand of product or service. 'While now central to the contemporary global economy and the reproduction of global production networks, it is only quite recently that _____ has been more than a marginal influence on patterns of sales and production. The formation of modern _____ was intimately bound up with the emergence of new forms of monopoly capitalism around the end of the 19th and beginning of the 20th century as one element in corporate strategies to create, organize and where possible control markets, especially for mass produced consumer goods.

    a. AMAX
    b. ADTECH
    c. ACNielsen
    d. Advertising

12. _____ is systematic determination of merit, worth, and significance of something or someone using criteria against a set of standards. _____ often is used to characterize and appraise subjects of interest in a wide range of human enterprises, including the arts, criminal justice, foundations and non-profit organizations, government, health care, and other human services.

Depending on the topic of interest, there are professional groups which look to the quality and rigor of the _____ process.

    a. AMAX
    b. Evaluation
    c. ADTECH
    d. ACNielsen

13. Cognition is the scientific term for 'the process of thought.' Its usage varies in different ways in accord with different disciplines: For example, in psychology and _____ science it refers to an information processing view of an individual's psychological functions. Other interpretations of the meaning of cognition link it to the development of concepts; individual minds, groups, organizations, and even larger coalitions of entities, can be modelled as 'societies' (Society of Mind), which cooperate to form concepts.

The autonomous elements of each 'society' would have the opportunity to demonstrate emergent behavior in the face of some crisis or opportunity.

    a. Cognitive
    b. Power III
    c. 6-3-5 Brainwriting
    d. 180SearchAssistant

14. _____ is an uncomfortable feeling caused by holding two contradictory ideas simultaneously. The 'ideas' or 'cognitions' in question may include attitudes and beliefs, and also the awareness of one's behavior. The theory of _____ proposes that people have a motivational drive to reduce dissonance by changing their attitudes, beliefs, and behaviors, or by justifying or rationalizing their attitudes, beliefs, and behaviors.

    a. 180SearchAssistant
    b. Perception
    c. Power III
    d. Cognitive dissonance

15. _____ is the activity that the selling organization undertakes to reduce customer account defections. The success of this activity is when the customer account places an additional order before a 12-month period has expired. Note that ideally these orders will need to contribute similar financial amounts to the previous 12 months.

    a. Customer retention
    b. Customer base
    c. First-mover advantage
    d. Customer centricity

Chapter 5. Consumer Behavior

16. _____, a business term, is a measure of how products and services supplied by a company meet or surpass customer expectation. It is seen as a key performance indicator within business and is part of the four perspectives of a Balanced Scorecard.

In a competitive marketplace where businesses compete for customers, _____ is seen as a key differentiator and increasingly has become a key element of business strategy.

  a. Customer base
  b. Psychological pricing
  c. Supplier diversity
  d. Customer satisfaction

17. In the field of marketing, demographics, opinion research, and social research in general, _____ variables are any attributes relating to personality, values, attitudes, interests, or lifestyles. They are also called IAO variables . They can be contrasted with demographic variables (such as age and gender), behavioral variables (such as usage rate or loyalty), and bizographic variables (such as industry, seniority and functional area.)
  a. Marketing myopia
  b. Business-to-business
  c. Lifetime value
  d. Psychographic

18. Maslow's _____ is a theory in psychology, proposed by Abraham Maslow in his 1943 paper A Theory of Human Motivation, which he subsequently extended to include his observations of humans' innate curiosity.

Maslow studied what he called exemplary people such as Albert Einstein, Jane Addams, Eleanor Roosevelt, and Frederick Douglass rather than mentally ill or neurotic people, writing that 'the study of crippled, stunted, immature, and unhealthy specimens can yield only a cripple psychology and a cripple philosophy.' Maslow also studied the healthiest one percent of the college student population. In his book, The Farther Reaches of Human Nature, Maslow writes, 'By ordinary standards of this kind of laboratory research...

  a. Power III
  b. 180SearchAssistant
  c. 6-3-5 Brainwriting
  d. Hierarchy of needs

19. _____ is the set of reasons that determines one to engage in a particular behavior. The term is generally used for human _____ but, theoretically, it can be used to describe the causes for animal behavior as well
  a. Role playing
  b. 180SearchAssistant
  c. Power III
  d. Motivation

20. _____ is a term that has been used in various psychology theories, often in slightly different ways (e.g., Goldstein, Maslow, Rogers.) The term was originally introduced by the organismic theorist Kurt Goldstein for the motive to realise all of one's potentialities. In his view, it is the master motive--indeed, the only real motive a person has, all others being merely manifestations of it.
  a. Power III
  b. Self-actualization
  c. 6-3-5 Brainwriting
  d. 180SearchAssistant

21. The _____ is an independent agency of the United States government, created, directed, and empowered by Congressional statute , and with the majority of its commissioners appointed by the current President.
  a. Power III
  b. 180SearchAssistant
  c. 6-3-5 Brainwriting
  d. Federal Communications Commission

22. _____ or self identity refers to the global understanding a sentient being has of him or herself. It presupposes but can be distinguished from self-consciousness, which is simply an awareness of one's self. It is also more general than self-esteem, which is the purely evaluative element of the _____.
   a. Power III
   b. Need for cognition
   c. Self-concept
   d. 180SearchAssistant

23. A _____ is a signal or message embedded in another medium, designed to pass below the normal limits of the human mind's perception. These messages are unrecognizable by the conscious mind, but in certain situations can affect the subconscious mind and can negatively or positively influence subsequent later thoughts, behaviors, actions, attitudes, belief systems and value systems. The term subliminal means 'beneath a limen' (sensory threshold.)
   a. 180SearchAssistant
   b. 6-3-5 Brainwriting
   c. Power III
   d. Subliminal message

24. _____ is the subjective judgment that people make about the characteristics and severity of a risk. The phrase is most commonly used in reference to natural hazards and threats to the environment or health, such as nuclear power. Several theories have been proposed to explain why different people make different estimates of the dangerousness of risks.
   a. 180SearchAssistant
   b. Power III
   c. Risk perception
   d. 6-3-5 Brainwriting

25. _____ is a concept that denotes the precise probability of specific eventualities. Technically, the notion of _____ is independent from the notion of value and, as such, eventualities may have both beneficial and adverse consequences. However, in general usage the convention is to focus only on potential negative impact to some characteristic of value that may arise from a future event.
   a. Risk
   b. 6-3-5 Brainwriting
   c. 180SearchAssistant
   d. Power III

26. _____ is the process when people remember messages that are closer to their interests, values and beliefs more accurately, than those that are in contrast with their values and beliefs, selecting what to keep in the memory, narrowing the informational flow.

Such examples could include:

- A person may gradually reflect more positively on their time at school as they grow older
- A consumer might remember only the positive health benefits of a product they enjoy
- People tending to omit problems and disputes in past relationships
- A conspiracy theorist paying less attention to facts which do not aid their standpoint

   a. 180SearchAssistant
   b. Power III
   c. 6-3-5 Brainwriting
   d. Selective retention

27. In environmental modeling and especially in hydrology, a _____ model means a model that is acceptably consistent with observed natural processes, i.e. that simulates well, for example, observed river discharge. It is a key concept of the so-called Generalized Likelihood Uncertainty Estimation (GLUE) methodology to quantify how uncertain environmental predictions are.

Chapter 5. Consumer Behavior

a. 6-3-5 Brainwriting
c. 180SearchAssistant
b. Power III
d. Behavioral

28. _____, in marketing, consists of a consumer's commitment to repurchase the brand and can be demonstrated by repeated buying of a product or service or other positive behaviors such as word of mouth advocacy. True _____ implies that the consumer is willing, at least on occasion, to put aside their own desires in the interest of the brand. _____ has been proclaimed by some to be the ultimate goal of marketing.
   a. Brand awareness
   c. Trade Symbols
   b. Brand implementation
   d. Brand loyalty

29. A _____ is a process that can allow an organization to concentrate its limited resources on the greatest opportunities to increase sales and achieve a sustainable competitive advantage. A _____ should be centered around the key concept that customer satisfaction is the main goal.

A _____ is most effective when it is an integral component of corporate strategy, defining how the organization will successfully engage customers, prospects, and competitors in the market arena.

   a. Psychographic
   c. Cyberdoc
   b. Societal marketing
   d. Marketing strategy

30. In operant conditioning, _____ occurs when an event following a response causes an increase in the probability of that response occurring in the future. Response strength can be assessed by measures such as the frequency with which the response is made (for example, a pigeon may peck a key more times in the session), or the speed with which it is made (for example, a rat may run a maze faster.) The environment change contingent upon the response is called a reinforcer.
   a. Completely randomized designs
   c. Generic brands
   b. Relationship Management Application
   d. Reinforcement

31. An _____ is quite usually a standard guarantee from the seller of a product that specifies the extent to which the quality or performance of the product is assured and states the conditions under which the product can be returned, replaced, or repaired. It is often given in the form of a specific, written 'Warranty' document. However, a warranty may also arise by operation of law based upon the seller's description of the goods, and perhaps their source and quality, and any material deviation from that specification would violate the guarantee.
   a. Imperial Group v. Philip Morris
   c. Energy Star
   b. Office for Harmonization in the Internal Market
   d. Express warranty

32. _____ can be regarded as an outcome of mental processes (cognitive process) leading to the selection of a course of action among several alternatives. Every _____ process produces a final choice. The output can be an action or an opinion of choice.
   a. 6-3-5 Brainwriting
   c. Power III
   b. Decision making
   d. 180SearchAssistant

33. A _____ is a plan of action designed to achieve a particular goal.

_____ is different from tactics. In military terms, tactics is concerned with the conduct of an engagement while _____ is concerned with how different engagements are linked.

Chapter 5. Consumer Behavior

a. 180SearchAssistant
b. Power III
c. 6-3-5 Brainwriting
d. Strategy

34. _____ was originally coined by Austrian psychologist Alfred Adler in 1929. The current broader sense of the word dates from 1961.

In sociology, a _____ is the way a person lives.

a. 180SearchAssistant
b. 6-3-5 Brainwriting
c. Power III
d. Lifestyle

35. The acronym _____, is a psychographic segmentation. It was developed in the 1970s to explain changing U.S. values and lifestyles. It has since been reworked to enhance its ability to predict consumer behavior.

According to the _____ Framework, groups of people are arranged in a rectangle and are based on two dimensions. The vertical dimension segments people based on the degree to which they are innovative and have resources such as income, education, self-confidence, intelligence, leadership skills, and energy.

a. 180SearchAssistant
b. Power III
c. 6-3-5 Brainwriting
d. VALS

36. _____ is a concept that arose out of the theory of two-step flow of communication propounded by Paul Lazarsfeld and Elihu Katz. This theory is one of several models that try to explain the diffusion of innovations, ideas, or commercial products.

The opinion leader is the agent who is an active media user and who interprets the meaning of media messages or content for lower-end media users.

a. Opinion leadership
b. Intellectual property
c. ACNielsen
d. Elasticity

37. _____ is difficult to define. For example, in 1952, Alfred Kroeber and Clyde Kluckhohn compiled a list of 164 definitions of '_____' in _____: A Critical Review of Concepts and Definitions. However, the word '_____' is most commonly used in three basic senses:

- excellence of taste in the fine arts and humanities
- an integrated pattern of human knowledge, belief, and behavior that depends upon the capacity for symbolic thought and social learning
- the set of shared attitudes, values, goals, and practices that characterizes an institution, organization or group.

When the concept first emerged in eighteenth- and nineteenth-century Europe, it connoted a process of cultivation or improvement, as in agriculture or horticulture. In the nineteenth century, it came to refer first to the betterment or refinement of the individual, especially through education, and then to the fulfillment of national aspirations or ideals.

a. Albert Einstein
b. Culture
c. AStore
d. African Americans

38. _____ is a reference to the passing of information from person to person. Originally the term referred specifically to oral communication (literally words from the mouth), but now includes any type of human communication, such as face to face, telephone, email, and text messaging.

Word-of-mouth marketing, which encompasses a variety of subcategories, including buzz, blog, viral, grassroots, cause influencers and social media marketing, as well as ambassador programs, work with consumer-generated media and more, can be highly valued by product marketers.

a. Merchandise
b. Marketing communication
c. New Media Strategies
d. Word of mouth

39. A _____ is a sociological concept referring to a group to which an individual or another group is compared.

_____s are used in order to evaluate and determine the nature of a given individual or other group's characteristics and sociological attributes. It is the group to which the individual relates or aspires relate himself or self psychologically.

a. Mociology
b. Reference group
c. Power III
d. Minority

40. In sociology, anthropology and cultural studies, a _____ is a group of people with a culture (whether distinct or hidden) which differentiates them from the larger culture to which they belong. If a particular _____ is characterized by a systematic opposition to the dominant culture, it may be described as a counterculture. As Ken Gelder notes, _____s are social, with their own shared conventions, values and rituals, but they can also seem 'immersed' or self-absorbed--another feature that distinguishes them from countercultures.

a. 180SearchAssistant
b. Power III
c. 6-3-5 Brainwriting
d. Subculture

41. _____ or consumer demand or consumption is also known as personal consumption expenditure. It is the largest part of aggregate demand or effective demand at the macroeconomic level. There are two variants of consumption in the aggregate demand model, including induced consumption and autonomous consumption.

a. Power III
b. Value added
c. Deregulation
d. Consumer spending

42. _____ is the variety of human societies or cultures in a specific region, or in the world as a whole. (The term is also sometimes used to refer to multiculturalism within an organisation)

a. Power III
b. 180SearchAssistant
c. 6-3-5 Brainwriting
d. Cultural diversity

43. _____s is the social science that studies the production, distribution, and consumption of goods and services. The term _____s comes from the Ancient Greek οἰκονομία from οἶκος (oikos, 'house') + νόμος (nomos, 'custom' or 'law'), hence 'rules of the house(hold)'. Current _____ models developed out of the broader field of political economy in the late 19th century, owing to a desire to use an empirical approach more akin to the physical sciences.

Chapter 5. Consumer Behavior

a. Industrial organization
c. ACNielsen
b. ADTECH
d. Economic

44. _____ is the increase in the amount of the goods and services produced by an economy over time. It is conventionally measured as the percent rate of increase in real gross domestic product, or real GDP. Growth is usually calculated in real terms, i.e. inflation-adjusted terms, in order to net out the effect of inflation on the price of the goods and services produced.

a. Economic Growth
c. ACNielsen
b. AMAX
d. ADTECH

45. The U.S. _____ is an agency of the United States Department of Health and Human Services and is responsible for regulating and supervising the safety of foods, dietary supplements, drugs, vaccines, biological medical products, blood products, medical devices, radiation-emitting devices, veterinary products, and cosmetics. The FDA also enforces section 361 of the Public Health Service Act and the associated regulations, including sanitation requirements on interstate travel as well as specific rules for control of disease on products ranging from pet turtles to semen donations for assisted reproductive medicine techniques.

The FDA is an agency within the United States Department of Health and Human Services responsible for protecting and promoting the nation's public health.

a. 6-3-5 Brainwriting
c. Food and Drug Administration
b. Power III
d. 180SearchAssistant

Chapter 6. Organizational Markets and Buyer Behavior

1. _____ is the practice of individuals including commercial businesses, governments and institutions, facilitating the sale of their products or services to other companies or organizations that in turn resell them, use them as components in products or services they offer _____ is also called business-to-_____ for short. (Note that while marketing to government entities shares some of the same dynamics of organizational marketing, B2G Marketing is meaningfully different.)
   a. Disruptive technology
   b. Mass marketing
   c. Law of disruption
   d. Business marketing

2. A _____ is a company or individual that purchases goods or services with the intention of reselling them rather than consuming or using them. This is usually done for profit (but could be resold at a loss.) One example can be found in the industry of telecommunications, where companies buy excess amounts of transmission capacity or call time from other carriers and resell it to smaller carriers.
   a. Discontinuation
   b. Jobbing house
   c. Value-based pricing
   d. Reseller

3. _____ is a measure of the strength of a brand, product, service relative to competitive offerings. There is often a geographic element to the competitive landscape. In defining _____, you must see to what extent a product, brand, or firm controls a product category in a given geographic area.
   a. Market system
   b. Productivity
   c. Discretionary spending
   d. Market dominance

4. An _____ is the manufacturing of a good or service within a category. Although _____ is a broad term for any kind of economic production, in economics and urban planning _____ is a synonym for the secondary sector, which is a type of economic activity involved in the manufacturing of raw materials into goods and products.

   There are four key industrial economic sectors: the primary sector, largely raw material extraction industries such as mining and farming; the secondary sector, involving refining, construction, and manufacturing; the tertiary sector, which deals with services (such as law and medicine) and distribution of manufactured goods; and the quaternary sector, a relatively new type of knowledge _____ focusing on technological research, design and development such as computer programming, and biochemistry.
   a. AMAX
   b. ADTECH
   c. ACNielsen
   d. Industry

5. _____ is defined by the American _____ Association as the activity, set of institutions, and processes for creating, communicating, delivering, and exchanging offerings that have value for customers, clients, partners, and society at large. The term developed from the original meaning which referred literally to going to market, as in shopping, or going to a market to sell goods or services.

   _____ practice tends to be seen as a creative industry, which includes advertising, distribution and selling.
   a. Marketing myopia
   b. Customer acquisition management
   c. Product naming
   d. Marketing

Chapter 6. Organizational Markets and Buyer Behavior

6. _____s is the social science that studies the production, distribution, and consumption of goods and services. The term _____s comes from the Ancient Greek oá¼°κονομῖα from oá¼¶κος (oikos, 'house') + vΐŒμος (nomos, 'custom' or 'law'), hence 'rules of the house(hold)'. Current _____ models developed out of the broader field of political economy in the late 19th century, owing to a desire to use an empirical approach more akin to the physical sciences.

   a. Economic
   b. Industrial organization
   c. ADTECH
   d. ACNielsen

7. The _____ is a trilateral trade bloc in North America created by the governments of the United States, Canada, and Mexico. It superseded the Canada-United States Free Trade Agreement between the US and Canada.

   Following diplomatic negotiations dating back to 1990 between the three nations, the leaders met in San Antonio, Texas on December 17, 1992 to sign _____.

   a. Power III
   b. 180SearchAssistant
   c. 6-3-5 Brainwriting
   d. North American Free Trade Agreement

8. The _____ or _____ is used by business and government to classify and measure economic activity in Canada, Mexico and the United States. It has largely replaced the older Standard Industrial Classification system; however, certain government departments and agencies, such as the U.S. Securities and Exchange Commission (SEC), still use the SIC codes.

   The _____ numbering system is a six-digit code.

   a. 180SearchAssistant
   b. 6-3-5 Brainwriting
   c. Power III
   d. North American Industry Classification System

9. The _____ is an international organization whose stated aims are to facilitate cooperation in international law, international security, economic development, social progress, human rights and achieving world peace. The _____ was founded in 1945 after World War II to replace the League of Nations, to stop wars between countries and to provide a platform for dialogue.

   There are currently 192 member states, including nearly every recognized independent state in the world.

   a. ADTECH
   b. United Nations
   c. AMAX
   d. ACNielsen

10. _____ is a broad label that refers to any individuals or households that use goods and services generated within the economy. The concept of a _____ is used in different contexts, so that the usage and significance of the term may vary.

    A _____ is a person who uses any product or service.

    a. 6-3-5 Brainwriting
    b. 180SearchAssistant
    c. Power III
    d. Consumer

Chapter 6. Organizational Markets and Buyer Behavior

11. _____ is the study of when, why, how, where and what people do or do not buy products. It blends elements from psychology, sociology, social psychology, anthropology and economics. It attempts to understand the buyer decision making process, both individually and in groups. It studies characteristics of individual consumers such as demographics and behavioural variables in an attempt to understand people's wants. It also tries to assess influences on the consumer from groups such as family, friends, reference groups, and society in general.
    a. Communal marketing
    b. Consumer confidence
    c. Multidimensional scaling
    d. Consumer behavior

12. _____ or consumer demand or consumption is also known as personal consumption expenditure. It is the largest part of aggregate demand or effective demand at the macroeconomic level. There are two variants of consumption in the aggregate demand model, including induced consumption and autonomous consumption.
    a. Deregulation
    b. Power III
    c. Value added
    d. Consumer spending

13. In economics, _____ is the desire to own something and the ability to pay for it. The term _____ signifies the ability or the willingness to buy a particular commodity at a given point of time.
    a. Demand
    b. Market system
    c. Discretionary spending
    d. Market dominance

14. _____ is a term in economics, where demand for one good or service occurs as a result of demand for another. This may occur as the former is a part of production of the second. For example, demand for coal leads to _____ for mining, as coal must be mined for coal to be consumed.
    a. Power III
    b. 180SearchAssistant
    c. 6-3-5 Brainwriting
    d. Derived demand

15. In research, and particularly psychology, _____ refers to an experimental artifact where participants form an interpretation of the experiment's purpose and unconsciously change their behavior accordingly. Pioneering research was conducted on _____ by Martin Orne. Typically, they are considered a confounding variable, exerting an effect on behavior other than that intended by the experimenter.
    a. 6-3-5 Brainwriting
    b. Power III
    c. 180SearchAssistant
    d. Demand characteristics

16. The _____ is generally accepted as the use and specification of the four p's describing the strategic position of a product in the marketplace. One version of the origins of the _____ starts in 1948 when James Culliton said that a marketing decision should be a result of something similar to a recipe. This version continued in 1953 when Neil Borden, in his American Marketing Association presidential address, took the recipe idea one step further and coined the term 'Marketing-Mix'.
    a. 180SearchAssistant
    b. Power III
    c. 6-3-5 Brainwriting
    d. Marketing mix

17. _____ refers to a business or organization attempting to acquire goods or services to accomplish the goals of the enterprise. Though there are several organizations that attempt to set standards in the _____ process, processes can vary greatly between organizations. Typically the word '_____' is not used interchangeably with the word 'procurement', since procurement typically includes Expediting, Supplier Quality, and Traffic and Logistics (T'L) in addition to _____.

Chapter 6. Organizational Markets and Buyer Behavior

a. Drop shipping
c. Purchasing
b. Supply chain
d. Supply network

18. A supply chain is the system of organizations, people, technology, activities, information and resources involved in moving a product or service from _____ to customer. Supply chain activities transform natural resources, raw materials and components into a finished product that is delivered to the end customer. In sophisticated supply chain systems, used products may re-enter the supply chain at any point where residual value is recyclable.
    a. Bringin' Home the Oil
    c. Supplier
    b. Rebate
    d. Product line extension

19. A _____ is a type of business entity in which partners (owners) share with each other the profits or losses of the business undertaking in which all have invested. _____s are often favored over corporations for taxation purposes, as the _____ structure does not generally incur a tax on profits before it is distributed to the partners (i.e. there is no dividend tax levied.) However, depending on the _____ structure and the jurisdiction in which it operates, owners of a _____ may be exposed to greater personal liability than they would as shareholders of a corporation.
    a. Brand piracy
    c. Competition law
    b. Partnership
    d. Fair Debt Collection Practices Act

20. A _____, in marketing, procurement, and organizational studies, is a group of employees, family members, or members of any type of organization responsible for purchasing an item for the organization. In a business setting, major purchases typically require input from various parts of the organization, including finance, accounting, purchasing, information technology management, and senior management. Highly technical purchases, such as information systems or production equipment, also require the expertise of technical specialists.
    a. Packshot
    c. Commercialization
    b. Marketing myopia
    d. Buying center

21. _____ is systematic determination of merit, worth, and significance of something or someone using criteria against a set of standards. _____ often is used to characterize and appraise subjects of interest in a wide range of human enterprises, including the arts, criminal justice, foundations and non-profit organizations, government, health care, and other human services.

Depending on the topic of interest, there are professional groups which look to the quality and rigor of the _____ process.

    a. Evaluation
    c. ACNielsen
    b. AMAX
    d. ADTECH

22. _____ is a term commonly used to describe commerce transactions between businesses like the one between a manufacturer and a wholesaler or a wholesaler and a retailer i.e both the buyer and the seller are business entity.This is unlike business-to-consumers (B2C) which involve a business entity and end consumer, or business-to-government (B2G) which involve a business entity and government.

The volume of B2B transactions is much higher than the volume of B2C transactions. The primary reason for this is that in a typical supply chain there will be many B2B transactions involving subcomponent or raw materials, and only one B2C transaction, specifically sale of the finished product to the end customer.

a. Disruptive technology
b. Customer relationship management
c. Social marketing
d. Business-to-business

23. The _____ business model is one in which participants bid for products and services over the Internet. The functionality of buying and selling in an auction format is made possible through auction software which regulates the various processes involved.

Several types of _____s are possible.

a. Online auction
b. ACNielsen
c. AMAX
d. ADTECH

24. Electronic commerce, commonly known as _____ or eCommerce, consists of the buying and selling of products or services over electronic systems such as the Internet and other computer networks. The amount of trade conducted electronically has grown extraordinarily with wide-spread Internet usage. A wide variety of commerce is conducted in this way, spurring and drawing on innovations in electronic funds transfer, supply chain management, Internet marketing, online transaction processing, electronic data interchange (EDI), inventory management systems, and automated data collection systems.

a. AMAX
b. ACNielsen
c. ADTECH
d. E-commerce

25. A _____ is a tool used in industrial business-to-business procurement. It is a type of auction in which the role of the buyer and seller are reversed, with the primary objective to drive purchase prices downward. In an ordinary auction, buyers compete to obtain a good or service.

a. Materials management
b. Reverse auction
c. Vendor Managed Inventory
d. Fulfillment house

26. A _____ is a relatively new executive level position at a corporation, company, organization typically reporting directly to the CEO or board of directors. The _____ is responsible for a brand's image, experience, and promise, and propagating it throughout all aspects of the company. The brand officer oversees marketing, advertising, design, public relations and customer service departments.

a. Chief brand officer
b. Power III
c. Financial analyst
d. Chief executive officer

Chapter 7. Reaching Global Markets

1. The Oxford University Press defines _____ as 'marketing on a worldwide scale reconciling or taking commercial advantage of global operational differences, similarities and opportunities in order to meet global objectives.' Oxford University Press' Glossary of Marketing Terms.

Here are three reasons for the shift from domestic to _____ as given by the authors of the textbook, _____ Management--3rd Edition by Masaaki Kotabe and Kristiaan Helsen, 2004.

One of the product categories in which global competition has been easy to track is in U.S. automotive sales.

   a. Digital marketing
   c. Diversity marketing
   b. Global marketing
   d. Guerrilla Marketing

2. _____ is defined by the American _____ Association as the activity, set of institutions, and processes for creating, communicating, delivering, and exchanging offerings that have value for customers, clients, partners, and society at large. The term developed from the original meaning which referred literally to going to market, as in shopping, or going to a market to sell goods or services.

_____ practice tends to be seen as a creative industry, which includes advertising, distribution and selling.

   a. Marketing
   c. Customer acquisition management
   b. Product naming
   d. Marketing myopia

3. Consumer market research is a form of applied sociology that concentrates on understanding the behaviours, whims and preferences, of consumers in a market-based economy, and aims to understand the effects and comparative success of marketing campaigns. The field of consumer _____ as a statistical science was pioneered by Arthur Nielsen with the founding of the ACNielsen Company in 1923.

Thus _____ is the systematic and objective identification, collection, analysis, and dissemination of information for the purpose of assisting management in decision making related to the identification and solution of problems and opportunities in marketing.

   a. Focus group
   c. Logit analysis
   b. Marketing research process
   d. Marketing research

4. An _____ is the manufacturing of a good or service within a category. Although _____ is a broad term for any kind of economic production, in economics and urban planning _____ is a synonym for the secondary sector, which is a type of economic activity involved in the manufacturing of raw materials into goods and products.

There are four key industrial economic sectors: the primary sector, largely raw material extraction industries such as mining and farming; the secondary sector, involving refining, construction, and manufacturing; the tertiary sector, which deals with services (such as law and medicine) and distribution of manufactured goods; and the quaternary sector, a relatively new type of knowledge _____ focusing on technological research, design and development such as computer programming, and biochemistry.

Chapter 7. Reaching Global Markets

a. AMAX
b. ADTECH
c. ACNielsen
d. Industry

5. _____s is the social science that studies the production, distribution, and consumption of goods and services. The term _____s comes from the Ancient Greek oá¼°κονομῖα from oá¼¶κος (oikos, 'house') + vĨŒμος (nomos, 'custom' or 'law'), hence 'rules of the house(hold)'. Current _____ models developed out of the broader field of political economy in the late 19th century, owing to a desire to use an empirical approach more akin to the physical sciences.

a. Industrial organization
b. ADTECH
c. Economic
d. ACNielsen

6. _____ is a term used to describe how different aspects between economies are integrated. The basics of this theory were written by the Hungarian Economist Béla Balassa in the 1960s. As _____ increases, the barriers of trade between markets diminishes.

a. Economic integration
b. Incoterms
c. ADTECH
d. ACNielsen

7. _____ is the economic policy of restraining trade between nations, through methods such as tariffs on imported goods, restrictive quotas, and a variety of other restrictive government regulations designed to discourage imports, and prevent foreign take-over of local markets and companies. This policy is closely aligned with anti-globalization, and contrasts with free trade, where government barriers to trade are kept to a minimum. The term is mostly used in the context of economics, where _____ refers to policies or doctrines which 'protect' businesses and workers within a country by restricting or regulating trade with foreign nations.

a. Protectionism
b. Market economy
c. Black market
d. Gift economy

8. A _____ is a tax imposed on goods when they are moved across a political boundary. They are usually associated with protectionism, the economic policy of restraining trade between nations. For political reasons, _____s are usually imposed on imported goods, although they may also be imposed on exported goods.

a. Tariff
b. Monetary policy
c. Power III
d. Fiscal policy

9. The _____ is an international organization designed to supervise and liberalize international trade. The _____ came into being on 1 January 1995, and is the successor to the General Agreement on Tariffs and Trade (GATT), which was created in 1947, and continued to operate for almost five decades as a de facto international organization.

The _____ deals with the rules of trade between nations at a near-global level; it is responsible for negotiating and implementing new trade agreements, and is in charge of policing member countries' adherence to all the _____ agreements, signed by the majority of the world's trading nations and ratified in their parliaments.

a. BSI Group
b. Merchandise Mart
c. Population Reference Bureau
d. World Trade Organization

10. A personal and cultural _____ is a relative ethic _____, an assumption upon which implementation can be extrapolated. A _____ system is a set of consistent _____s and measures that is soo not true. A principle _____ is a foundation upon which other _____s and measures of integrity are based.

Chapter 7. Reaching Global Markets

a. Package-on-Package
b. Perceptual maps
c. Supreme Court of the United States
d. Value

11. _____ refer to a collection of facts usually collected as the result of experience, observation or experiment or a set of premises. This may consist of numbers, words particularly as measurements or observations of a set of variables. _____ are often viewed as a lowest level of abstraction from which information and knowledge are derived.

a. Mean
b. Sample size
c. Pearson product-moment correlation coefficient
d. Data

12. The _____ is the official currency of 16 out of 27 member states of the European Union (EU.) The states, known collectively as the Eurozone are: Austria, Belgium, Cyprus, Finland, France, Germany, Greece, Ireland, Italy, Luxembourg, Malta, the Netherlands, Portugal, Slovakia, Slovenia, and Spain. The currency is also used in a further five European countries, with and without formal agreements and is consequently used daily by some 327 million Europeans.

a. ACNielsen
b. ADTECH
c. Eurozone
d. Euro

13. The _____ is an economic and political union of 27 member states, located primarily in Europe. It was established by the Treaty of Maastricht on 1 November 1993 upon the foundations of the pre-existing European Economic Community. With almost 500 million citizens, the _____ combined generates an estimated 30% share (US$16.8 trillion in 2007) of the nominal gross world product.

a. ACNielsen
b. ADTECH
c. European Union
d. Eurozone

14. A _____ is a process that can allow an organization to concentrate its limited resources on the greatest opportunities to increase sales and achieve a sustainable competitive advantage. A _____ should be centered around the key concept that customer satisfaction is the main goal.

A _____ is most effective when it is an integral component of corporate strategy, defining how the organization will successfully engage customers, prospects, and competitors in the market arena.

a. Cyberdoc
b. Marketing strategy
c. Societal marketing
d. Psychographic

15. The _____ is a trilateral trade bloc in North America created by the governments of the United States, Canada, and Mexico. It superseded the Canada-United States Free Trade Agreement between the US and Canada.

Following diplomatic negotiations dating back to 1990 between the three nations, the leaders met in San Antonio, Texas on December 17, 1992 to sign _____.

a. Power III
b. North American Free Trade Agreement
c. 6-3-5 Brainwriting
d. 180SearchAssistant

16. A _____ is a plan of action designed to achieve a particular goal.

_____ is different from tactics. In military terms, tactics is concerned with the conduct of an engagement while _____ is concerned with how different engagements are linked.

Chapter 7. Reaching Global Markets

a. Strategy
b. 6-3-5 Brainwriting
c. 180SearchAssistant
d. Power III

17. _____ is a rivalry between individuals, groups, nations for territory, a niche, or allocation of resources. It arises whenever two or more parties strive for a goal which cannot be shared. _____ occurs naturally between living organisms which co-exist in the same environment.
    a. Price fixing
    b. Price competition
    c. Non-price competition
    d. Competition

18. _____ is a designated group of countries that have agreed to eliminate tariffs, quotas and preferences on most (if not all) goods and services traded between them. It can be considered the second stage of economic integration. Countries choose this kind of economic integration form if their economical structures are complementary.
    a. 180SearchAssistant
    b. Free trade area
    c. 6-3-5 Brainwriting
    d. Power III

19. A _____ is a wide ranging tax, tariff and _____ that often includes investment guarantees. _____s are frequently politically contentious since they may change economic customs and deepen interdependence with trade partners. Increasing efficiency through 'free trade' is a common goal.
    a. Power III
    b. General Agreement on Tariffs and Trade
    c. General Agreement on Trade in Services
    d. Trade pact

20. A _____ or transnational corporation is a corporation or enterprise that manages production or delivers services in more than one country. It can also be referred to as an international corporation.

The first modern MNC is generally thought to be the British East India Company, established in 1600.

    a. Checkoff
    b. HD share
    c. Hechsher
    d. Multinational corporation

21. Foreign _____ in its classic form is defined as a company from one country making a physical investment into building a factory in another country. It is the establishment of an enterprise by a foreigner. Its definition can be extended to include investments made to acquire lasting interest in enterprises operating outside of the economy of the investor.
    a. Fountain Fresh International
    b. Brash Brands
    c. VideoJug
    d. Direct investment

22. _____ is a measure of the strength of a brand, product, service relative to competitive offerings. There is often a geographic element to the competitive landscape. In defining _____, you must see to what extent a product, brand, or firm controls a product category in a given geographic area.
    a. Discretionary spending
    b. Market dominance
    c. Productivity
    d. Market system

23. A _____ is a collection of symbols, experiences and associations connected with a product, a service, a person or any other artifact or entity.

_____s have become increasingly important components of culture and the economy, now being described as 'cultural accessories and personal philosophies'.

Some people distinguish the psychological aspect of a _____ from the experiential aspect.

a. Store brand
b. Brand
c. Brand equity
d. Brandable software

24. _____ is a term commonly used to describe commerce transactions between businesses like the one between a manufacturer and a wholesaler or a wholesaler and a retailer i.e both the buyer and the seller are business entity.This is unlike business-to-consumers (B2C) which involve a business entity and end consumer, or business-to-government (B2G) which involve a business entity and government.

The volume of B2B transactions is much higher than the volume of B2C transactions. The primary reason for this is that in a typical supply chain there will be many B2B transactions involving subcomponent or raw materials, and only one B2C transaction, specifically sale of the finished product to the end customer.

a. Disruptive technology
b. Customer relationship management
c. Business-to-business
d. Social marketing

25. _____ is a broad label that refers to any individuals or households that use goods and services generated within the economy. The concept of a _____ is used in different contexts, so that the usage and significance of the term may vary.

A _____ is a person who uses any product or service.

a. 6-3-5 Brainwriting
b. 180SearchAssistant
c. Power III
d. Consumer

26. _____ or consumer demand or consumption is also known as personal consumption expenditure. It is the largest part of aggregate demand or effective demand at the macroeconomic level. There are two variants of consumption in the aggregate demand model, including induced consumption and autonomous consumption.

a. Consumer spending
b. Deregulation
c. Power III
d. Value added

27. _____ - an information and communication based electronic exchange environment - is a relatively new concept in marketing. Since physical boundaries no longer interfere with buy/sell decisions, the world has grown into several industry specific _____s which are integration of marketplaces through sophisticated computer and telecommunication technologies. The term _____ was introduced by Rayport and Sviokla in 1994 (see Rayport, Jeffrey F.

a. Kano model
b. Value chain
c. Market segment
d. Marketspace

28. _____ is the variety of human societies or cultures in a specific region, or in the world as a whole. (The term is also sometimes used to refer to multiculturalism within an organisation)

a. 180SearchAssistant
b. 6-3-5 Brainwriting
c. Power III
d. Cultural diversity

Chapter 7. Reaching Global Markets

29. _____ is an authority or agency in a country responsible for collecting and safeguarding _____ duties and for controlling the flow of goods including animals, personal effects and hazardous items in and out of a country. Depending on local legislation and regulations, the import or export of some goods may be restricted or forbidden, and the _____ agency enforces these rules. The _____ agency may be different from the immigration authority, which monitors persons who leave or enter the country, checking for appropriate documentation, apprehending people wanted by international arrest warrants, and impeding the entry of others deemed dangerous to the country.

   a. Registered trademark symbol
   b. Specific Performance
   c. Madrid system for the international registration of marks
   d. Customs

30. _____ is a process of gathering, analyzing, and dispensing information for tactical or strategic purposes. The _____ process entails obtaining both factual and subjective information on the business environments in which a company is operating or considering entering.

There are three ways of scanning the business environment:

- Ad-hoc scanning - Short term, infrequent examinations usually initiated by a crisis
- Regular scanning - Studies done on a regular schedule (say, once a year)
- Continuous scanning(also called continuous learning) - continuous structured data collection and processing on a broad range of environmental factors

Most commentators feel that in today's turbulent business environment the best scanning method available is continuous scanning.This allows the firm to :

-act quickly-take advantage of opportunities before competitors do-respond to environmental threats before significant damage is done

The Macro Environment

_____ usually refers just to the macro environment, but it can also include:-industry -competitor analysis -marketing research(consumer analysis) -New Product Development(product innovations)- the company's internal environment

Macro _____ involves analysing:

- The Economy

GDP per capitaeconomic growthunemployment]] rateinflation]] rateconsumer and investor confidenceinventory levelscurrency exchange ratesmerchandise trade balancefinancial and political health of trading partnersbalance of paymentsfuture trends

- Government

political climate - amount of government activitypolitical stability and riskgovernment debtbudget deficit or surpluscorporate and personal tax ratespayroll taxesimport tariffs and quotasexport restrictionsrestrictions on international financial flows

- Legal

minimum wage lawsenvironmental protection lawsworker safety lawsunion lawscopyright and patent lawsanti- monopoly lawsSunday closing lawsmunicipal licenceslaws that favour business investment

- Technology

efficiency of infrastructure, including: roads, ports, airports, rolling stock, hospitals, education, healthcare, communication, etc.industrial productivitynew manufacturing processesnew products and services of competitorsnew products and services of supply chain partnersany new technology that could impact the companycost and accessibility of electrical power

- Ecology
    - ecological concerns that affect the firms production processes
    - ecological concerns that affect customers' buying habits
    - ecological concerns that affect customers' perception of the company or product
- Socio-Cultural
    - demographic factors such as:
        - population size and distribution
        - age distribution
        - education levels
        - income levels
        - ethnic origins
        - religious affiliations
    - attitudes towards:
        - materialism, capitalism, free enterprise
        - individualism, role of family, role of government, collectivism
        - role of church and religion
        - consumerism
        - environmentalism
        - importance of work, pride of accomplishment
    - cultural structures including:
        - diet and nutrition
        - housing conditions
- Potential Suppliers
    - Labour supply
        - quantity of labour available
        - quality of labour available
        - stability of labour supply
        - wage expectations
        - employee turn-over rate
        - strikes and labour relations
        - educational facilities
    - Material suppliers
        - quality, quantity, price, and stability of material inputs
        - delivery delays
        - proximity of bulky or heavy material inputs
        - level of competition among suppliers
    - Service Providers
        - quantity, quality, price, and stability of service facilitators
        - special requirements
- Stakeholders
    - Lobbyists
    - Shareholders
    - Employees
    - Partners

Scanning these macro environmental variables for threats and opportunities requires that each issue be rated on two dimensions. It must be rated on its potential impact on the company, and rated on its likeliness of occurrence.

   a. ADTECH
   b. ACNielsen
   c. AMAX
   d. Environmental scanning

31. _____ is the use of governmental powers by government officials for illegitimate private gain. Misuse of government power for other purposes, such as repression of political opponents and general police brutality, is not considered _____. Neither are illegal acts by private persons or corporations not directly involved with the government.
   a. Political corruption
   b. Albert Einstein
   c. AStore
   d. African Americans

32. _____ is a form of communication that typically attempts to persuade potential customers to purchase or to consume more of a particular brand of product or service. 'While now central to the contemporary global economy and the reproduction of global production networks, it is only quite recently that _____ has been more than a marginal influence on patterns of sales and production. The formation of modern _____ was intimately bound up with the emergence of new forms of monopoly capitalism around the end of the 19th and beginning of the 20th century as one element in corporate strategies to create, organize and where possible control markets, especially for mass produced consumer goods.
   a. ACNielsen
   b. ADTECH
   c. AMAX
   d. Advertising

33. The _____ of 1977 (15 U.S.C. §§ 78dd-1, et seq.) is a United States federal law known primarily for two of its main provisions, one that addresses accounting transparency requirements under the Securities Exchange Act of 1934 and another concerning bribery of foreign officials.
   a. Copyright
   b. Trademark dilution
   c. Tenth Amendment
   d. Foreign Corrupt Practices Act

34. _____ means how much each individual receives, in monetary terms, of the yearly income generated in the country. This is what each citizen is to receive if the yearly national income is divided equally among everyone. _____ is usually reported in units of currency per year (e.g. US$20,000 per year.)
   a. 180SearchAssistant
   b. Power III
   c. 6-3-5 Brainwriting
   d. Per capita income

35. _____ refers to a business or organization attempting to acquire goods or services to accomplish the goals of the enterprise. Though there are several organizations that attempt to set standards in the _____ process, processes can vary greatly between organizations. Typically the word '_____' is not used interchangeably with the word 'procurement', since procurement typically includes Expediting, Supplier Quality, and Traffic and Logistics (T'L) in addition to _____.
   a. Drop shipping
   b. Supply chain
   c. Supply network
   d. Purchasing

36. _____ is the number of goods/services that can be purchased with a unit of currency. For example, if you had taken one dollar to a store in the 1950s, you would have been able to buy a greater number of items than you would today, indicating that you would have had a greater _____ in the 1950s. Currency can be either a commodity money, like gold or silver, or fiat currency like US dollars which are the world reserve currency.

Chapter 7. Reaching Global Markets

a. Power III
b. Purchasing power
c. 6-3-5 Brainwriting
d. 180SearchAssistant

37. In economics, _____ is the desire to own something and the ability to pay for it. The term _____ signifies the ability or the willingness to buy a particular commodity at a given point of time .

a. Market system
b. Market dominance
c. Demand
d. Discretionary spending

38. In finance, the _____s between two currencies specifies how much one currency is worth in terms of the other. It is the value of a foreign nation's currency in terms of the home nation's currency. For example an _____ of 102 Japanese yen to the United States dollar means that JPY 102 is worth the same as USD 1.

a. ACNielsen
b. ADTECH
c. Exchange rate
d. AMAX

39. Regulation refers to 'controlling human or societal behaviour by rules or restrictions.' Regulation can take many forms: legal restrictions promulgated by a government authority, self-regulation, social regulation (e.g. norms), co-regulation and market regulation. One can consider regulation as actions of conduct imposing sanctions (such as a fine.) This action of administrative law, or implementing _____ law, may be contrasted with statutory or case law.

a. Robinson-Patman Act
b. Regulatory
c. Right to Financial Privacy Act
d. Privacy law

40. _____ is exchange of capital, goods, and services across international borders or territories. In most countries, it represents a significant share of gross domestic product (GDP.) While _____ has been present throughout much of history , its economic, social, and political importance has been on the rise in recent centuries.

a. ADTECH
b. International trade
c. Incoterms
d. ACNielsen

41. _____ refers to 'controlling human or societal behaviour by rules or restrictions.' _____ can take many forms: legal restrictions promulgated by a government authority, self-_____, social _____, co-_____ and market _____. One can consider _____ as actions of conduct imposing sanctions (such as a fine.) This action of administrative law, or implementing regulatory law, may be contrasted with statutory or case law.

a. Non-conventional trademark
b. Rule of four
c. CAN-SPAM
d. Regulation

42. _____ are legal property rights over creations of the mind, both artistic and commercial, and the corresponding fields of law. Under _____ law, owners are granted certain exclusive rights to a variety of intangible assets, such as musical, literary, and artistic works; ideas, discoveries and inventions; and words, phrases, symbols, and designs. Common types of _____ include copyrights, trademarks, patents, industrial design rights and trade secrets.

a. Opinion leadership
b. ACNielsen
c. Elasticity
d. Intellectual property

43. The verb _____ or grant _____ means to give permission. The noun _____ refers to that permission as well as to the document memorializing that permission. _____ may be granted by a party to another party as an element of an agreement between those parties.

a. License
b. Power III
c. 180SearchAssistant
d. 6-3-5 Brainwriting

44. In economics, an _____ is any good or commodity, transported from one country to another country in a legitimate fashion, typically for use in trade. _____ goods or services are provided to foreign consumers by domestic producers. _____ is an important part of international trade.
   a. AMAX
   b. ADTECH
   c. ACNielsen
   d. Export

45. _____ refers to the methods of practicing and using another person's philosophy of business. The franchisor grants the independent operator the right to distribute its products, techniques, and trademarks for a percentage of gross monthly sales and a royalty fee. Various tangibles and intangibles such as national or international advertising, training, and other support services are commonly made available by the franchisor.
   a. Franchising
   b. Power III
   c. 180SearchAssistant
   d. Franchise fee

46. A _____ is an entity formed between two or more parties to undertake economic activity together. The parties agree to create a new entity by both contributing equity, and they then share in the revenues, expenses, and control of the enterprise. The venture can be for one specific project only, or a continuing business relationship such as the Fuji Xerox _____.
   a. Trademark attorney
   b. Consumer protection
   c. Joint venture
   d. Gripe site

47. _____s are versions of the same parent product that serve a segment of the target market and increase the variety of an offering. An example of a _____ is Coke vs. Diet Coke in same product category of soft drinks. This tactic is undertaken due to the brand loyalty and brand awareness they enjoy consumers are more likely to buy a new product that has a tried and trusted brand name on it.
   a. Product extension
   b. Brand recognition
   c. Web 2.0
   d. Distinctiveness

48. _____ is one of the four elements of marketing mix. An organization or set of organizations (go-betweens) involved in the process of making a product or service available for use or consumption by a consumer or business user.

The other three parts of the marketing mix are product, pricing, and promotion.

   a. Distribution
   b. Better Living Through Chemistry
   c. Japan Advertising Photographers' Association
   d. Comparison-Shopping agent

Chapter 7. Reaching Global Markets

49. _____ involves disseminating information about a product, product line, brand, or company. It is one of the four key aspects of the marketing mix. (The other three elements are product marketing, pricing, and distribution). P>_____ is generally sub-divided into two parts:

- Above the line _____: Promotion in the media (e.g. TV, radio, newspapers, Internet and Mobile Phones) in which the advertiser pays an advertising agency to place the ad
- Below the line _____: All other _____. Much of this is intended to be subtle enough for the consumer to be unaware that _____ is taking place. E.g. sponsorship, product placement, endorsements, sales _____, merchandising, direct mail, personal selling, public relations, trade shows

   a. Davie Brown Index
   b. Cashmere Agency
   c. Bottling lines
   d. Promotion

50. In economics, '_____' can refer to any kind of predatory pricing. However, the word is now generally used only in the context of international trade law, where _____ is defined as the act of a manufacturer in one country exporting a product to another country at a price which is either below the price it charges in its home market or is below its costs of production. The term has a negative connotation, but advocates of free markets see '_____' as beneficial for consumers and believe that protectionism to prevent it would have net negative consequences.

   a. Gold Key Matching Service
   b. Sample sales
   c. Hawkers
   d. Dumping

51. A grey market or _____ is the trade of a commodity through distribution channels which, while legal, are unofficial, unauthorized, or unintended by the original manufacturer. In contrast, a black market is the trade of goods and services that are illegal in themselves and/or distributed through illegal channels, such as the selling of stolen goods or illegal items such as heroin or unregistered handguns.

The two main types of grey market are imported manufactured goods that would be normally unavailable or more expensive in a certain country and unissued securities that are not yet traded in official markets.

   a. Customs union
   b. Green market
   c. Zone pricing
   d. Gray market

52. _____ is one of the four Ps of the marketing mix. The other three aspects are product, promotion, and place. It is also a key variable in microeconomic price allocation theory.
   a. Competitor indexing
   b. Price
   c. Relationship based pricing
   d. Pricing

Chapter 8. Marketing Research: From Information to Action

1. _____ is defined by the American _____ Association as the activity, set of institutions, and processes for creating, communicating, delivering, and exchanging offerings that have value for customers, clients, partners, and society at large. The term developed from the original meaning which referred literally to going to market, as in shopping, or going to a market to sell goods or services.

_____ practice tends to be seen as a creative industry, which includes advertising, distribution and selling.

- a. Customer acquisition management
- b. Marketing
- c. Product naming
- d. Marketing myopia

2. Consumer market research is a form of applied sociology that concentrates on understanding the behaviours, whims and preferences, of consumers in a market-based economy, and aims to understand the effects and comparative success of marketing campaigns. The field of consumer _____ as a statistical science was pioneered by Arthur Nielsen with the founding of the ACNielsen Company in 1923.

Thus _____ is the systematic and objective identification, collection, analysis, and dissemination of information for the purpose of assisting management in decision making related to the identification and solution of problems and opportunities in marketing.

- a. Marketing research process
- b. Focus group
- c. Marketing research
- d. Logit analysis

3. An _____ is the manufacturing of a good or service within a category. Although _____ is a broad term for any kind of economic production, in economics and urban planning _____ is a synonym for the secondary sector, which is a type of economic activity involved in the manufacturing of raw materials into goods and products.

There are four key industrial economic sectors: the primary sector, largely raw material extraction industries such as mining and farming; the secondary sector, involving refining, construction, and manufacturing; the tertiary sector, which deals with services (such as law and medicine) and distribution of manufactured goods; and the quaternary sector, a relatively new type of knowledge _____ focusing on technological research, design and development such as computer programming, and biochemistry.

- a. ACNielsen
- b. ADTECH
- c. AMAX
- d. Industry

4. _____ is a concept that denotes the precise probability of specific eventualities. Technically, the notion of _____ is independent from the notion of value and, as such, eventualities may have both beneficial and adverse consequences. However, in general usage the convention is to focus only on potential negative impact to some characteristic of value that may arise from a future event.
- a. 180SearchAssistant
- b. 6-3-5 Brainwriting
- c. Power III
- d. Risk

5. _____ is a method of direct marketing in which a salesperson solicits to prospective customers to buy products or services, either over the phone or through a subsequent face to face or Web conferencing appointment scheduled during the call.

Chapter 8. Marketing Research: From Information to Action

_____ can also include recorded sales pitches programmed to be played over the phone via automatic dialing. _____ has come under fire in recent years, being viewed as an annoyance by many.

a. Phishing
c. Directory Harvest Attack

b. Joe job
d. Telemarketing

6. _____ refer to a collection of facts usually collected as the result of experience, observation or experiment or a set of premises. This may consist of numbers, words particularly as measurements or observations of a set of variables. _____ are often viewed as a lowest level of abstraction from which information and knowledge are derived.

a. Mean
c. Sample size

b. Pearson product-moment correlation coefficient
d. Data

7. _____ is a process of gathering, modeling, and transforming data with the goal of highlighting useful information, suggesting conclusions, and supporting decision making. _____ has multiple facets and approaches, encompassing diverse techniques under a variety of names, in different business, science, and social science domains.

Data mining is a particular _____ technique that focuses on modeling and knowledge discovery for predictive rather than purely descriptive purposes.

a. Data analysis
c. Power III

b. 6-3-5 Brainwriting
d. 180SearchAssistant

8. _____ is a term used to describe a process of preparing and collecting data - for example as part of a process improvement or similar project.

_____ usually takes place early on in an improvement project, and is often formalised through a _____ Plan which often contains the following activity.

1. Pre collection activity - Agree goals, target data, definitions, methods
2. Collection - _____
3. Present Findings - usually involves some form of sorting analysis and/or presentation.

A formal _____ process is necessary as it ensures that data gathered is both defined and accurate and that subsequent decisions based on arguments embodied in the findings are valid . The process provides both a baseline from which to measure from and in certain cases a target on what to improve. Types of _____ 1-By mail questionnaires 2-By personal interview

- Six sigma
- Sampling (statistics)

a. Power III
c. 6-3-5 Brainwriting

b. Data collection
d. 180SearchAssistant

Chapter 8. Marketing Research: From Information to Action

9. _____ - an information and communication based electronic exchange environment - is a relatively new concept in marketing. Since physical boundaries no longer interfere with buy/sell decisions, the world has grown into several industry specific _____s which are integration of marketplaces through sophisticated computer and telecommunication technologies. The term _____ was introduced by Rayport and Sviokla in 1994 (see Rayport, Jeffrey F.
   a. Marketspace
   b. Market segment
   c. Kano model
   d. Value chain

10. The _____ is a project of the U.S. Census Bureau that replaces the long form in the decennial census. It is an ongoing statistical survey, and thus more current than information obtained by the long form. Many Americans found filling out the long form to be burdensome, intrusive, and its unpopularity was a factor in the declining response rate to the decennial census.
    a. American Community Survey
    b. AMAX
    c. ACNielsen
    d. ADTECH

11. The _____ is a professional association for marketers. As of 2008 it had approximately 40,000 members. There are collegiate chapters on 250 campuses.
    a. AMAX
    b. ADTECH
    c. ACNielsen
    d. American Marketing Association

12. The United States _____ is the government agency that is responsible for the United States Census. It also gathers other national demographic and economic data.
    a. 6-3-5 Brainwriting
    b. 180SearchAssistant
    c. Census Bureau
    d. Power III

13. In economics, an externality or spillover of an economic transaction is an impact on a party that is not directly involved in the transaction. In such a case, prices do not reflect the full costs or benefits in production or consumption of a product or service. A positive impact is called an _____ benefit, while a negative impact is called an _____ cost.
    a. ADTECH
    b. ACNielsen
    c. AMAX
    d. External

14. _____ is a term for unprocessed data, it is also known as primary data. It is a relative term _____ can be input to a computer program or used in manual analysis procedures such as gathering statistics from a survey.
    a. Shoppers Food ' Pharmacy
    b. Product manager
    c. Raw data
    d. Chief marketing officer

15. _____ is that part of statistical practice concerned with the selection of individual observations intended to yield some knowledge about a population of concern, especially for the purposes of statistical inference. Each observation measures one or more properties (weight, location, etc.) of an observable entity enumerated to distinguish objects or individuals.
    a. Sampling
    b. AStore
    c. Richard Buckminster 'Bucky' Fuller
    d. Sports Marketing Group

16. Combining Existing _____ Sources with New Primary Data Sources

Imagine that we could get hold of a good collection of surveys taken in earlier years, such as detailed studies about changes going on in this phase and hopefully additional studies in the years to come. Analyzing this data base over time could give us a good picture of what changes actually have taken place in the orientation of the population and of the extent to which new technical concepts did have an impact on subgroups of the population. Furthermore, data archives can help to prepare studies on change over time by monitoring what questions have been asked in earlier years and alerting principal investigators to important questions which should be repeated in planned research projects.

a. 6-3-5 Brainwriting
b. 180SearchAssistant
c. Secondary data
d. Power III

17. _____ or statistical induction comprises the use of statistics to make inferences concerning some unknown aspect of a population. It is distinguished from descriptive statistics.

Two schools of _____ are frequency probability and Bayesian inference.

a. Statistical inference
b. Probability sampling
c. Moving average
d. Standard score

18. The _____ is the government agency that is responsible for the United States Census. It also gathers other national demographic and economic data.
a. ADTECH
b. ACNielsen
c. United States Census Bureau
d. AMAX

19. _____s is the social science that studies the production, distribution, and consumption of goods and services. The term _____s comes from the Ancient Greek oá¼°κονομῖα from oá¼¶κος (oikos, 'house') + vĩŒµος (nomos, 'custom' or 'law'), hence 'rules of the house(hold)'. Current _____ models developed out of the broader field of political economy in the late 19th century, owing to a desire to use an empirical approach more akin to the physical sciences.
a. ACNielsen
b. Economic
c. ADTECH
d. Industrial organization

20. A _____ is a type of wholesale merchant business that buys goods and bulk products from importers, other wholesalers and then sells to retailers. _____s can deal in any commodity destined for the retail market. Typical categories are food, lumber, hardware, fuel, and textiles.
a. Tacit collusion
b. Chief privacy officer
c. Refusal to deal
d. Jobbing house

21. The _____ or _____ is used by business and government to classify and measure economic activity in Canada, Mexico and the United States. It has largely replaced the older Standard Industrial Classification system; however, certain government departments and agencies, such as the U.S. Securities and Exchange Commission (SEC), still use the SIC codes.

The _____ numbering system is a six-digit code.

a. 180SearchAssistant
b. Power III
c. 6-3-5 Brainwriting
d. North American Industry Classification System

22. A _____ is a structured collection of records or data that is stored in a computer system. The structure is achieved by organizing the data according to a _____ model. The model in most common use today is the relational model.
   a. 180SearchAssistant
   b. 6-3-5 Brainwriting
   c. Power III
   d. Database

23. In statistics, an _____ draws inferences about the effect of a treatment on subjects, where the assignment of subjects into a treated group versus a control group is outside the control of the investigator. This is in contrast with controlled experiments, such as randomized controlled trials, where each subject is randomly assigned to a treated group or a control group before the start of the treatment.

The assignment of treatments may be beyond the control of the investigator for a variety of reasons:

- A randomized experiment would violate ethical standards. Suppose one wanted to investigate the abortion-breast cancer hypothesis, which postulates a causal link between induced abortion and the incidence of breast cancer. In a hypothetical controlled experiment, one would start with a large subject pool of pregnant women and divide them randomly into a treatment group (receiving induced abortions) and a control group (bearing children), and then conduct regular cancer screenings for women from both groups. Needless to say, such an experiment would run counter to common ethical principles. (It would also suffer from various confounds and sources of bias, e.g., it would be impossible to conduct it as a blind experiment.) The published studies investigating the abortion-breast cancer hypothesis generally start with a group of women who already have received abortions. Membership in this 'treated' group is not controlled by the investigator: the group is formed after the 'treatment' has been assigned.

- The investigator may simply lack the requisite influence. Suppose a scientist wants to study the public health effects of a community-wide ban on smoking in public indoor areas.

   a. AMAX
   b. Observational study
   c. ACNielsen
   d. ADTECH

24. A _____ is a tool used to measure the viewing habits of TV and cable audiences.

The _____ is a 'box', about the size of a paperback book. The box is hooked up to each television set and is accompanied by a remote control unit.

   a. 180SearchAssistant
   b. 6-3-5 Brainwriting
   c. Power III
   d. People meter

25. In economics, business, retail, and accounting, a _____ is the value of money that has been used up to produce something, and hence is not available for use anymore. In economics, a _____ is an alternative that is given up as a result of a decision. In business, the _____ may be one of acquisition, in which case the amount of money expended to acquire it is counted as _____.

a. Variable cost
b. Fixed costs
c. Transaction cost
d. Cost

26. Mystery shopping or Mystery Consumer is a tool used by market research companies to measure quality of retail service or gather specific information about products and services. _____ posing as normal customers perform specific tasks-- such as purchasing a product, asking questions, registering complaints or behaving in a certain way - and then provide detailed reports or feedback about their experiences.

Mystery shopping began in the 1940s as a way to measure employee integrity.

a. Questionnaire
b. Market research
c. Mystery shoppers
d. Mystery shopping

27. _____ is either an activity of a living being (such as a human), consisting of receiving knowledge of the outside world through the senses, or the recording of data using scientific instruments. The term may also refer to any datum collected during this activity.

The scientific method requires _____s of nature to formulate and test hypotheses.

a. ACNielsen
b. ADTECH
c. AMAX
d. Observation

28. A _____ is a research instrument consisting of a series of questions and other prompts for the purpose of gathering information from respondents. Although they are often designed for statistical analysis of the responses, this is not always the case. The _____ was invented by Sir Francis Galton.

a. Mystery shopping
b. Mystery shoppers
c. Market research
d. Questionnaire

29. _____ is a broad label that refers to any individuals or households that use goods and services generated within the economy. The concept of a _____ is used in different contexts, so that the usage and significance of the term may vary.

A _____ is a person who uses any product or service.

a. Power III
b. 180SearchAssistant
c. 6-3-5 Brainwriting
d. Consumer

30. A _____ is a form of qualitative research in which a group of people are asked about their attitude towards a product, service, concept, advertisement, idea, or packaging. Questions are asked in an interactive group setting where participants are free to talk with other group members.

Ernest Dichter originated the idea of having a 'group therapy' for products and this process is what became known as a _____.

a. Focus group
b. Cross tabulation
c. Logit analysis
d. Marketing research process

31. _____ is systematic determination of merit, worth, and significance of something or someone using criteria against a set of standards. _____ often is used to characterize and appraise subjects of interest in a wide range of human enterprises, including the arts, criminal justice, foundations and non-profit organizations, government, health care, and other human services.

Depending on the topic of interest, there are professional groups which look to the quality and rigor of the _____ process.

a. ADTECH
b. ACNielsen
c. Evaluation
d. AMAX

32. A _____, in the field of business and marketing, is a geographic region or demographic group used to gauge the viability of a product or service in the mass market prior to a wide scale roll-out. The criteria used to judge the acceptability of a _____ region or group include:

1. a population that is demographically similar to the proposed target market; and
2. relative isolation from densely populated media markets so that advertising to the test audience can be efficient and economical.

The _____ ideally aims to duplicate 'everything' - promotion and distribution as well as `product' - on a smaller scale. The technique replicates, typically in one area, what is planned to occur in a national launch; and the results are very carefully monitored, so that they can be extrapolated to projected national results. The `area' may be any one of the following:

- Television area
- Test town
- Residential neighborhood
- Test site

A number of decisions have to be taken about any _____:

- Which _____?
- What is to be tested?
- How long a test?
- What are the success criteria?

The simple go or no-go decision, together with the related reduction of risk, is normally the main justification for the expense of _____s. At the same time, however, such _____s can be used to test specific elements of a new product's marketing mix; possibly the version of the product itself, the promotional message and media spend, the distribution channels and the price.

a. Power III
b. Preadolescence
c. Test market
d. 180SearchAssistant

33. _____ is the process of extracting hidden patterns from data. As more data is gathered, with the amount of data doubling every three years, _____ is becoming an increasingly important tool to transform this data into information. It is commonly used in a wide range of profiling practices, such as marketing, surveillance, fraud detection and scientific discovery.

a. Data mining
b. Power III
c. 180SearchAssistant
d. Structure mining

34. _____ is the use of an object (typically referred to as an RFID tag) applied to or incorporated into a product, animal, or person for the purpose of identification and tracking using radio waves. Some tags can be read from several meters away and beyond the line of sight of the reader.

Most RFID tags contain at least two parts.

a. 6-3-5 Brainwriting
b. Radio-frequency identification
c. Power III
d. 180SearchAssistant

35. _____ is the process of estimation in unknown situations. Prediction is a similar, but more general term. Both can refer to estimation of time series, cross-sectional or longitudinal data.

a. Forecasting
b. Power III
c. 6-3-5 Brainwriting
d. 180SearchAssistant

Chapter 9. Identifying Market Segments and Targets

1. _____ is defined by the American _____ Association as the activity, set of institutions, and processes for creating, communicating, delivering, and exchanging offerings that have value for customers, clients, partners, and society at large. The term developed from the original meaning which referred literally to going to market, as in shopping, or going to a market to sell goods or services.

_____ practice tends to be seen as a creative industry, which includes advertising, distribution and selling.

- a. Customer acquisition management
- b. Marketing myopia
- c. Product naming
- d. Marketing

2. _____ is a rivalry between individuals, groups, nations for territory, a niche, or allocation of resources. It arises whenever two or more parties strive for a goal which cannot be shared. _____ occurs naturally between living organisms which co-exist in the same environment.
- a. Non-price competition
- b. Price competition
- c. Competition
- d. Price fixing

3. _____ was originally coined by Austrian psychologist Alfred Adler in 1929. The current broader sense of the word dates from 1961.

In sociology, a _____ is the way a person lives.

- a. 180SearchAssistant
- b. 6-3-5 Brainwriting
- c. Power III
- d. Lifestyle

4. A _____ is a subgroup of people or organizations sharing one or more characteristics that cause them to have similar product and/or service needs. A true _____ meets all of the following criteria: it is distinct from other segments (different segments have different needs), it is homogeneous within the segment (exhibits common needs); it responds similarly to a market stimulus, and it can be reached by a market intervention. The term is also used when consumers with identical product and/or service needs are divided up into groups so they can be charged different amounts.
- a. Customer insight
- b. Production orientation
- c. Commercial planning
- d. Market segment

5. _____ in economics and business is the result of an exchange and from that trade we assign a numerical monetary value to a good, service or asset. If I trade 4 apples for an orange, the _____ of an orange is 4 - apples. Inversely, the _____ of an apple is 1/4 oranges.
- a. Pricing
- b. Discounts and allowances
- c. Contribution margin-based pricing
- d. Price

6. Competitiveness is a comparative concept of the ability and performance of a firm, sub-sector or country to sell and supply goods and/or services in a given market. Although widely used in economics and business management, the usefulness of the concept, particularly in the context of national competitiveness, is vigorously disputed by economists, such as Paul Krugman .

The term may also be applied to markets, where it is used to refer to the extent to which the market structure may be regarded as perfectly _____.

Chapter 9. Identifying Market Segments and Targets

a. Free trade zone
b. Geographical pricing
c. Customs union
d. Competitive

7. In marketing, _____ is the process of distinguishing the differences of a product or offering from others, to make it more attractive to a particular target market. This involves differentiating it from competitors' products as well as one's own product offerings.

Differentiation is a source of competitive advantage.

a. Marketing myopia
b. Corporate image
c. Product differentiation
d. Packshot

8. _____ is a lightweight markup language, originally created by John Gruber and Aaron Swartz to help maximum readability and 'publishability' of both its input and output forms. The language takes many cues from existing conventions for marking up plain text in email. _____ converts its marked-up text input to valid, well-formed XHTML and replaces left-pointing angle brackets ('<') and ampersands with their corresponding character entity references.

a. Power III
b. 6-3-5 Brainwriting
c. 180SearchAssistant
d. Markdown

9. On an intranet or B2E Enterprise Web portals, personalization is often based on user attributes such as department, functional area, or role. The term _____ in this context refers to the ability of users to modify the page layout or specify what content should be displayed.

There are two categories of personalizations:

1. Rule-based
2. Content-based

Web personalization models include rules-based filtering, based on 'if this, then that' rules processing, and collaborative filtering, which serves relevant material to customers by combining their own personal preferences with the preferences of like-minded others. Collaborative filtering works well for books, music, video, etc.

a. Cashmere Agency
b. Movin'
c. Self branding
d. Customization

10. _____ is a market coverage strategy in which a firm decides to ignore market segment differences and go after the whole market with one offer.it is type of marketing (or attempting to sell through persuasion) of a product to a wide audience. The idea is to broadcast a message that will reach the largest number of people possible. Traditionally _____ has focused on radio, television and newspapers as the medium used to reach this broad audience.

a. Cyberdoc
b. Mass marketing
c. Marketspace
d. Business-to-consumer

11. _____, in marketing, manufacturing, and management, is the use of flexible computer-aided manufacturing systems to produce custom output. Those systems combine the low unit costs of mass production processes with the flexibility of individual customization.

Chapter 9. Identifying Market Segments and Targets

'_____' is the new frontier in business competition for both manufacturing and service industries.

    a. Flanking marketing warfare strategies
    b. Vertical integration
    c. Power III
    d. Mass customization

12. _____ is the term used to describe a situation where different entities cooperate advantageously for a final outcome. Simply defined, it means that the whole is greater than the sum of its parts. The essence of _____ is to value differences.
    a. 180SearchAssistant
    b. Power III
    c. 6-3-5 Brainwriting
    d. Synergy

13. _____ is a form of marketing developed from direct response marketing campaigns conducted in the 1970's and 1980's which emphasizes customer retention and satisfaction, rather than a dominant focus on 'point of sale' transactions.

_____ differs from other forms of marketing in that it recognizes the long term value to the firm of keeping customers, as opposed to direct or 'Intrusion' marketing, which focuses upon acquisition of new clients by targeting majority demographics based upon prospective client lists.

_____ refers to long-term and mutually beneficial arrangement wherein both buyer and seller focus on value enhancement through the certain of more satisfying exchange. This approach attempts to transcend the simple purchase exchange process with customer to make more meaningful and richer contact by providing a more holistic, personalized purchase, and use orn consumption experience to create stronger ties.

    a. Global marketing
    b. Relationship marketing
    c. Diversity marketing
    d. Guerrilla Marketing

14. A personal and cultural _____ is a relative ethic _____, an assumption upon which implementation can be extrapolated. A _____ system is a set of consistent _____s and measures that is soo not true. A principle _____ is a foundation upon which other _____s and measures of integrity are based.
    a. Supreme Court of the United States
    b. Package-on-Package
    c. Perceptual maps
    d. Value

15. In marketing and strategy, _____ refers to a reduction in the sales volume, sales revenue, or market share of one product as a result of the introduction of a new product by the same producer.

For example, if Coca Cola were to introduce a similar product (say, Diet Coke or Cherry Coke), this new product could take some of the sales away from the original Coke. _____ is a key consideration in product portfolio analysis.

    a. Business-to-consumer
    b. Co-marketing
    c. Marketing
    d. Cannibalization

16. _____ is a broad label that refers to any individuals or households that use goods and services generated within the economy. The concept of a _____ is used in different contexts, so that the usage and significance of the term may vary.

Chapter 9. Identifying Market Segments and Targets

A _____ is a person who uses any product or service.

a. 6-3-5 Brainwriting
b. 180SearchAssistant
c. Power III
d. Consumer

17. In economics, business, retail, and accounting, a _____ is the value of money that has been used up to produce something, and hence is not available for use anymore. In economics, a _____ is an alternative that is given up as a result of a decision. In business, the _____ may be one of acquisition, in which case the amount of money expended to acquire it is counted as _____.

a. Fixed costs
b. Transaction cost
c. Variable cost
d. Cost

18. The break-even point for a product is the point where total revenue received equals the total costs associated with the sale of the product (TR=TC.) A break-even point is typically calculated in order for businesses to determine if it would be profitable to sell a proposed product, as opposed to attempting to modify an existing product instead so it can be made lucrative. _____ can also be used to analyse the potential profitability of an expenditure in a sales-based business.

In _____, margin of safety is how much output or sales level can fall before a business reaches its break-even point (BEP).

a. Price skimming
b. Contribution margin-based pricing
c. Break even analysis
d. Pay Per Sale

19. _____ or _____ data refers to selected population characteristics as used in government, marketing or opinion research, or the _____ profiles used in such research. Note the distinction from the term 'demography' Commonly-used _____ include race, age, income, disabilities, mobility (in terms of travel time to work or number of vehicles available), educational attainment, home ownership, employment status, and even location.

a. AStore
b. Demographic
c. African Americans
d. Albert Einstein

20. _____ is the study of the Earth and its lands, features, inhabitants, and phenomena. A literal translation would be 'to describe or write about the Earth'. The first person to use the word '_____' was Eratosthenes.

a. 6-3-5 Brainwriting
b. Power III
c. 180SearchAssistant
d. Geography

21. In the field of marketing, demographics, opinion research, and social research in general, _____ variables are any attributes relating to personality, values, attitudes, interests, or lifestyles. They are also called IAO variables. They can be contrasted with demographic variables (such as age and gender), behavioral variables (such as usage rate or loyalty), and bizographic variables (such as industry, seniority and functional area.)

a. Lifetime value
b. Business-to-business
c. Marketing myopia
d. Psychographic

Chapter 9. Identifying Market Segments and Targets

22. _____ is the process or cycle of introducing a new product into the market. The actual launch of a new product is the final stage of new product development, and the one where the most money will have to be spent for advertising, sales promotion, and other marketing efforts. In the case of a new consumer packaged good, costs will be at least $ 10 million, but can reach up to $ 200 million.
   a. Confusion marketing
   b. Customer Interaction Tracker
   c. Commercialization
   d. Sweepstakes

23. An _____ is the manufacturing of a good or service within a category. Although _____ is a broad term for any kind of economic production, in economics and urban planning _____ is a synonym for the secondary sector, which is a type of economic activity involved in the manufacturing of raw materials into goods and products.

   There are four key industrial economic sectors: the primary sector, largely raw material extraction industries such as mining and farming; the secondary sector, involving refining, construction, and manufacturing; the tertiary sector, which deals with services (such as law and medicine) and distribution of manufactured goods; and the quaternary sector, a relatively new type of knowledge _____ focusing on technological research, design and development such as computer programming, and biochemistry.

   a. AMAX
   b. ADTECH
   c. ACNielsen
   d. Industry

24. _____s are used in open sentences. For instance, in the formula x + 1 = 5, x is a _____ which represents an 'unknown' number. _____s are often represented by letters of the Roman alphabet, or those of other alphabets, such as Greek, and use other special symbols.
   a. Book of business
   b. Variable
   c. Personalization
   d. Quantitative

25. _____ is a contract between two parties, one being the employer and the other being the employee. An employee may be defined as: 'A person in the service of another under any contract of hire, express or implied, oral or written, where the employer has the power or right to control and direct the employee in the material details of how the work is to be performed.' Black's Law Dictionary page 471 (5th ed. 1979.)
   a. AMAX
   b. ACNielsen
   c. ADTECH
   d. Employment

26. In the United States, the Office of Management and Budget (OMB) has produced a formal definition of metropolitan areas. These are referred to as '_____s' (_____s) and 'Combined Statistical Areas.' An earlier version of the _____ was the 'Standard _____' (SMetropolitan statistical area.) _____s are composed of counties and for some county equivalents.
   a. Power III
   b. 180SearchAssistant
   c. Metropolitan statistical area
   d. Race and ethnicity in the United States Census

27. The _____ or _____ is used by business and government to classify and measure economic activity in Canada, Mexico and the United States. It has largely replaced the older Standard Industrial Classification system; however, certain government departments and agencies, such as the U.S. Securities and Exchange Commission (SEC), still use the SIC codes.

   The _____ numbering system is a six-digit code.

Chapter 9. Identifying Market Segments and Targets

a. 180SearchAssistant
b. 6-3-5 Brainwriting
c. Power III
d. North American Industry Classification System

28. _____ is a form of communication that typically attempts to persuade potential customers to purchase or to consume more of a particular brand of product or service. 'While now central to the contemporary global economy and the reproduction of global production networks, it is only quite recently that _____ has been more than a marginal influence on patterns of sales and production. The formation of modern _____ was intimately bound up with the emergence of new forms of monopoly capitalism around the end of the 19th and beginning of the 20th century as one element in corporate strategies to create, organize and where possible control markets, especially for mass produced consumer goods.

a. ACNielsen
b. Advertising
c. AMAX
d. ADTECH

29. _____ is a business term meaning the market segment to which a particular good or service is marketed. It is mainly defined by age, gender, geography, socio-economic grouping, technographic, or any other combination of demographics. It is generally studied and mapped by an organization through lists and reports containing demographic information that may have an effect on the marketing of key products or services.

a. Brando
b. Category Development Index
c. Distribution
d. Market specialization

30. A _____ is a process that can allow an organization to concentrate its limited resources on the greatest opportunities to increase sales and achieve a sustainable competitive advantage. A _____ should be centered around the key concept that customer satisfaction is the main goal.

A _____ is most effective when it is an integral component of corporate strategy, defining how the organization will successfully engage customers, prospects, and competitors in the market arena.

a. Societal marketing
b. Cyberdoc
c. Psychographic
d. Marketing strategy

31. In marketing, _____ has come to mean the process by which marketers try to create an image or identity in the minds of their target market for its product, brand, or organization. It is the 'relative competitive comparison' their product occupies in a given market as perceived by the target market.

Re-_____ involves changing the identity of a product, relative to the identity of competing products, in the collective minds of the target market.

a. Containerization
b. GE matrix
c. Moratorium
d. Positioning

32. A _____ is a plan of action designed to achieve a particular goal.

_____ is different from tactics. In military terms, tactics is concerned with the conduct of an engagement while _____ is concerned with how different engagements are linked.

Chapter 9. Identifying Market Segments and Targets

a. Strategy
c. 180SearchAssistant

b. 6-3-5 Brainwriting
d. Power III

33. A _____ is a collection of symbols, experiences and associations connected with a product, a service, a person or any other artifact or entity.

_____s have become increasingly important components of culture and the economy, now being described as 'cultural accessories and personal philosophies'.

Some people distinguish the psychological aspect of a _____ from the experiential aspect.

a. Store brand
c. Brand equity

b. Brandable software
d. Brand

34. Perceptual mapping is a graphics technique used by asset marketers that attempts to visually display the perceptions of customers or potential customers. Typically the position of a product, product line, brand, or company is displayed relative to their competition.

_____ can have any number of dimensions but the most common is two dimensions.

a. Comparison-Shopping agent
c. Developed country

b. Retail floor planning
d. Perceptual maps

35. There are many important decisions about product and service development and marketing. In the process of product development and marketing we should focus on strategic decisions about product attributes, product branding, product packaging, product labeling and product support services. But product strategy also calls for building a _____.

a. Macromarketing
c. Pinstorm

b. Technology acceptance model
d. Product line

Chapter 10. Developing New Products and Services

1. _____ - an information and communication based electronic exchange environment - is a relatively new concept in marketing. Since physical boundaries no longer interfere with buy/sell decisions, the world has grown into several industry specific _____s which are integration of marketplaces through sophisticated computer and telecommunication technologies. The term _____ was introduced by Rayport and Sviokla in 1994 (see Rayport, Jeffrey F.
   a. Market segment
   b. Kano model
   c. Value chain
   d. Marketspace

2. There are many important decisions about product and service development and marketing. In the process of product development and marketing we should focus on strategic decisions about product attributes, product branding, product packaging, product labeling and product support services. But product strategy also calls for building a _____.
   a. Pinstorm
   b. Technology acceptance model
   c. Product line
   d. Macromarketing

3. _____ is defined by the American _____ Association as the activity, set of institutions, and processes for creating, communicating, delivering, and exchanging offerings that have value for customers, clients, partners, and society at large. The term developed from the original meaning which referred literally to going to market, as in shopping, or going to a market to sell goods or services.

   _____ practice tends to be seen as a creative industry, which includes advertising, distribution and selling.

   a. Product naming
   b. Marketing
   c. Customer acquisition management
   d. Marketing myopia

4. In business and engineering, _____ is the term used to describe the complete process of bringing a new product or service to market. There are two parallel paths involved in the _____ process: one involves the idea generation, product design, and detail engineering; the other involves market research and marketing analysis. Companies typically see _____ as the first stage in generating and commercializing new products within the overall strategic process of product life cycle management used to maintain or grow their market share.
   a. New product development
   b. Product optimization
   c. Specification
   d. Product development

5. In business and engineering, new _____ is the term used to describe the complete process of bringing a new product or service to market. There are two parallel paths involved in the Nproduct development process: one involves the idea generation, product design, and detail engineering; the other involves market research and marketing analysis. Companies typically see new _____ as the first stage in generating and commercializing new products within the overall strategic process of product life cycle management used to maintain or grow their market share.
   a. Product development
   b. New product development
   c. New product screening
   d. Specification tree

6. _____ is a term commonly used to describe commerce transactions between businesses like the one between a manufacturer and a wholesaler or a wholesaler and a retailer i.e both the buyer and the seller are business entity.This is unlike business-to-consumers (B2C) which involve a business entity and end consumer, or business-to-government (B2G) which involve a business entity and government.

The volume of B2B transactions is much higher than the volume of B2C transactions. The primary reason for this is that in a typical supply chain there will be many B2B transactions involving subcomponent or raw materials, and only one B2C transaction, specifically sale of the finished product to the end customer.

Chapter 10. Developing New Products and Services

a. Social marketing
b. Customer relationship management
c. Disruptive technology
d. Business-to-business

7. _____ is a broad label that refers to any individuals or households that use goods and services generated within the economy. The concept of a _____ is used in different contexts, so that the usage and significance of the term may vary.

A _____ is a person who uses any product or service.

a. 6-3-5 Brainwriting
b. 180SearchAssistant
c. Power III
d. Consumer

8. _____ are final goods specifically intended for the mass market. For instance, _____ do not include investment assets, like precious antiques, even though these antiques are final goods.

Manufactured goods are goods that have been processed by way of machinery.

a. Consumer goods
b. Free good
c. Power III
d. Durable good

9. In economics, a _____ or a hard good is a good which does not quickly wear out it yields services or utility over time rather than being completely used up when used once. Most goods are therefore _____s to a certain degree. These are goods that can last for a relatively long time, such as refrigerators, cars, and DVD players.

a. Durable good
b. Power III
c. Free good
d. Luxury good

10. _____ is used in marketing to describe the inability to assess the value gained from engaging in an activity using any tangible evidence. It is often used to describe services where there isn't a tangible product that the customer can purchase, that can be seen, tasted or touched.

Other key characteristics of services include perishability, inseparability and variability.

a. Individual branding
b. Inseparability
c. Intangibility
d. Automated surveys

11. _____ is an advertisement in which a particular product specifically mentions a competitor by name for the express purpose of showing why the competitor is inferior to the product naming it.

This should not be confused with parody advertisements, where a fictional product is being advertised for the purpose of poking fun at the particular advertisement, nor should it be confused with the use of a coined brand name for the purpose of comparing the product without actually naming an actual competitor. ("Wikipedia tastes better and is less filling than the Encyclopedia Galactica.')

In the 1980s, during what has been referred to as the cola wars, soft-drink manufacturer Pepsi ran a series of advertisements where people, caught on hidden camera, in a blind taste test, chose Pepsi over rival Coca-Cola.

Chapter 10. Developing New Products and Services

a. Comparative advertising
b. GL-70
c. Heavy-up
d. Cost per conversion

12. _____ is used in marketing to describe a key quality of services as distinct from goods. _____ is the characteristic that a service has which renders it impossible to divorce the supply or production of the service from its consumption.

Other key characteristics of services include perishability, intangibility and variability.

a. Individual branding
b. Engagement
c. Online focus group
d. Inseparability

13. _____ is a list for goods and materials held available in stock by a business. It is also used for a list of the contents of a household and for a list for testamentary purposes of the possessions of someone who has died. In accounting _____ is considered an asset.

a. ACNielsen
b. Ending Inventory
c. Inventory
d. ADTECH

14. _____ is anything that is intended to save time, energy or frustration. A _____ store at a petrol station, for example, sells items that have nothing to do with gasoline/petrol, but it saves the consumer from having to go to a grocery store. '_____' is a very relative term and its meaning tends to change over time.

a. Convenience
b. MaxDiff
c. Demographic profile
d. Marketing buzz

15. In economics, _____ is the desire to own something and the ability to pay for it. The term _____ signifies the ability or the willingness to buy a particular commodity at a given point of time.

a. Market dominance
b. Discretionary spending
c. Market system
d. Demand

16. _____ is a term in economics, where demand for one good or service occurs as a result of demand for another. This may occur as the former is a part of production of the second. For example, demand for coal leads to _____ for mining, as coal must be mined for coal to be consumed.

a. Power III
b. 6-3-5 Brainwriting
c. 180SearchAssistant
d. Derived demand

17. _____ is the examining of goods or services from retailers with the intent to purchase at that time. _____ is an activity of selection and/or purchase. In some contexts it is considered a leisure activity as well as an economic one.

a. Discount store
b. Hawkers
c. Khodebshchik
d. Shopping

Chapter 10. Developing New Products and Services 87

18. _____ is the practice of individuals including commercial businesses, governments and institutions, facilitating the sale of their products or services to other companies or organizations that in turn resell them, use them as components in products or services they offer _____ is also called business-to-_____ for short. (Note that while marketing to government entities shares some of the same dynamics of organizational marketing, B2G Marketing is meaningfully different.)

   a. Law of disruption
   b. Mass marketing
   c. Disruptive technology
   d. Business marketing

19. _____ is a cohort which consists of those people born after the Generation X cohort. Its name is controversial and is synonymous with several alternative names including The Net Generation, Millennials, Echo Boomers, and iGeneration. _____ consists primarily of the offspring of the Generation Jones and Baby Boomers cohorts.

   a. Generation X
   b. AStore
   c. Generation Y
   d. Greatest Generation

20. The _____ is generally accepted as the use and specification of the four p's describing the strategic position of a product in the marketplace. One version of the origins of the _____ starts in 1948 when James Culliton said that a marketing decision should be a result of something similar to a recipe. This version continued in 1953 when Neil Borden, in his American Marketing Association presidential address, took the recipe idea one step further and coined the term 'Marketing-Mix'.

   a. 6-3-5 Brainwriting
   b. 180SearchAssistant
   c. Power III
   d. Marketing mix

21. _____ is a lightweight markup language, originally created by John Gruber and Aaron Swartz to help maximum readability and 'publishability' of both its input and output forms. The language takes many cues from existing conventions for marking up plain text in email. _____ converts its marked-up text input to valid, well-formed XHTML and replaces left-pointing angle brackets ('<') and ampersands with their corresponding character entity references.

   a. 6-3-5 Brainwriting
   b. Power III
   c. 180SearchAssistant
   d. Markdown

22. _____ is a business management strategy, originally developed by Motorola, that today enjoys widespread application in many sectors of industry.

   _____ seeks to identify and remove the causes of defects and errors in manufacturing and business processes. It uses a set of quality management methods, including statistical methods, and creates a special infrastructure of people within the organization ('Black Belts' etc.)

   a. Six Sigma
   b. Power III
   c. 6-3-5 Brainwriting
   d. 180SearchAssistant

23. A _____ is a group of employees from various functional areas of the organization - research, engineering, marketing, finance. human resources, and operations, for example - who are all focused on a specific objective and are responsible to work as a team to improve coordination and innovation across divisions and resolve mutual problems.

   a. 180SearchAssistant
   b. Power III
   c. Job analysis
   d. Cross-functional team

24. A _____ is a plan of action designed to achieve a particular goal.

_____ is different from tactics. In military terms, tactics is concerned with the conduct of an engagement while _____ is concerned with how different engagements are linked.

a. 180SearchAssistant
b. 6-3-5 Brainwriting
c. Power III
d. Strategy

25. _____ is a contract between two parties, one being the employer and the other being the employee. An employee may be defined as: 'A person in the service of another under any contract of hire, express or implied, oral or written, where the employer has the power or right to control and direct the employee in the material details of how the work is to be performed.' Black's Law Dictionary page 471 (5th ed. 1979.)

a. ACNielsen
b. ADTECH
c. Employment
d. AMAX

26. A supply chain is the system of organizations, people, technology, activities, information and resources involved in moving a product or service from _____ to customer. Supply chain activities transform natural resources, raw materials and components into a finished product that is delivered to the end customer. In sophisticated supply chain systems, used products may re-enter the supply chain at any point where residual value is recyclable.

a. Bringin' Home the Oil
b. Rebate
c. Product line extension
d. Supplier

27. An _____ is the manufacturing of a good or service within a category. Although _____ is a broad term for any kind of economic production, in economics and urban planning _____ is a synonym for the secondary sector, which is a type of economic activity involved in the manufacturing of raw materials into goods and products.

There are four key industrial economic sectors: the primary sector, largely raw material extraction industries such as mining and farming; the secondary sector, involving refining, construction, and manufacturing; the tertiary sector, which deals with services (such as law and medicine) and distribution of manufactured goods; and the quaternary sector, a relatively new type of knowledge _____ focusing on technological research, design and development such as computer programming, and biochemistry.

a. ACNielsen
b. ADTECH
c. Industry
d. AMAX

28. Competitiveness is a comparative concept of the ability and performance of a firm, sub-sector or country to sell and supply goods and/or services in a given market. Although widely used in economics and business management, the usefulness of the concept, particularly in the context of national competitiveness, is vigorously disputed by economists, such as Paul Krugman .

The term may also be applied to markets, where it is used to refer to the extent to which the market structure may be regarded as perfectly _____.

a. Geographical pricing
b. Customs union
c. Competitive
d. Free trade zone

Chapter 10. Developing New Products and Services

29. _____ is systematic determination of merit, worth, and significance of something or someone using criteria against a set of standards. _____ often is used to characterize and appraise subjects of interest in a wide range of human enterprises, including the arts, criminal justice, foundations and non-profit organizations, government, health care, and other human services.

Depending on the topic of interest, there are professional groups which look to the quality and rigor of the _____ process.

a. Evaluation
c. ACNielsen
b. AMAX
d. ADTECH

30. In economics, an externality or spillover of an economic transaction is an impact on a party that is not directly involved in the transaction. In such a case, prices do not reflect the full costs or benefits in production or consumption of a product or service. A positive impact is called an _____ benefit, while a negative impact is called an _____ cost.

a. ACNielsen
c. AMAX
b. ADTECH
d. External

31. The phrase _____, according to the Organization for Economic Co-operation and Development, refers to 'creative work undertaken on a systematic basis in order to increase the stock of knowledge, including knowledge of man, culture and society, and the use of this stock of knowledge to devise new applications [sic]' Though it is questionable that an organization is needed for this definition, as it is quite obvious that _____ refers to the _____ of something.

New product design and development is more often than not a crucial factor in the survival of a company. In an industry that is fast changing, firms must continually revise their design and range of products.

a. Power III
c. 6-3-5 Brainwriting
b. 180SearchAssistant
d. Research and development

32. Proof-of-Principle _____ This type of _____ is used to test some aspect of the intended design without attempting to exactly simulate the visual appearance, choice of materials or intended manufacturing process. Such _____s can be used to 'prove' out a potential design approach such as range of motion, mechanics, sensors, architecture, etc.

a. Power III
c. 6-3-5 Brainwriting
b. 180SearchAssistant
d. Prototype

33. _____ is the set of tasks, knowledge, and techniques required to identify business needs and determine solutions to business problems. Solutions often include a systems development component, but may also consist of process improvement or organizational change. The person who carries out this task is called a business analyst or _____.

a. Business analysis
c. Fast moving consumer goods
b. Door-to-door
d. Marketing management

34. _____ is a mathematical science pertaining to the collection, analysis, interpretation or explanation, and presentation of data. It also provides tools for prediction and forecasting based on data. It is applicable to a wide variety of academic disciplines, from the natural and social sciences to the humanities, government and business.

a. Type I error
b. Median
c. Null hypothesis
d. Statistics

35. In economics, _____ is a measure of the relative satisfaction from consumption of various goods and services. Given this measure, one may speak meaningfully of increasing or decreasing _____, and thereby explain economic behavior in terms of attempts to increase one's _____. For illustrative purposes, changes in _____ are sometimes expressed in units called utils.
   a. Utility
   b. AMAX
   c. ACNielsen
   d. ADTECH

36. A _____, in the field of business and marketing, is a geographic region or demographic group used to gauge the viability of a product or service in the mass market prior to a wide scale roll-out. The criteria used to judge the acceptability of a _____ region or group include:

   1. a population that is demographically similar to the proposed target market; and
   2. relative isolation from densely populated media markets so that advertising to the test audience can be efficient and economical.

The _____ ideally aims to duplicate 'everything' - promotion and distribution as well as `product' - on a smaller scale. The technique replicates, typically in one area, what is planned to occur in a national launch; and the results are very carefully monitored, so that they can be extrapolated to projected national results. The `area' may be any one of the following:

- Television area
- Test town
- Residential neighborhood
- Test site

A number of decisions have to be taken about any _____:

- Which _____?
- What is to be tested?
- How long a test?
- What are the success criteria?

The simple go or no-go decision, together with the related reduction of risk, is normally the main justification for the expense of _____s. At the same time, however, such _____s can be used to test specific elements of a new product's marketing mix; possibly the version of the product itself, the promotional message and media spend, the distribution channels and the price.

   a. Preadolescence
   b. 180SearchAssistant
   c. Test market
   d. Power III

Chapter 10. Developing New Products and Services 91

37. _____ or _____ data refers to selected population characteristics as used in government, marketing or opinion research, or the _____ profiles used in such research. Note the distinction from the term 'demography' Commonly-used _____ include race, age, income, disabilities, mobility (in terms of travel time to work or number of vehicles available), educational attainment, home ownership, employment status, and even location.
 a. AStore
 b. African Americans
 c. Albert Einstein
 d. Demographic

38. A personal and cultural _____ is a relative ethic _____, an assumption upon which implementation can be extrapolated. A _____ system is a set of consistent _____s and measures that is soo not true. A principle _____ is a foundation upon which other _____s and measures of integrity are based.
 a. Perceptual maps
 b. Supreme Court of the United States
 c. Value
 d. Package-on-Package

39. _____ is the process or cycle of introducing a new product into the market. The actual launch of a new product is the final stage of new product development, and the one where the most money will have to be spent for advertising, sales promotion, and other marketing efforts. In the case of a new consumer packaged good, costs will be at least $ 10 million, but can reach up to $ 200 million.
 a. Confusion marketing
 b. Customer Interaction Tracker
 c. Sweepstakes
 d. Commercialization

40. A _____ is a process that can allow an organization to concentrate its limited resources on the greatest opportunities to increase sales and achieve a sustainable competitive advantage. A _____ should be centered around the key concept that customer satisfaction is the main goal.

A _____ is most effective when it is an integral component of corporate strategy, defining how the organization will successfully engage customers, prospects, and competitors in the market arena.

 a. Societal marketing
 b. Marketing strategy
 c. Psychographic
 d. Cyberdoc

41. _____ is marketing based on relationship and value. It may be used to market a service or a product.

Marketing a service-base business is different from marketing a goods-base business.

 a. Power III
 b. 180SearchAssistant
 c. 6-3-5 Brainwriting
 d. Services Marketing

42. In commerce, _____ is the length of time it takes from a product being conceived until its being available for sale. _____ is important in industries where products are outmoded quickly. A common assumption is that _____ matters most for first-of-a-kind products, but actually the leader often has the luxury of time, while the clock is clearly running for the followers.
 a. Product life cycle management
 b. Customer centricity
 c. Product support
 d. Time to market

Chapter 11. Managing Products, Services, and Brands

1. A _____ is a collection of symbols, experiences and associations connected with a product, a service, a person or any other artifact or entity.

_____s have become increasingly important components of culture and the economy, now being described as 'cultural accessories and personal philosophies'.

Some people distinguish the psychological aspect of a _____ from the experiential aspect.

  a. Store brand
  c. Brandable software
  b. Brand equity
  d. Brand

2. _____ Management is the succession of strategies used by management as a product goes through its _____. The conditions in which a product is sold changes over time and must be managed as it moves through its succession of stages.

The _____ goes through many phases, involves many professional disciplines, and requires many skills, tools and processes.

  a. Customer satisfaction
  c. Supplier diversity
  b. Product life cycle
  d. Chain stores

3. In economics, _____ is the desire to own something and the ability to pay for it. The term _____ signifies the ability or the willingness to buy a particular commodity at a given point of time .

  a. Discretionary spending
  c. Market dominance
  b. Demand
  d. Market system

4. _____ is defined by the American _____ Association as the activity, set of institutions, and processes for creating, communicating, delivering, and exchanging offerings that have value for customers, clients, partners, and society at large. The term developed from the original meaning which referred literally to going to market, as in shopping, or going to a market to sell goods or services.

_____ practice tends to be seen as a creative industry, which includes advertising, distribution and selling.

  a. Marketing myopia
  c. Marketing
  b. Customer acquisition management
  d. Product naming

5. The _____ is generally accepted as the use and specification of the four p's describing the strategic position of a product in the marketplace. One version of the origins of the _____ starts in 1948 when James Culliton said that a marketing decision should be a result of something similar to a recipe. This version continued in 1953 when Neil Borden, in his American Marketing Association presidential address, took the recipe idea one step further and coined the term 'Marketing-Mix'.

  a. Marketing mix
  c. Power III
  b. 180SearchAssistant
  d. 6-3-5 Brainwriting

Chapter 11. Managing Products, Services, and Brands

6. _____ - an information and communication based electronic exchange environment - is a relatively new concept in marketing. Since physical boundaries no longer interfere with buy/sell decisions, the world has grown into several industry specific _____s which are integration of marketplaces through sophisticated computer and telecommunication technologies. The term _____ was introduced by Rayport and Sviokla in 1994 (see Rayport, Jeffrey F.

   a. Value chain
   b. Kano model
   c. Marketspace
   d. Market segment

7. _____ is a broad label that refers to any individuals or households that use goods and services generated within the economy. The concept of a _____ is used in different contexts, so that the usage and significance of the term may vary.

A _____ is a person who uses any product or service.

   a. 6-3-5 Brainwriting
   b. 180SearchAssistant
   c. Power III
   d. Consumer

8. _____ is one of the four elements of marketing mix. An organization or set of organizations (go-betweens) involved in the process of making a product or service available for use or consumption by a consumer or business user.

The other three parts of the marketing mix are product, pricing, and promotion.

   a. Distribution
   b. Comparison-Shopping agent
   c. Japan Advertising Photographers' Association
   d. Better Living Through Chemistry

9. _____ is one of the four Ps of the marketing mix. The other three aspects are product, promotion, and place. It is also a key variable in microeconomic price allocation theory.
   a. Price
   b. Relationship based pricing
   c. Pricing
   d. Competitor indexing

10. A _____ is a plan of action designed to achieve a particular goal.

_____ is different from tactics. In military terms, tactics is concerned with the conduct of an engagement while _____ is concerned with how different engagements are linked.

   a. 180SearchAssistant
   b. 6-3-5 Brainwriting
   c. Strategy
   d. Power III

11. _____ is the pricing technique of setting a relatively low initial entry price, often lower than the eventual market price, to attract new customers. The strategy works on the expectation that customers will switch to the new brand because of the lower price. _____ is most commonly associated with a marketing objective of increasing market share or sales volume, rather than to make profit in the short term.
   a. Price war
   b. Fee
   c. Competitor indexing
   d. Penetration pricing

Chapter 11. Managing Products, Services, and Brands

12. In marketing, _____ is the process of distinguishing the differences of a product or offering from others, to make it more attractive to a particular target market. This involves differentiating it from competitors' products as well as one's own product offerings.

Differentiation is a source of competitive advantage.

a. Corporate image
c. Packshot

b. Marketing myopia
d. Product differentiation

13. _____ is a foundational element of logic and human reasoning. _____ posits the existence of a domain or set of elements, as well as one or more common characteristics shared by those elements. As such, it is the essential basis of all valid deductive inference.

a. 6-3-5 Brainwriting
c. 180SearchAssistant

b. Power III
d. Generalization

14. _____ is the process by which a new idea or new product is accepted by the market. The rate of _____ is the speed that the new idea spreads from one consumer to the next. Adoption is similar to _____ except that it deals with the psychological processes an individual goes through, rather than an aggregate market process.

a. Perceptual maps
c. Market development

b. Diffusion
d. Kano model

15. _____ is a theory of how, why, and at what rate new ideas and technology spread through cultures. Everett Rogers introduced it in his 1962 book, _____s, writing that 'Diffusion is the process by which an innovation is communicated through certain channels over time among the members of a social system.' The adoption curve becomes an s-curve when cumulative adoption is used.

Rogers theorized that innovations would spread through a community in an S curve, as the early adopters select the innovation (which may be a technology) first, followed by the majority, until a technology or innovation has reached its saturation point in a community.

According to Rogers, diffusion research centers on the conditions which increase or decrease the likelihood that a new idea, product, or practice will be adopted by members of a given culture.

a. Diffusion of innovation
c. 6-3-5 Brainwriting

b. 180SearchAssistant
d. Power III

16. A craze is a product, idea, cultural movement, or model that gains popularity among a small section of the populace then quickly migrates to the mainstream. Crazes are characterized by their lightning fast adoption and swift departure from public awareness. Crazes and _____s are also characterized by their unusually high interest and sales figures relative to the time they are active in the marketplace, as compared with other similar products, ideas, cultural movements or models.

a. 6-3-5 Brainwriting
c. Power III

b. 180SearchAssistant
d. Fad

Chapter 11. Managing Products, Services, and Brands

17. _____ is a cohort which consists of those people born after the Generation X cohort. Its name is controversial and is synonymous with several alternative names including The Net Generation, Millennials, Echo Boomers, and iGeneration. _____ consists primarily of the offspring of the Generation Jones and Baby Boomers cohorts.
   a. Generation X
   b. Generation Y
   c. AStore
   d. Greatest Generation

18. _____ is the succession of strategies used by management as a product goes through its product life cycle. The conditions in which a product is sold changes over time and must be managed as it moves through its succession of stages.

The product life cycle goes through many phases, involves many professional disciplines, and requires many skills, tools and processes.

   a. Small business
   b. Cross-docking
   c. Product life cycle
   d. Product life cycle management

19. In calculus, a function f defined on a subset of the real numbers with real values is called _____, if for all x and y such that x ≤ y one has f(x) ≤ f(y), so f preserves the order. In layman's terms, the sign of the slope is always positive (the curve tending upwards) or zero (i.e., non-decreasing, or asymptotic, or depicted as a horizontal, flat line) Likewise, a function is called monotonically decreasing (non-increasing) if, whenever x ≤ y, then f(x) ≥ f(y), so it reverses the order.
   a. 6-3-5 Brainwriting
   b. Power III
   c. 180SearchAssistant
   d. Monotonic

20. The U.S. _____ is an agency of the United States Department of Health and Human Services and is responsible for regulating and supervising the safety of foods, dietary supplements, drugs, vaccines, biological medical products, blood products, medical devices, radiation-emitting devices, veterinary products, and cosmetics. The FDA also enforces section 361 of the Public Health Service Act and the associated regulations, including sanitation requirements on interstate travel as well as specific rules for control of disease on products ranging from pet turtles to semen donations for assisted reproductive medicine techniques.

The FDA is an agency within the United States Department of Health and Human Services responsible for protecting and promoting the nation's public health.

   a. 6-3-5 Brainwriting
   b. Power III
   c. Food and Drug Administration
   d. 180SearchAssistant

21. A personal and cultural _____ is a relative ethic _____, an assumption upon which implementation can be extrapolated. A _____ system is a set of consistent _____s and measures that is soo not true. A principle _____ is a foundation upon which other _____s and measures of integrity are based.
   a. Perceptual maps
   b. Supreme Court of the United States
   c. Value
   d. Package-on-Package

22. _____ is the application of marketing techniques to a specific product, product line, or brand. It seeks to increase the product's perceived value to the customer and thereby increase brand franchise and brand equity. Marketers see a brand as an implied promise that the level of quality people have come to expect from a brand will continue with future purchases of the same product.

a. Trademark distinctiveness	b. Store brand
c. Brand management	d. Naming rights

23. _____ is a form of communication that typically attempts to persuade potential customers to purchase or to consume more of a particular brand of product or service. 'While now central to the contemporary global economy and the reproduction of global production networks, it is only quite recently that _____ has been more than a marginal influence on patterns of sales and production. The formation of modern _____ was intimately bound up with the emergence of new forms of monopoly capitalism around the end of the 19th and beginning of the 20th century as one element in corporate strategies to create, organize and where possible control markets, especially for mass produced consumer goods.

a. ACNielsen	b. Advertising
c. AMAX	d. ADTECH

24. _____ is a marketing concept that refers to a consumer knowing of a brand's existence; at aggregate (brand) level it refers to the proportion of consumers who know of the brand.

_____ can be measured by showing a consumer the brand and asking whether or not they knew of it beforehand. However, in common market research practice a variety of recognition and recall measures of _____ are employed all of which test the brand name's association to a product category cue, this came about because most market research in the 20th Century was conducted by post or telephone, actually showing the brand to consumers usually required more expensive face-to-face interviews (until web-based interviews became possible.)

a. Brand awareness	b. Brand equity
c. Fitting Group	d. Brand orientation

25. _____ refers to the marketing effects or outcomes that accrue to a product with its brand name compared with those that would accrue if the same product did not have the brand name . And, at the root of these marketing effects is consumers' knowledge. In other words, consumers' knowledge about a brand makes manufacturers/advertisers respond differently or adopt appropriately adapt measures for the marketing of the brand .

a. Brand equity	b. Brand image
c. Product extension	d. Brand aversion

26. _____ is the process of creating and managing contracts between the owner of a brand and a company or individual who wants to use the brand in association with a product, for an agreed period of time, within an agreed territory. Licensing is used by brand owners to extend a trademark or character onto products of a completely different nature.

_____ a is well-established business, both in the area of patents and trademarks.

a. Brand loyalty	b. Brand culture
c. Brand strength analysis	d. Brand licensing

27. The verb _____ or grant _____ means to give permission. The noun _____ refers to that permission as well as to the document memorializing that permission. _____ may be granted by a party to another party as an element of an agreement between those parties.

a. 6-3-5 Brainwriting
b. Power III
c. 180SearchAssistant
d. License

28. _____ or brand stretching is a marketing strategy in which a firm marketing a product with a well-developed image uses the same brand name in a different product category. Organizations use this strategy to increase and leverage brand equity (definition: the net worth and long-term sustainability just from the renowned name.) An example of a _____ is Jello-gelatin creating Jello pudding pops.

a. Brand awareness
b. Brand orientation
c. Web 2.0
d. Brand extension

29. _____ is a rivalry between individuals, groups, nations for territory, a niche, or allocation of resources. It arises whenever two or more parties strive for a goal which cannot be shared. _____ occurs naturally between living organisms which co-exist in the same environment.

a. Non-price competition
b. Price fixing
c. Price competition
d. Competition

30. _____ is the practice of using a company's name as a product brand name. It is an attempt to leverage corporate brand equity to create product brand recognition. It is a type of family branding or umbrella brand.

a. Foreign branding
b. Nation branding
c. Rebranding
d. Corporate branding

31. _____ is a marketing strategy that involves selling several related products under one brand name. It is contrasted with individual branding in which each product in a portfolio is given a unique identity and brand name.

There are often economies of scope associated with _____ since several products can efficiently be promoted with a single advertisement or campaign.

a. 180SearchAssistant
b. 6-3-5 Brainwriting
c. Power III
d. Family branding

32. A product _____ is the use of an established product's brand name for a new item in the same product category. _____s occur when a company introduces additional items in the same product category under the same brand name such as new flavors, forms, colors, added ingredients, package sizes.Examples includei) Zen LXI, Zen VXIii) Surf, Surf Excel, Surf Excel Blueiii) Splendour, Splendour Plusiv) Coke, Diet Coke, Vanilla Cokev) Clinic All Clear, Clinic Plus

- brand
- brand management
- marketing
- product management
- Product lining

a. Perishability
b. Line extension
c. Brand Development Index
d. Targeted advertising

Chapter 11. Managing Products, Services, and Brands

33. A _____ is the use of an established product's brand name for a new item in the same product category. _____s occur when a company introduces additional items in the same product category under the same brand name such as new flavors, forms, colors, added ingredients, package sizes.
   a. Retail floor planning
   b. Pearson's chi-square
   c. Comparison-Shopping agent
   d. Product line extension

34. _____ is the marketing strategy of giving each product in a product portfolio its own unique brand name. This is contrasted with family branding in which the products in a product line are given the same brand name. The advantage of _____ is that each product has a self image and identity that's unique.
   a. Online focus group
   b. Engagement
   c. Intangibility
   d. Individual branding

35. There are many important decisions about product and service development and marketing. In the process of product development and marketing we should focus on strategic decisions about product attributes, product branding, product packaging, product labeling and product support services. But product strategy also calls for building a _____.
   a. Technology acceptance model
   b. Macromarketing
   c. Pinstorm
   d. Product line

36. _____ is when a large distribution channel member (usually a retailer), buys from a manufacturer in bulk and puts its own name on the product. This strategy is only practical when the retailer does very high levels of volume. The advantages to the retailer are:

   - more freedom and flexibility in pricing
   - more control over product attributes and quality
   - higher margins (or lower selling price)
   - eliminates much of the manufacturer's promotional costs

The advantages to the manufacturer are:

   - reduced promotional costs
   - stability of sales volume (at least while the contract is operative)

   - Kumar, Nirmalya; Steenkamp, Jan-Benedict E.M., Private Label Strategy - How to Meet the Store Brand Challenge. Harvard Business Press 2007

   - private label
   - brand management
   - brand
   - product management
   - marketing

   a. Promotion
   b. Customization
   c. Rural market
   d. Private branding

Chapter 11. Managing Products, Services, and Brands

37. A _____ is a company or individual that purchases goods or services with the intention of reselling them rather than consuming or using them. This is usually done for profit (but could be resold at a loss.) One example can be found in the industry of telecommunications, where companies buy excess amounts of transmission capacity or call time from other carriers and resell it to smaller carriers.
   a. Discontinuation
   b. Jobbing house
   c. Value-based pricing
   d. Reseller

38. In economics, business, retail, and accounting, a _____ is the value of money that has been used up to produce something, and hence is not available for use anymore. In economics, a _____ is an alternative that is given up as a result of a decision. In business, the _____ may be one of acquisition, in which case the amount of money expended to acquire it is counted as _____.
   a. Fixed costs
   b. Cost
   c. Transaction cost
   d. Variable cost

39. The break-even point for a product is the point where total revenue received equals the total costs associated with the sale of the product (TR=TC.) A break-even point is typically calculated in order for businesses to determine if it would be profitable to sell a proposed product, as opposed to attempting to modify an existing product instead so it can be made lucrative. _____ can also be used to analyse the potential profitability of an expenditure in a sales-based business.

In _____, margin of safety is how much output or sales level can fall before a business reaches its break-even point (BEP).

   a. Pay Per Sale
   b. Price skimming
   c. Contribution margin-based pricing
   d. Break even analysis

40. _____ is a form of government regulation which protects the interests of consumers. For example, a government may require businesses to disclose detailed information about products--particularly in areas where safety or public health is an issue, such as food. _____ is linked to the idea of consumer rights (that consumers have various rights as consumers), and to the formation of consumer organizations which help consumers make better choices in the marketplace.
   a. Consumer protection
   b. Sound trademark
   c. Trademark dilution
   d. Federal Bureau of Investigation

41. _____ is anything that is intended to save time, energy or frustration. A _____ store at a petrol station, for example, sells items that have nothing to do with gasoline/petrol, but it saves the consumer from having to go to a grocery store. '_____' is a very relative term and its meaning tends to change over time.
   a. Convenience
   b. Demographic profile
   c. MaxDiff
   d. Marketing buzz

42. The _____ Act of 2003 (15 U.S.C. 7701, et seq., Public Law No. 108-187, was S.877 of the 108th United States Congress), signed into law by President George W. Bush on December 16, 2003, establishes the United States' first national standards for the sending of commercial e-mail and requires the Federal Trade Commission (FTC) to enforce its provisions.
   a. Singapore Treaty on the Law of Trademarks
   b. Denominazione di origine controllata
   c. Non-conventional trademark
   d. CAN-SPAM

43. A _____ is the fee paid by a traveler allowing him or her to make use of a public transport system: rail, bus, taxi, etc. In the case of air transport, the term airfare is often used.

The _____ paid is a contribution to the operational costs of the transport system involved, either partial (as is frequently the case with publicly supported systems) or total.

    a. 180SearchAssistant
    b. Power III
    c. 6-3-5 Brainwriting
    d. Fare

44. A _____ is the price one pays as remuneration for services, especially the honorarium paid to a doctor, lawyer, consultant, or other member of a learned profession. _____s usually allow for overhead, wages, costs, and markup.

Traditionally, professionals in Great Britain received a _____ in contradistinction to a payment, salary, or wage, and would often use guineas rather than pounds as units of account.

    a. Fee
    b. Price shading
    c. Price war
    d. Transfer pricing

45. A _____ is a set of exclusive rights granted by a State to an inventor or his assignee for a limited period of time in exchange for a disclosure of an invention.

The procedure for granting _____s, the requirements placed on the _____ee and the extent of the exclusive rights vary widely between countries according to national laws and international agreements. Typically, however, a _____ application must include one or more claims defining the invention which must be new, inventive, and useful or industrially applicable.

    a. Product liability
    b. Foreign Corrupt Practices Act
    c. Reasonable person standard
    d. Patent

46. _____ in economics and business is the result of an exchange and from that trade we assign a numerical monetary value to a good, service or asset. If I trade 4 apples for an orange, the _____ of an orange is 4 - apples. Inversely, the _____ of an apple is 1/4 oranges.

    a. Contribution margin-based pricing
    b. Discounts and allowances
    c. Pricing
    d. Price

47. _____ is an advertisement in which a particular product specifically mentions a competitor by name for the express purpose of showing why the competitor is inferior to the product naming it.

This should not be confused with parody advertisements, where a fictional product is being advertised for the purpose of poking fun at the particular advertisement, nor should it be confused with the use of a coined brand name for the purpose of comparing the product without actually naming an actual competitor. ('Wikipedia tastes better and is less filling than the Encyclopedia Galactica.')

In the 1980s, during what has been referred to as the cola wars, soft-drink manufacturer Pepsi ran a series of advertisements where people, caught on hidden camera, in a blind taste test, chose Pepsi over rival Coca-Cola.

Chapter 11. Managing Products, Services, and Brands 101

a. GL-70
b. Cost per conversion
c. Comparative advertising
d. Heavy-up

48. A _____ or logistics network is the system of organizations, people, technology, activities, information and resources involved in moving a product or service from supplier to customer. _____ activities transform natural resources, raw materials and components into a finished product that is delivered to the end customer. In sophisticated _____ systems, used products may re-enter the _____ at any point where residual value is recyclable.
   a. Supply chain network
   b. Purchasing
   c. Demand chain management
   d. Supply chain

49. _____ is a process used to manage information technology (IT.) Its primary goal is to ensure that IT capacity meets current and future business requirements in a cost-effective manner. One common interpretation of _____ is described in the ITIL framework .
   a. Project Portfolio Management
   b. Power III
   c. Pop-up ads
   d. Capacity management

50. _____ is marketing based on relationship and value. It may be used to market a service or a product.

Marketing a service-base business is different from marketing a goods-base business.

   a. 6-3-5 Brainwriting
   b. 180SearchAssistant
   c. Power III
   d. Services Marketing

51. _____ are infrequent, technical, or unique functions performed by independent contractors or consultants whose occupation is the rendering of such services. Examples of _____ contracts include: accountants, actuaries, appraisers, archaeologists, architects, attorneys, brokerage firms, business consultants, business development managers, copywriters, engineers, law firms, physicians, public relations professionals, recruiters, researchers, real estate brokers, translators, software engineers and web designers. While not limited to licentiates (individuals holding professional licenses), the services are considered 'professional' and the contract may run to partnerships, firms, or corporations as well as to individuals.
   a. Power III
   b. Professional services
   c. Spokesperson
   d. 180SearchAssistant

52. A _____ or community service announcement (CSA) is a non-commercial advertisement broadcast on radio or television, ostensibly for the public interest. _____s are intended to modify public attitudes by raising awareness about specific issues.

The most common topics of _____s are health and safety.

   a. 180SearchAssistant
   b. Public service announcement
   c. Power III
   d. 6-3-5 Brainwriting

53. _____ is the deliberate attempt to manage the public's perception of a subject. The subjects of _____ include people (for example, politicians and performing artists), goods and services, organizations of all kinds, and works of art or entertainment.

Chapter 11. Managing Products, Services, and Brands

From a marketing perspective, _____ is one component of promotion.

a. Brando
b. Pearson's chi-square
c. Little value placed on potential benefits
d. Publicity

54. _____ is the practice of individuals including commercial businesses, governments and institutions, facilitating the sale of their products or services to other companies or organizations that in turn resell them, use them as components in products or services they offer _____ is also called business-to-_____ for short. (Note that while marketing to government entities shares some of the same dynamics of organizational marketing, B2G Marketing is meaningfully different.)

a. Mass marketing
b. Disruptive technology
c. Business marketing
d. Law of disruption

55. _____ involves disseminating information about a product, product line, brand, or company. It is one of the four key aspects of the marketing mix. (The other three elements are product marketing, pricing, and distribution). P>_____ is generally sub-divided into two parts:

- Above the line _____: Promotion in the media (e.g. TV, radio, newspapers, Internet and Mobile Phones) in which the advertiser pays an advertising agency to place the ad
- Below the line _____: All other _____. Much of this is intended to be subtle enough for the consumer to be unaware that _____ is taking place. E.g. sponsorship, product placement, endorsements, sales _____, merchandising, direct mail, personal selling, public relations, trade shows

a. Davie Brown Index
b. Bottling lines
c. Cashmere Agency
d. Promotion

56. _____ is an organizational lifecycle function within a company dealing with the planning or marketing of a product or products at all stages of the product lifecycle.

_____ and product marketing (outbound focused) are different yet complementary efforts with the objective of maximizing sales revenues, market share, and profit margins. The role of _____ spans many activities from strategic to tactical and varies based on the organizational structure of the company.

a. Product information management
b. Service product management
c. Requirement prioritization
d. Product management

Chapter 12. Pricing Products and Services

1. _____ is a type of trade in which goods or services are directly exchanged for other goods and/or services, without the use of money. It can be bilateral or multilateral, and usually exists parallel to monetary systems in most developed countries, though to a very limited extent. _____ usually replaces money as the method of exchange in times of monetary crisis, when the currency is unstable and devalued by hyperinflation.

   a. Black market
   b. Mixed economy
   c. Market economy
   d. Barter

2. A _____ is the fee paid by a traveler allowing him or her to make use of a public transport system: rail, bus, taxi, etc. In the case of air transport, the term airfare is often used.

   The _____ paid is a contribution to the operational costs of the transport system involved, either partial (as is frequently the case with publicly supported systems) or total.

   a. Power III
   b. 180SearchAssistant
   c. Fare
   d. 6-3-5 Brainwriting

3. A _____ is the price one pays as remuneration for services, especially the honorarium paid to a doctor, lawyer, consultant, or other member of a learned profession. _____s usually allow for overhead, wages, costs, and markup.

   Traditionally, professionals in Great Britain received a _____ in contradistinction to a payment, salary, or wage, and would often use guineas rather than pounds as units of account.

   a. Price shading
   b. Fee
   c. Price war
   d. Transfer pricing

4. _____ is a fee paid on borrowed assets. It is the price paid for the use of borrowed money , or, money earned by deposited funds . Assets that are sometimes lent with _____ include money, shares, consumer goods through hire purchase, major assets such as aircraft, and even entire factories in finance lease arrangements.

   a. ACNielsen
   b. AMAX
   c. Interest
   d. ADTECH

5. _____ in economics and business is the result of an exchange and from that trade we assign a numerical monetary value to a good, service or asset. If I trade 4 apples for an orange, the _____ of an orange is 4 - apples. Inversely, the _____ of an apple is 1/4 oranges.

   a. Contribution margin-based pricing
   b. Discounts and allowances
   c. Pricing
   d. Price

6. The _____ is a covariance equation which is a mathematical description of evolution and natural selection. The _____ was derived by George R. Price, working in London to rederive W.D. Hamilton's work on kin selection.

   Suppose there is a population of n individuals over which the amount of a particular characteristic varies.

   a. Range
   b. Good things come to those who wait
   c. Madrid system for the international registration of marks
   d. Price equation

Chapter 12. Pricing Products and Services

7. An overprint is the addition of text (and sometimes graphics) to the face of a postage stamp (or banknote) after it has been printed (although some overprints are solely in the selvedge area of souvenir sheets.) Overprints have been used for many purposes over the years. They have been used as _____s, commemorations, and control marks.
   a. Consumption Map
   b. Moratorium
   c. Surcharge
   d. Comparison-Shopping agent

8. An _____ is the manufacturing of a good or service within a category. Although _____ is a broad term for any kind of economic production, in economics and urban planning _____ is a synonym for the secondary sector, which is a type of economic activity involved in the manufacturing of raw materials into goods and products.

   There are four key industrial economic sectors: the primary sector, largely raw material extraction industries such as mining and farming; the secondary sector, involving refining, construction, and manufacturing; the tertiary sector, which deals with services (such as law and medicine) and distribution of manufactured goods; and the quaternary sector, a relatively new type of knowledge _____ focusing on technological research, design and development such as computer programming, and biochemistry.

   a. ADTECH
   b. AMAX
   c. ACNielsen
   d. Industry

9. _____ is defined by the American _____ Association as the activity, set of institutions, and processes for creating, communicating, delivering, and exchanging offerings that have value for customers, clients, partners, and society at large. The term developed from the original meaning which referred literally to going to market, as in shopping, or going to a market to sell goods or services.

   _____ practice tends to be seen as a creative industry, which includes advertising, distribution and selling.

   a. Marketing myopia
   b. Customer acquisition management
   c. Product naming
   d. Marketing

10. _____ is a cohort which consists of those people born after the Generation X cohort. Its name is controversial and is synonymous with several alternative names including The Net Generation, Millennials, Echo Boomers, and iGeneration. _____ consists primarily of the offspring of the Generation Jones and Baby Boomers cohorts.
    a. Generation Y
    b. Generation X
    c. AStore
    d. Greatest Generation

11. The (manufacturer's) suggested retail price (MSRP or SRP), _____ or recommended retail price (RRP) of a product is the price the manufacturer recommends that the retailer sell it for. The intention was to help to standardize prices among locations. While some stores always sell at, or below, the suggested retail price, others do so only when items are on sale or closeout.
    a. Power III
    b. List price
    c. Predatory pricing
    d. 180SearchAssistant

12. A personal and cultural _____ is a relative ethic _____, an assumption upon which implementation can be extrapolated. A _____ system is a set of consistent _____s and measures that is soo not true. A principle _____ is a foundation upon which other _____s and measures of integrity are based.

a. Supreme Court of the United States
b. Package-on-Package
c. Value
d. Perceptual maps

13. _____ is one of the four Ps of the marketing mix. The other three aspects are product, promotion, and place. It is also a key variable in microeconomic price allocation theory.
    a. Pricing
    b. Price
    c. Competitor indexing
    d. Relationship based pricing

14. The _____ is generally accepted as the use and specification of the four p's describing the strategic position of a product in the marketplace. One version of the origins of the _____ starts in 1948 when James Culliton said that a marketing decision should be a result of something similar to a recipe. This version continued in 1953 when Neil Borden, in his American Marketing Association presidential address, took the recipe idea one step further and coined the term 'Marketing-Mix'.
    a. 6-3-5 Brainwriting
    b. Marketing mix
    c. Power III
    d. 180SearchAssistant

15. _____ is the practice of individuals including commercial businesses, governments and institutions, facilitating the sale of their products or services to other companies or organizations that in turn resell them, use them as components in products or services they offer _____ is also called business-to-_____ for short. (Note that while marketing to government entities shares some of the same dynamics of organizational marketing, B2G Marketing is meaningfully different.)
    a. Disruptive technology
    b. Mass marketing
    c. Law of disruption
    d. Business marketing

16. _____ is a marketing strategy that involves offering several products for sale as one combined product. This strategy is very common in the software business (for example: bundle a word processor, a spreadsheet, and a database into a single office suite), in the cable television industry (for example, basic cable in the United States generally offers many channels at one price), and in the fast food industry in which multiple items are combined into a complete meal. A bundle of products is sometimes referred to as a package deal or a compilation or an anthology.
    a. Product bundling
    b. Primary research
    c. Psychographic
    d. Technology acceptance model

17. A _____ is a written document that details the necessary actions to achieve one or more marketing objectives. It can be for a product or service, a brand, or a product line. _____s cover between one and five years.
    a. Disruptive technology
    b. Prosumer
    c. Marketing strategy
    d. Marketing plan

18. A _____ is a plan of action designed to achieve a particular goal.

_____ is different from tactics. In military terms, tactics is concerned with the conduct of an engagement while _____ is concerned with how different engagements are linked.

   a. 180SearchAssistant
   b. Power III
   c. Strategy
   d. 6-3-5 Brainwriting

19. _____ is the pricing technique of setting a relatively low initial entry price, often lower than the eventual market price, to attract new customers. The strategy works on the expectation that customers will switch to the new brand because of the lower price. _____ is most commonly associated with a marketing objective of increasing market share or sales volume, rather than to make profit in the short term.

   a. Price war
   b. Fee
   c. Competitor indexing
   d. Penetration pricing

20. _____ is a pricing method used by companies. It is used primarily because it is easy to calculate and requires little information. There are several varieties, but the common thread in all of them is that one first calculates the cost of the product, then includes an additional amount to represent profit.

   a. Break even analysis
   b. Relationship based pricing
   c. Cost-plus pricing
   d. Loss leader

21. _____ is the process of understanding, anticipating and influencing consumer behavior in order to maximize revenue or profits from a fixed, perishable resource This process was first discovered by Dr. Matt H. Keller. The challenge is to sell the right resources to the right customer at the right time for the right price. This process can result in price discrimination, where a firm charges customers consuming otherwise identical goods or services a different price for doing so.

   a. Multi-level marketing
   b. Cross-selling
   c. Service provider
   d. Yield management

22. In economics, _____ is the desire to own something and the ability to pay for it. The term _____ signifies the ability or the willingness to buy a particular commodity at a given point of time.

   a. Market dominance
   b. Market system
   c. Discretionary spending
   d. Demand

23. _____ is an advertisement in which a particular product specifically mentions a competitor by name for the express purpose of showing why the competitor is inferior to the product naming it.

This should not be confused with parody advertisements, where a fictional product is being advertised for the purpose of poking fun at the particular advertisement, nor should it be confused with the use of a coined brand name for the purpose of comparing the product without actually naming an actual competitor. ('Wikipedia tastes better and is less filling than the Encyclopedia Galactica.')

In the 1980s, during what has been referred to as the cola wars, soft-drink manufacturer Pepsi ran a series of advertisements where people, caught on hidden camera, in a blind taste test, chose Pepsi over rival Coca-Cola.

   a. Comparative advertising
   b. Heavy-up
   c. GL-70
   d. Cost per conversion

24. _____ is a broad label that refers to any individuals or households that use goods and services generated within the economy. The concept of a _____ is used in different contexts, so that the usage and significance of the term may vary.

A _____ is a person who uses any product or service.

a. Power III
b. Consumer
c. 180SearchAssistant
d. 6-3-5 Brainwriting

25. _____ or price ending is a marketing practice based on the theory that certain prices have a psychological impact. The retail prices are often expressed as 'odd prices': a little less than a round number, e.g. $19.99 or Â£6.95 (but not necessarily mathematically odd, it could also be 2.98.) The theory is this drives demand greater than would be expected if consumers were perfectly rational.
a. Supplier diversity
b. Psychological pricing
c. First-mover advantage
d. Chain stores

26. A _____ or leader is a product sold at a low price (at cost or below cost) to stimulate other, profitable sales. It is a kind of sales promotion, in other words marketing concentrating on a pricing strategy. The price can even be so low that the product is sold at a loss.
a. Price shading
b. Penetration pricing
c. Loss leader
d. Resale price maintenance

27. _____ is an economic concept with commonplace familiarity. It is the price that a good or service is offered at, or will fetch, in the marketplace. It is of interest mainly in the study of microeconomics.
a. Forward market
b. Market maker
c. Market price
d. Power III

28. In economics, the _____ can be defined as the graph depicting the relationship between the price of a certain commodity, and the amount of it that consumers are willing and able to purchase at that given price. It is a graphic representation of a demand schedule The _____ for all consumers together follows from the _____ of every individual consumer: the individual demands at each price are added together.

_____s are used to estimate behaviors in competitive markets, and are often combined with supply curves to estimate the equilibrium price (the price at which sellers together are willing to sell the same amount as buyers together are willing to buy, also known as market clearing price) and the equilibrium quantity (the amount of that good or service that will be produced and bought without surplus/excess supply or shortage/excess demand) of that market.

a. Demand curve
b. Power III
c. 6-3-5 Brainwriting
d. 180SearchAssistant

29. In economics, _____ describes demand that is not very sensitive to a change in price.
a. ADTECH
b. Inelastic
c. ACNielsen
d. AMAX

30. _____ is defined as the measure of responsiveness in the quantity demanded for a commodity as a result of change in price of the same commodity. It is a measure of how consumers react to a change in price. In other words, it is percentage change in quantity demanded as per the percentage change in price of the same commodity.

a. 6-3-5 Brainwriting
b. Power III
c. Price elasticity of demand
d. 180SearchAssistant

31. _____ is a form of communication that typically attempts to persuade potential customers to purchase or to consume more of a particular brand of product or service. 'While now central to the contemporary global economy and the reproduction of global production networks, it is only quite recently that _____ has been more than a marginal influence on patterns of sales and production. The formation of modern _____ was intimately bound up with the emergence of new forms of monopoly capitalism around the end of the 19th and beginning of the 20th century as one element in corporate strategies to create, organize and where possible control markets, especially for mass produced consumer goods.
a. AMAX
b. ADTECH
c. ACNielsen
d. Advertising

32. In economics, _____ is the ratio of the percent change in one variable to the percent change in another variable. It is a tool for measuring the responsiveness of a function to changes in parameters in a relative way. Commonly analyzed are _____ of substitution, price and wealth.
a. Opinion leadership
b. Intellectual property
c. ACNielsen
d. Elasticity

33. Price _____ is defined as the measure of responsiveness in the quantity demanded for a commodity as a result of change in price of the same commodity. It is a measure of how consumers react to a change in price. In other words, it is percentage change in quantity demanded as per the percentage change in price of the same commodity.
a. ACNielsen
b. ADTECH
c. AMAX
d. Elasticity of demand

34. In economics, business, retail, and accounting, a _____ is the value of money that has been used up to produce something, and hence is not available for use anymore. In economics, a _____ is an alternative that is given up as a result of a decision. In business, the _____ may be one of acquisition, in which case the amount of money expended to acquire it is counted as _____.
a. Transaction cost
b. Cost
c. Variable cost
d. Fixed costs

35. In economics, and cost accounting, _____ describes the total economic cost of production and is made up of variable costs, which vary according to the quantity of a good produced and include inputs such as labor and raw materials, plus fixed costs, which are independent of the quantity of a good produced and include inputs (capital) that cannot be varied in the short term, such as buildings and machinery. _____ in economics includes the total opportunity cost of each factor of production in addition to fixed and variable costs.

The rate at which _____ changes as the amount produced changes is called marginal cost.

a. Product proliferation
b. Hoarding
c. Household production function
d. Total cost

36. In microeconomics, _____ is the total number of dollars received by a firm from the sale of a product.
a. 180SearchAssistant
b. Total revenue
c. Nonmarket
d. Power III

Chapter 12. Pricing Products and Services

37. _____s are used in open sentences. For instance, in the formula x + 1 = 5, x is a _____ which represents an 'unknown' number. _____s are often represented by letters of the Roman alphabet, or those of other alphabets, such as Greek, and use other special symbols.
   a. Book of business
   b. Quantitative
   c. Variable
   d. Personalization

38. _____s are expenses that change in proportion to the activity of a business. In other words, _____ is the sum of marginal costs. It can also be considered normal costs.
   a. Marginal cost
   b. Transaction cost
   c. Fixed costs
   d. Variable cost

39. The break-even point for a product is the point where total revenue received equals the total costs associated with the sale of the product (TR=TC.) A break-even point is typically calculated in order for businesses to determine if it would be profitable to sell a proposed product, as opposed to attempting to modify an existing product instead so it can be made lucrative. _____ can also be used to analyse the potential profitability of an expenditure in a sales-based business.

In _____, margin of safety is how much output or sales level can fall before a business reaches its break-even point (BEP).

   a. Contribution margin-based pricing
   b. Break even analysis
   c. Price skimming
   d. Pay Per Sale

40. In economics ' business, specifically cost accounting, the _____ is the point at which cost or expenses and revenue are equal: there is no net loss or gain, and one has 'broken even'. A profit or a loss has not been made, although opportunity costs have been paid, and capital has received the risk-adjusted, expected return.

For example, if the business sells less than 200 tables each month, it will make a loss, if it sells more, it will be a profit.

   a. Total revenue
   b. 180SearchAssistant
   c. Break-even point
   d. Power III

41. _____ or goals give direction to the whole pricing process. Determining what your objectives are is the first step in pricing. When deciding on _____ you must consider: 1) the overall financial, marketing, and strategic objectives of the company; 2) the objectives of your product or brand; 3) consumer price elasticity and price points; and 4) the resources you have available.
   a. Transfer pricing
   b. Discounts and allowances
   c. Pricing objectives
   d. Competitor indexing

42. In economics, _____ is the process by which a firm determines the price and output level that returns the greatest profit. There are several approaches to this problem. The total revenue--total cost method relies on the fact that profit equals revenue minus cost, and the marginal revenue--marginal cost method is based on the fact that total profit in a perfectly competitive market reaches its maximum point where marginal revenue equals marginal cost.
   a. Power III
   b. Profit margin
   c. 180SearchAssistant
   d. Profit maximization

Chapter 12. Pricing Products and Services

43. In economic models, the _____ time frame assumes no fixed factors of production. Firms can enter or leave the marketplace, and the cost (and availability) of land, labor, raw materials, and capital goods can be assumed to vary. In contrast, in the short-run time frame, certain factors are assumed to be fixed, because there is not sufficient time for them to change.

   a. Power III
   b. Long-run
   c. 6-3-5 Brainwriting
   d. 180SearchAssistant

44. _____, in strategic management and marketing, is the percentage or proportion of the total available market or market segment that is being serviced by a company. It can be expressed as a company's sales revenue (from that market) divided by the total sales revenue available in that market. It can also be expressed as a company's unit sales volume (in a market) divided by the total volume of units sold in that market.

   a. Demand generation
   b. Customer relationship management
   c. Cyberdoc
   d. Market share

45. _____, known in the United States as antitrust law, has three main elements:

   - prohibiting agreements or practices that restrict free trading and competition between business entities. This includes in particular the repression of cartels.
   - banning abusive behaviour by a firm dominating a market, or anti-competitive practices that tend to lead to such a dominant position. Practices controlled in this way may include predatory pricing, tying, price gouging, refusal to deal, and many others.
   - supervising the mergers and acquisitions of large corporations, including some joint ventures. Transactions that are considered to threaten the competitive process can be prohibited altogether, or approved subject to 'remedies' such as an obligation to divest part of the merged business or to offer licences or access to facilities to enable other businesses to continue competing.

   The substance and practice of _____ varies from jurisdiction to jurisdiction. Protecting the interests of consumers (consumer welfare) and ensuring that entrepreneurs have an opportunity to compete in the market economy are often treated as important objectives. _____ is closely connected with law on deregulation of access to markets, state aids and subsidies, the privatisation of state owned assets and the establishment of independent sector regulators. In recent decades, _____ has been viewed as a way to provide better public services.

   a. Right to Financial Privacy Act
   b. Covenant not to compete
   c. Denominazione di origine controllata
   d. Competition law

46. _____ is a form of government regulation which protects the interests of consumers. For example, a government may require businesses to disclose detailed information about products--particularly in areas where safety or public health is an issue, such as food. _____ is linked to the idea of consumer rights (that consumers have various rights as consumers), and to the formation of consumer organizations which help consumers make better choices in the marketplace.

   a. Federal Bureau of Investigation
   b. Trademark dilution
   c. Sound trademark
   d. Consumer protection

Chapter 12. Pricing Products and Services

47. A craze is a product, idea, cultural movement, or model that gains popularity among a small section of the populace then quickly migrates to the mainstream. Crazes are characterized by their lightning fast adoption and swift departure from public awareness. Crazes and _____s are also characterized by their unusually high interest and sales figures relative to the time they are active in the marketplace, as compared with other similar products, ideas, cultural movements or models.
   a. Power III
   b. 180SearchAssistant
   c. 6-3-5 Brainwriting
   d. Fad

48. _____ is an agreement between business competitors to sell the same product or service at the same price. In general, it is an agreement intended to ultimately push the price of a product as high as possible, leading to profits for all the sellers. _____ can also involve any agreement to fix, peg, discount or stabilize prices.
   a. Price fixing
   b. Non-price competition
   c. Price competition
   d. Direct competition

49. _____ Management is the succession of strategies used by management as a product goes through its _____. The conditions in which a product is sold changes over time and must be managed as it moves through its succession of stages.

   The _____ goes through many phases, involves many professional disciplines, and requires many skills, tools and processes.

   a. Chain stores
   b. Customer satisfaction
   c. Product life cycle
   d. Supplier diversity

50. Regulation refers to 'controlling human or societal behaviour by rules or restrictions.' Regulation can take many forms: legal restrictions promulgated by a government authority, self-regulation, social regulation (e.g. norms), co-regulation and market regulation. One can consider regulation as actions of conduct imposing sanctions (such as a fine.) This action of administrative law, or implementing _____ law, may be contrasted with statutory or case law.
   a. Right to Financial Privacy Act
   b. Robinson-Patman Act
   c. Privacy law
   d. Regulatory

51. The _____ requires the Federal government to investigate and pursue trusts, companies and organizations suspected of violating the Act. It was the first United States Federal statute to limit cartels and monopolies, and today still forms the basis for most antitrust litigation by the federal government.
   a. 180SearchAssistant
   b. Sherman Antitrust Act
   c. Power III
   d. 6-3-5 Brainwriting

52. In retail sales, a _____ is a form of fraud in which the party putting forth the fraud lures in customers by advertising a product or service at an unprofitably low price, then reveals to potential customers that the advertised good is not available but that a substitute is.

The goal of the bait-and-switch is to convince some buyers to purchase the substitute good as a means of avoiding disappointment over not getting the bait, or as a way to recover sunk costs expended to try to obtain the bait. It suggests that the seller will not show the original product or product advertised but instead will demonstrate a more expensive product.

Chapter 12. Pricing Products and Services

a. Roll-in
b. Promotional products
c. Transpromotional
d. Bait and switch

53. _____ are final goods specifically intended for the mass market. For instance, _____ do not include investment assets, like precious antiques, even though these antiques are final goods.

Manufactured goods are goods that have been processed by way of machinery.

a. Power III
b. Free good
c. Durable good
d. Consumer Goods

54. False advertising or _____ is the use of false or misleading statements in advertising. As advertising has the potential to persuade people into commercial transactions that they might otherwise avoid, many governments around the world use regulations to control false, deceptive or misleading advertising. Truth in labeling refers to essentially the same concept, that customers have the right to know what they are buying, and that all necessary information should be on the label.

a. Power III
b. Fine print
c. Misleading advertising
d. Deceptive advertising

55. The _____ is an independent agency of the United States government, established in 1914 by the _____ Act. Its principal mission is the promotion of 'consumer protection' and the elimination and prevention of what regulators perceive to be harmfully 'anti-competitive' business practices, such as coercive monopoly.

The _____ Act was one of President Wilson's major acts against trusts.

a. Federal Trade Commission
b. 6-3-5 Brainwriting
c. Power III
d. 180SearchAssistant

56. The _____ is a marketing term and refers to all of the forces outside of marketing that affect marketing management's ability to build and maintain successful relationships with target customers. The _____ consists of both the macroenvironment and the microenvironment.

The microenvironment refers to the forces that are close to the company and affect its ability to serve its customers.

a. Customer franchise
b. Business-to-consumer
c. Psychographic
d. Market environment

57. _____ is the practice of selling a product or service at a very low price, intending to drive competitors out of the market, or create barriers to entry for potential new competitors. If competitors or potential competitors cannot sustain equal or lower prices without losing money, they go out of business or choose not to enter the business. The predatory merchant then has fewer competitors or is even a de facto monopoly, and can then raise prices above what the market would otherwise bear.

a. List price
b. 180SearchAssistant
c. Power III
d. Predatory pricing

Chapter 12. Pricing Products and Services

58. _____ exists when sales of identical goods or services are transacted at different prices from the same provider. In a theoretical market with perfect information, no transaction costs or prohibition on secondary exchange (or re-selling) to prevent arbitrage, _____ can only be a feature of monopoly and oligopoly markets, where market power can be exercised. Otherwise, the moment the seller tries to sell the same good at different prices, the buyer at the lower price can arbitrage by selling to the consumer buying at the higher price but with a tiny discount.
   a. Price
   b. Price discrimination
   c. Penetration pricing
   d. Resale price maintenance

59. _____ is the practice whereby a manufacturer and its distributors agree that the latter will sell the former's product at certain prices (_____), at or above a price floor (minimum _____) or at or below a price ceiling (maximum _____.) These rules prevent resellers from competing too fiercely on price and thus driving down profits. Some argue that the manufacturer may do this because it wishes to keep resellers profitable, and thus keeping the manufacturer profitable.
   a. Price discrimination
   b. Break even analysis
   c. Price skimming
   d. Resale price maintenance

60. The _____ of 1936 (or Anti-Price Discrimination Act, 15 U.S.C. § 13) is a United States federal law that prohibits what were considered, at the time of passage, to be anticompetitive practices by producers, specifically price discrimination. It grew out of practices in which chain stores were allowed to purchase goods at lower prices than other retailers.
   a. Fair Debt Collection Practices Act
   b. Trademark infringement
   c. Registered trademark symbol
   d. Robinson-Patman Act

61. Resale _____ is the practice whereby a manufacturer and its distributors agree that the latter will sell the former's product at certain prices (resale _____), at or above a price floor (minimum resale _____) or at or below a price ceiling (maximum resale _____.) These rules prevent resellers from competing too fiercely on price and thus drive down profits. Some argue that the manufacturer may do this because it wishes to keep resellers profitable, and thus keeping the manufacturer profitable.
   a. Price points
   b. Transfer pricing
   c. Pricing
   d. Price maintenance

62. The _____ is a term used in economics to describe a good that is not scarce. A _____ is available in as great a quantity as desired with zero opportunity cost to society.

A good that is made available at zero price is not necessarily a _____.

   a. Free good
   b. Durable good
   c. Power III
   d. Luxury good

63. A _____ is a type of wholesale merchant business that buys goods and bulk products from importers, other wholesalers and then sells to retailers. _____s can deal in any commodity destined for the retail market. Typical categories are food, lumber, hardware, fuel, and textiles.
   a. Refusal to deal
   b. Chief privacy officer
   c. Tacit collusion
   d. Jobbing house

Chapter 13. Managing Marketing Channels and Supply Chains

1. _____ is a broad label that refers to any individuals or households that use goods and services generated within the economy. The concept of a _____ is used in different contexts, so that the usage and significance of the term may vary.

A _____ is a person who uses any product or service.

   a. 180SearchAssistant   b. Power III
   c. 6-3-5 Brainwriting   d. Consumer

2. _____ is defined by the American _____ Association as the activity, set of institutions, and processes for creating, communicating, delivering, and exchanging offerings that have value for customers, clients, partners, and society at large. The term developed from the original meaning which referred literally to going to market, as in shopping, or going to a market to sell goods or services.

_____ practice tends to be seen as a creative industry, which includes advertising, distribution and selling.

   a. Marketing myopia   b. Product naming
   c. Customer acquisition management   d. Marketing

3. A _____ is a party that mediates between a buyer and a seller. A _____ who also acts as a seller or as a buyer becomes a principal party to the deal. Distinguish agent: one who acts on behalf of a principal.
   a. 180SearchAssistant   b. Power III
   c. Spokesperson   d. Broker

4. _____ is one of the four elements of marketing mix. An organization or set of organizations (go-betweens) involved in the process of making a product or service available for use or consumption by a consumer or business user.

The other three parts of the marketing mix are product, pricing, and promotion.

   a. Japan Advertising Photographers' Association   b. Distribution
   c. Better Living Through Chemistry   d. Comparison-Shopping agent

5. A personal and cultural _____ is a relative ethic _____, an assumption upon which implementation can be extrapolated. A _____ system is a set of consistent _____s and measures that is soo not true. A principle _____ is a foundation upon which other _____s and measures of integrity are based.
   a. Value   b. Supreme Court of the United States
   c. Perceptual maps   d. Package-on-Package

6. _____ is the management of the flow of goods, information and other resources, including energy and people, between the point of origin and the point of consumption in order to meet the requirements of consumers (frequently, and originally, military organizations.) _____ involves the integration of information, transportation, inventory, warehousing, material-handling, and packaging. _____ is a channel of the supply chain which adds the value of time and place utility.
   a. Power III   b. 6-3-5 Brainwriting
   c. 180SearchAssistant   d. Logistics

Chapter 13. Managing Marketing Channels and Supply Chains

7. _____ is a concept that denotes the precise probability of specific eventualities. Technically, the notion of _____ is independent from the notion of value and, as such, eventualities may have both beneficial and adverse consequences. However, in general usage the convention is to focus only on potential negative impact to some characteristic of value that may arise from a future event.
   a. Power III
   b. 180SearchAssistant
   c. 6-3-5 Brainwriting
   d. Risk

8. In economics, _____ is a measure of the relative satisfaction from consumption of various goods and services. Given this measure, one may speak meaningfully of increasing or decreasing _____, and thereby explain economic behavior in terms of attempts to increase one's _____. For illustrative purposes, changes in _____ are sometimes expressed in units called utils.
   a. ADTECH
   b. ACNielsen
   c. AMAX
   d. Utility

9. _____ is a form of communication that typically attempts to persuade potential customers to purchase or to consume more of a particular brand of product or service. 'While now central to the contemporary global economy and the reproduction of global production networks, it is only quite recently that _____ has been more than a marginal influence on patterns of sales and production. The formation of modern _____ was intimately bound up with the emergence of new forms of monopoly capitalism around the end of the 19th and beginning of the 20th century as one element in corporate strategies to create, organize and where possible control markets, especially for mass produced consumer goods.
   a. AMAX
   b. ACNielsen
   c. Advertising
   d. ADTECH

10. A _____ is a list of the general tasks and responsibilities of a position. Typically, it also includes to whom the position reports, specifications such as the qualifications needed by the person in the job, salary range for the position, etc. A _____ is usually developed by conducting a job analysis, which includes examining the tasks and sequences of tasks necessary to perform the job.
    a. Job description
    b. 180SearchAssistant
    c. Power III
    d. 6-3-5 Brainwriting

11. _____ are final goods specifically intended for the mass market. For instance, _____ do not include investment assets, like precious antiques, even though these antiques are final goods.

Manufactured goods are goods that have been processed by way of machinery.

   a. Free good
   b. Durable good
   c. Power III
   d. Consumer goods

12. _____ is an advertisement in which a particular product specifically mentions a competitor by name for the express purpose of showing why the competitor is inferior to the product naming it.

This should not be confused with parody advertisements, where a fictional product is being advertised for the purpose of poking fun at the particular advertisement, nor should it be confused with the use of a coined brand name for the purpose of comparing the product without actually naming an actual competitor. ('Wikipedia tastes better and is less filling than the Encyclopedia Galactica.')

Chapter 13. Managing Marketing Channels and Supply Chains

In the 1980s, during what has been referred to as the cola wars, soft-drink manufacturer Pepsi ran a series of advertisements where people, caught on hidden camera, in a blind taste test, chose Pepsi over rival Coca-Cola.

a. Comparative advertising
b. Cost per conversion
c. Heavy-up
d. GL-70

13. An _____ is the manufacturing of a good or service within a category. Although _____ is a broad term for any kind of economic production, in economics and urban planning _____ is a synonym for the secondary sector, which is a type of economic activity involved in the manufacturing of raw materials into goods and products.

There are four key industrial economic sectors: the primary sector, largely raw material extraction industries such as mining and farming; the secondary sector, involving refining, construction, and manufacturing; the tertiary sector, which deals with services (such as law and medicine) and distribution of manufactured goods; and the quaternary sector, a relatively new type of knowledge _____ focusing on technological research, design and development such as computer programming, and biochemistry.

a. ACNielsen
b. ADTECH
c. Industry
d. AMAX

14. The Oxford University Press defines _____ as 'marketing on a worldwide scale reconciling or taking commercial advantage of global operational differences, similarities and opportunities in order to meet global objectives.' Oxford University Press' Glossary of Marketing Terms.

Here are three reasons for the shift from domestic to _____ as given by the authors of the textbook, _____ Management--3rd Edition by Masaaki Kotabe and Kristiaan Helsen, 2004.

One of the product categories in which global competition has been easy to track is in U.S. automotive sales.

a. Diversity marketing
b. Digital marketing
c. Guerrilla Marketing
d. Global marketing

15. A _____ or logistics network is the system of organizations, people, technology, activities, information and resources involved in moving a product or service from supplier to customer. _____ activities transform natural resources, raw materials and components into a finished product that is delivered to the end customer. In sophisticated _____ systems, used products may re-enter the _____ at any point where residual value is recyclable.
a. Purchasing
b. Demand chain management
c. Supply chain network
d. Supply chain

16. The most important feature of a contract is that one party makes an _____ for an arrangement that another accepts. This can be called a 'concurrence of wills' or 'ad idem' (meeting of the minds) of two or more parties. The concept is somewhat contested.
a. AMAX
b. ACNielsen
c. ADTECH
d. Offer

Chapter 13. Managing Marketing Channels and Supply Chains

17. _____ refers to the methods of practicing and using another person's philosophy of business. The franchisor grants the independent operator the right to distribute its products, techniques, and trademarks for a percentage of gross monthly sales and a royalty fee. Various tangibles and intangibles such as national or international advertising, training, and other support services are commonly made available by the franchisor.
   a. 180SearchAssistant
   b. Power III
   c. Franchise fee
   d. Franchising

18. A _____ is defined by the International Co-operative Alliance's Statement on the Co-operative Identity as an autonomous association of persons united voluntarily to meet their common economic, social, and cultural needs and aspirations through a jointly-owned and democratically-controlled enterprise. It is a business organization owned and operated by a group of individuals for their mutual benefit. A _____ may also be defined as a business owned and controlled equally by the people who use its services or who work at it.
   a. Power III
   b. 6-3-5 Brainwriting
   c. 180SearchAssistant
   d. Cooperative

19. Wholesaling, historically called jobbing, is the sale of goods or merchandise to retailers, to industrial, commercial, institutional or to other wholesalers and related subordinated services.

According to the United Nations Statistics Division, '_____' is the resale (sale without transformation) of new and used goods to retailers, to industrial, commercial, institutional or professional users or involves acting as an agent or broker in buying merchandise for such persons or companies. Wholesalers frequently physically assemble, sort and grade goods in large lots, break bulk, repack and redistribute in smaller lots.

   a. Supply chain network
   b. Purchasing
   c. Supply network
   d. Wholesale

20. _____ is anything that is intended to save time, energy or frustration. A _____ store at a petrol station, for example, sells items that have nothing to do with gasoline/petrol, but it saves the consumer from having to go to a grocery store. '_____' is a very relative term and its meaning tends to change over time.
   a. Convenience
   b. Marketing buzz
   c. MaxDiff
   d. Demographic profile

21. _____ occurs when manufacturers (brands) disintermediate their channel partners, such as distributors, retailers, dealers, and sales representatives, by selling their products direct to consumers through general marketing methods and/or over the internet through eCommerce.

Some manufacturers want their brands to capture the power of the internet but do not want to create conflict with their other distribution channels, as these partners are necessary and viable for any manufacturer to maintain and gain success. The Census Bureau of the U.S. Department of Commerce reported that online sales in 2005 grew 24.6 percent over 2004 to reach 86.3 billion dollars.

   a. Channel conflict
   b. Retail design
   c. Trade Symbols
   d. Store brand

118 *Chapter 13. Managing Marketing Channels and Supply Chains*

22. In economics, business, retail, and accounting, a _____ is the value of money that has been used up to produce something, and hence is not available for use anymore. In economics, a _____ is an alternative that is given up as a result of a decision. In business, the _____ may be one of acquisition, in which case the amount of money expended to acquire it is counted as _____.

   a. Cost
   b. Transaction cost
   c. Variable cost
   d. Fixed costs

23. The break-even point for a product is the point where total revenue received equals the total costs associated with the sale of the product (TR=TC.) A break-even point is typically calculated in order for businesses to determine if it would be profitable to sell a proposed product, as opposed to attempting to modify an existing product instead so it can be made lucrative. _____ can also be used to analyse the potential profitability of an expenditure in a sales-based business.

   In _____, margin of safety is how much output or sales level can fall before a business reaches its break-even point (BEP).

   a. Contribution margin-based pricing
   b. Break even analysis
   c. Price skimming
   d. Pay Per Sale

24. _____ is the provision of service to customers before, during and after a purchase.

   According to Turban et al., '_____ is a series of activities designed to enhance the level of customer satisfaction - that is, the feeling that a product or service has met the customer expectation.'

   Its importance varies by product, industry and customer.

   a. Customer experience
   b. COPC Inc.
   c. Facing
   d. Customer service

25. In economics, _____ is the removal of intermediaries in a supply chain: 'cutting out the middleman'. Instead of going through traditional distribution channels, which had some type of intermediate (such as a distributor, wholesaler, broker, or agent), companies may now deal with every customer directly, for example via the Internet. One important factor is a drop in the cost of servicing customers directly.

   a. Consumer-to-consumer
   b. Social shopping
   c. Spamvertising
   d. Disintermediation

26. _____s is the social science that studies the production, distribution, and consumption of goods and services. The term _____s comes from the Ancient Greek oá¼°κονομῖα from oá¼¶κος (oikos, 'house') + vĪŒµος (nomos, 'custom' or 'law'), hence 'rules of the house(hold)'. Current _____ models developed out of the broader field of political economy in the late 19th century, owing to a desire to use an empirical approach more akin to the physical sciences.

   a. ACNielsen
   b. ADTECH
   c. Industrial organization
   d. Economic

27. In environmental modeling and especially in hydrology, a _____ model means a model that is acceptably consistent with observed natural processes, i.e. that simulates well, for example, observed river discharge. It is a key concept of the so-called Generalized Likelihood Uncertainty Estimation (GLUE) methodology to quantify how uncertain environmental predictions are.

Chapter 13. Managing Marketing Channels and Supply Chains

a. 180SearchAssistant
b. 6-3-5 Brainwriting
c. Power III
d. Behavioral

28. the term _____ is that part of Supply Chain Management that plans, implements, and controls the efficient, effective, forward, and reverse flow and storage of goods, services, and related information between the point of origin and the point of consumption in order to meet customers' requirements.

Software is used for logistics automation which helps the supply chain industry in automating the work flow as well as management of the system. There are very few generalized software available in the new market in the said topology.

a. Digital strategy
b. Logistics management
c. Corporate transparency
d. Crisis management

29. A supply chain is the system of organizations, people, technology, activities, information and resources involved in moving a product or service from _____ to customer. Supply chain activities transform natural resources, raw materials and components into a finished product that is delivered to the end customer. In sophisticated supply chain systems, used products may re-enter the supply chain at any point where residual value is recyclable.

a. Supplier
b. Bringin' Home the Oil
c. Product line extension
d. Rebate

30. A _____ is a process that can allow an organization to concentrate its limited resources on the greatest opportunities to increase sales and achieve a sustainable competitive advantage. A _____ should be centered around the key concept that customer satisfaction is the main goal.

A _____ is most effective when it is an integral component of corporate strategy, defining how the organization will successfully engage customers, prospects, and competitors in the market arena.

a. Marketing strategy
b. Psychographic
c. Cyberdoc
d. Societal marketing

31. A _____ is a plan of action designed to achieve a particular goal.

_____ is different from tactics. In military terms, tactics is concerned with the conduct of an engagement while _____ is concerned with how different engagements are linked.

a. 180SearchAssistant
b. 6-3-5 Brainwriting
c. Strategy
d. Power III

32. _____ is a practice in logistics of unloading materials from an incoming semi-trailer truck or rail car and loading these materials in outbound trailers or rail cars, with little or no storage in between. This may be done to change type of conveyance, or to sort material intended for different destinations, or to combine material from different origins.

In purest form this is done directly, with minimal or no warehousing.

a. Customer base
c. Product support
b. Cross-docking
d. Product life cycle management

33. _____ is a list for goods and materials held available in stock by a business. It is also used for a list of the contents of a household and for a list for testamentary purposes of the possessions of someone who has died. In accounting _____ is considered an asset.

a. Ending Inventory
c. Inventory
b. ACNielsen
d. ADTECH

34. _____ is a value showing the reliability of a person to others because of his/her integrity, truthfulness, and trustfulness, traits that can encourage someone to depend on him/her.

The wider use of this noun is in Systems engineering.

_____ as applied to a computer system is defined by the IFIP 10.4 Working Group on Dependable Computing and Fault Tolerance as:

'[..] the trustworthiness of a computing system which allows reliance to be justifiably placed on the service it delivers [..]'

an alternative and broader definition is provided by IEC IEV 191-02-03:

'_____ the collective term used to describe the availability performance and its influencing factors : reliability performance, maintainability performance and maintenance support performance'

This concept can be further extended to encompass mechanisms to increase and maintain the _____ of a system .

a. Power III
c. 180SearchAssistant
b. Dependability
d. 6-3-5 Brainwriting

35. _____ is a family of business models in which the buyer of a product provides certain information to a supplier of that product and the supplier takes full responsibility for maintaining an agreed inventory of the material, usually at the buyer's consumption location (usually a store.) A third party logistics provider can also be involved to make sure that the buyer have the required level of inventory by adjusting the demand and supply gaps.

As a symbiotic relationship, _____ makes it less likely that a business will unintentionally become out of stock of a good and reduces inventory in the supply chain.

a. Customer driven supply chain
c. Reverse auction
b. Merchandise management system
d. Vendor Managed Inventory

36. A _____ is a subgroup of people or organizations sharing one or more characteristics that cause them to have similar product and/or service needs. A true _____ meets all of the following criteria: it is distinct from other segments (different segments have different needs), it is homogeneous within the segment (exhibits common needs); responds similarly to a market stimulus, and it can be reached by a market intervention. The term is also used when consumers with identical product and/or service needs are divided up into groups so they can be charged different amounts.
   a. Commercial planning
   b. Production orientation
   c. Customer insight
   d. Market segment

Chapter 14. Retailing and Wholesaling

1. _____ consists of the sale of goods or merchandise from a fixed location, such as a department store or kiosk in small or individual lots for direct consumption by the purchaser. _____ may include subordinated services, such as delivery. Purchasers may be individuals or businesses.
   a. Warehouse store
   b. Charity shop
   c. Thrifting
   d. Retailing

2. A personal and cultural _____ is a relative ethic _____, an assumption upon which implementation can be extrapolated. A _____ system is a set of consistent _____s and measures that is soo not true. A principle _____ is a foundation upon which other _____s and measures of integrity are based.
   a. Package-on-Package
   b. Perceptual maps
   c. Value
   d. Supreme Court of the United States

3. _____ is the state or fact of exclusive rights and control over property, which may be an object, land/real estate, or some other kind of property (like government-granted monopolies collectively referred to as intellectual property.) It is embodied in an _____ right also referred to as title.

   _____ is the key building block in the development of the capitalist socio-economic system.

   a. ACNielsen
   b. ADTECH
   c. AMAX
   d. Ownership

4. _____ is a broad label that refers to any individuals or households that use goods and services generated within the economy. The concept of a _____ is used in different contexts, so that the usage and significance of the term may vary.

   A _____ is a person who uses any product or service.

   a. 180SearchAssistant
   b. Consumer
   c. 6-3-5 Brainwriting
   d. Power III

5. The most important feature of a contract is that one party makes an _____ for an arrangement that another accepts. This can be called a 'concurrence of wills' or 'ad idem' (meeting of the minds) of two or more parties. The concept is somewhat contested.
   a. AMAX
   b. ACNielsen
   c. ADTECH
   d. Offer

6. _____s is the social science that studies the production, distribution, and consumption of goods and services. The term _____s comes from the Ancient Greek oá¼°κονομῖα from oá¼¶κος (oikos, 'house') + vÏŒμος (nomos, 'custom' or 'law'), hence 'rules of the house(hold)'. Current _____ models developed out of the broader field of political economy in the late 19th century, owing to a desire to use an empirical approach more akin to the physical sciences.
   a. ACNielsen
   b. Industrial organization
   c. ADTECH
   d. Economic

7. _____, in strategic management and marketing, is the percentage or proportion of the total available market or market segment that is being serviced by a company. It can be expressed as a company's sales revenue (from that market) divided by the total sales revenue available in that market. It can also be expressed as a company's unit sales volume (in a market) divided by the total volume of units sold in that market.

a. Market share
b. Cyberdoc
c. Customer relationship management
d. Demand generation

8. A _____ is an optical machine-readable representation of data. Originally, _____s represented data in the widths (lines) and the spacings of parallel lines and may be referred to as linear or 1D (1 dimensional) barcodes or symbologies. But they also come in patterns of squares, dots, hexagons and other geometric patterns within images termed 2D (2 dimensional) matrix codes or symbologies.

a. Power III
b. Bar code
c. 6-3-5 Brainwriting
d. 180SearchAssistant

9. _____ are retail outlets, usually corporate owned businesses, that share brands and central management, often with standardized business methods and practices, and these may include stores, restaurants, and some service-oriented businesses.

The displacement of independent businesses by chains has generated controversy in many countries, and has sparked increased collaboration among independent businesses and communities to prevent chain proliferation. Such efforts occur within national trade groups such as the American Booksellers Association, as well as community-based coalitions such as Independent Business Alliances.

a. Chain stores
b. Customer base
c. Product life cycle management
d. Supplier diversity

10. Level-of-service is a measure-of-effectiveness by which traffic engineers determine the quality of service on elements of transportation infrastructure. Whilst the motorist is, in general, interested in speed of his journey, _____ is a more holistic approach, taking into account several other factors.

_____ may be used for other public facilities as a tool to measure changes in condition or availability, such as water supply.

a. Power III
b. Level of service
c. 6-3-5 Brainwriting
d. 180SearchAssistant

11. Merchandising refers to the methods, practices and operations conducted to promote and sustain certain categories of commercial activity. The term is understood to have different specific meanings depending on the context. _____ is a sale goods at a store

In marketing, one of the definitions of merchandising is the practice in which the brand or image from one product or service is used to sell another.

a. Sales promotion
b. Merchandising
c. New Media Strategies
d. Merchandise

12. _____ is the use of an object (typically referred to as an RFID tag) applied to or incorporated into a product, animal, or person for the purpose of identification and tracking using radio waves. Some tags can be read from several meters away and beyond the line of sight of the reader.

Most RFID tags contain at least two parts.

a. Radio-frequency identification
b. Power III
c. 6-3-5 Brainwriting
d. 180SearchAssistant

13. _____ is an advertisement in which a particular product specifically mentions a competitor by name for the express purpose of showing why the competitor is inferior to the product naming it.

This should not be confused with parody advertisements, where a fictional product is being advertised for the purpose of poking fun at the particular advertisement, nor should it be confused with the use of a coined brand name for the purpose of comparing the product without actually naming an actual competitor. ('Wikipedia tastes better and is less filling than the Encyclopedia Galactica.')

In the 1980s, during what has been referred to as the cola wars, soft-drink manufacturer Pepsi ran a series of advertisements where people, caught on hidden camera, in a blind taste test, chose Pepsi over rival Coca-Cola.

a. Cost per conversion
b. GL-70
c. Comparative advertising
d. Heavy-up

14. A _____ is the price one pays as remuneration for services, especially the honorarium paid to a doctor, lawyer, consultant, or other member of a learned profession. _____s usually allow for overhead, wages, costs, and markup.

Traditionally, professionals in Great Britain received a _____ in contradistinction to a payment, salary, or wage, and would often use guineas rather than pounds as units of account.

a. Price shading
b. Price war
c. Fee
d. Transfer pricing

15. A _____ is a fee that a person pays to operate a franchise branch of a larger company and enjoy the profits therefrom.

By joining a franchise an investor or franchisee is able to run a business under the umbrella of the franchise.

The franchisee must pay a _____, which may become costly.

a. 180SearchAssistant
b. Power III
c. Franchising
d. Franchise fee

16. _____ refers to the methods of practicing and using another person's philosophy of business. The franchisor grants the independent operator the right to distribute its products, techniques, and trademarks for a percentage of gross monthly sales and a royalty fee. Various tangibles and intangibles such as national or international advertising, training, and other support services are commonly made available by the franchisor.

a. Franchise fee
b. Power III
c. 180SearchAssistant
d. Franchising

17. In the Mediterranean Basin and the Near East, a _____ is a small, separated garden pavilion open on some or all sides. _____s were common in Persia, India, Pakistan, and in the Ottoman Empire from the 13th century onward. Today, there are many _____s in and around the TopkapÄ± Palace in Istanbul, and they are still a relatively common sight in Greece.
   a. 180SearchAssistant
   b. 6-3-5 Brainwriting
   c. Power III
   d. Kiosk

18. A _____ is a commercial building for storage of goods. _____s are used by manufacturers, importers, exporters, wholesalers, transport businesses, customs, etc. They are usually large plain buildings in industrial areas of cities and towns.
   a. Power III
   b. 180SearchAssistant
   c. 6-3-5 Brainwriting
   d. Warehouse

19. A _____, as opposed to a warehouse club, is a retail location with a limited variety of merchandise sold in bulk at a discount to customers. Unlike a warehouse club, _____s do not require their patrons to obtain a membership nor do they require the payment of any fees.

This type of store is also referred to as a 'Big Box' or 'Price-Impact' store because of the spartan, warehouse style of the interior and the low prices.

   a. Khodebshchik
   b. History of pawnbroking
   c. Warehouse store
   d. Closeout store

20. A _____ is defined by the International Co-operative Alliance's Statement on the Co-operative Identity as an autonomous association of persons united voluntarily to meet their common economic, social, and cultural needs and aspirations through a jointly-owned and democratically-controlled enterprise. It is a business organization owned and operated by a group of individuals for their mutual benefit. A _____ may also be defined as a business owned and controlled equally by the people who use its services or who work at it.
   a. Cooperative
   b. 6-3-5 Brainwriting
   c. 180SearchAssistant
   d. Power III

21. _____ measures the performance of a system. Certain goals are defined and the _____ gives the percentage to which they should be achieved.

Examples

- Percentage of calls answered in a call center.
- Percentage of customers waiting less than a given fixed time.
- Percentage of customers that do not experience a stock out.

_____ is used in supply chain management and in inventory management to measure the performance of inventory systems.

Chapter 14. Retailing and Wholesaling

Under stochastic conditions it is unavoidable that in some periods the inventory on hand is not sufficient to deliver the complete demand and, as a consequence, that part of the demand is filled only after an inventory-related waiting time.

a. Nielsen SoundScan
b. False designation of origin
c. Symbol group
d. Service Level

22. _____ is a term used in marketing and strategic management to describe a product, service, brand, or company that has such a distinct sustainable competitive advantage that competing firms find it almost impossible to operate profitably in that industry. The existence of a _____ will eliminate almost all market entities, whether real or virtual. Many existing firms will leave the industry, thereby increasing the industry's concentration ratio.
a. 6-3-5 Brainwriting
b. Power III
c. 180SearchAssistant
d. Category killer

23. A _____ is a retail establishment which specializes in selling a wide range of products without a single predominant merchandise line. _____s usually sell products including apparel, furniture, appliances, electronics, and additionally select other lines of products such as paint, hardware, toiletries, cosmetics, photographic equipment, jewelery, toys, and sporting goods. Certain _____s are further classified as discount _____s.
a. Department store
b. 6-3-5 Brainwriting
c. Power III
d. 180SearchAssistant

24. There are many important decisions about product and service development and marketing. In the process of product development and marketing we should focus on strategic decisions about product attributes, product branding, product packaging, product labeling and product support services. But product strategy also calls for building a _____.
a. Product line
b. Pinstorm
c. Macromarketing
d. Technology acceptance model

25. _____ are small stores which specialize in a specific range of merchandise and related items. Most stores have an extensive width and depth of stock in the item that they specify in and provide high levels of service and expertise. The pricing policy is generally in the medium to high range, depending on factors like the type and exclusivity of merchandise and ownership, that is, whether they are owner operated or a chain operation which has the advantage of bulk purchasing and centralized warehousing system.
a. Wardrobing
b. Catalog merchant
c. Brick and mortar business
d. Specialty stores

26. _____ is the transfer of information over a distance without the use of electrical conductors or 'wires'. The distances involved may be short (a few meters as in television remote control) or long (thousands or millions of kilometers for radio communications.) When the context is clear, the term is often shortened to 'wireless'.
a. Power III
b. 6-3-5 Brainwriting
c. Wireless communication
d. 180SearchAssistant

27. _____ refers to the methods, practices and operations conducted to promote and sustain certain categories of commercial activity. The term is understood to have different specific meanings depending on the context. Merchandise is a sale goods at a store

In marketing, one of the definitions of _____ is the practice in which the brand or image from one product or service is used to sell another.

a. New Media Strategies
b. Marketing communication
c. Word of mouth
d. Merchandising

28. Advertising mail junk mail is the delivery of advertising material to recipients of postal mail. The delivery of advertising mail forms a large and growing service for many postal services, and _____ marketing forms a significant portion of the direct marketing industry. Some organizations attempt to help people opt-out of receiving advertising mail, in many cases motivated by a concern over its negative environmental impact.

a. Telemarketing
b. Directory Harvest Attack
c. Direct mail
d. Phishing

29. _____ commonly refers to the electronic retailing / _____ channels industry, which includes such billion dollar companies as Home shoppingN, QVC, eBay, ShopNBC, Buy.com, and Amazon.com. _____ allows consumers to shop for goods while in the privacy of their own home, as opposed to traditional shopping, which requires you to visit brick and mortar stores and shopping malls.

The _____ / electronic retailing industry was created in 1977 when small market radio talk show host Bob Circosta was asked to sell avocado-green-colored can openers live on the air by station owner Bud Paxson when an advertiser traded 112 units of product instead of paying his advertising bill.

a. Home shopping
b. Power III
c. 6-3-5 Brainwriting
d. 180SearchAssistant

30. _____ is the examining of goods or services from retailers with the intent to purchase at that time. _____ is an activity of selection and/or purchase. In some contexts it is considered a leisure activity as well as an economic one.

a. Discount store
b. Hawkers
c. Khodebshchik
d. Shopping

31. _____ laws and regulations seek to protect any individual from loss of privacy due to failures or limitations of corporate customer privacy measures. They recognize that the damage done by privacy loss is typically not measurable, nor can it be undone, and that commercial organizations have little or no interest in taking unprofitable measures to drastically increase privacy of customers - indeed, their motivation is very often quite the opposite, to share data for commercial advantage, and to fail to officially recognize it as sensitive, so as to avoid legal liability for lapses of security that may occur.

_____ concerns date back to the first commercial couriers and bankers, who in every culture took strong measures to protect customer privacy, but also in every culture tended to be subject to very harsh punitive measures for failures to keep a customer's information private.

a. Personalized marketing
b. Locator software
c. Consumer privacy
d. Business-to-government

Chapter 14. Retailing and Wholesaling

32. Electronic commerce, commonly known as _____ or eCommerce, consists of the buying and selling of products or services over electronic systems such as the Internet and other computer networks. The amount of trade conducted electronically has grown extraordinarily with wide-spread Internet usage. A wide variety of commerce is conducted in this way, spurring and drawing on innovations in electronic funds transfer, supply chain management, Internet marketing, online transaction processing, electronic data interchange (EDI), inventory management systems, and automated data collection systems.

   a. ADTECH
   b. ACNielsen
   c. AMAX
   d. E-commerce

33. The _____ is an independent agency of the United States government, established in 1914 by the _____ Act. Its principal mission is the promotion of 'consumer protection' and the elimination and prevention of what regulators perceive to be harmfully 'anti-competitive' business practices, such as coercive monopoly.

   The _____ Act was one of President Wilson's major acts against trusts.

   a. Federal Trade Commission
   b. 180SearchAssistant
   c. Power III
   d. 6-3-5 Brainwriting

34. The _____ business model is one in which participants bid for products and services over the Internet. The functionality of buying and selling in an auction format is made possible through auction software which regulates the various processes involved.

   Several types of _____s are possible.

   a. ADTECH
   b. AMAX
   c. Online auction
   d. ACNielsen

35. _____ is a method of direct marketing in which a salesperson solicits to prospective customers to buy products or services, either over the phone or through a subsequent face to face or Web conferencing appointment scheduled during the call.

   _____ can also include recorded sales pitches programmed to be played over the phone via automatic dialing. _____ has come under fire in recent years, being viewed as an annoyance by many.

   a. Telemarketing
   b. Joe job
   c. Directory Harvest Attack
   d. Phishing

36. _____ is the ability of an individual or group to seclude themselves or information about themselves and thereby reveal themselves selectively. The boundaries and content of what is considered private differ among cultures and individuals, but share basic common themes. _____ is sometimes related to anonymity, the wish to remain unnoticed or unidentified in the public realm.

   a. Privacy
   b. Power III
   c. 180SearchAssistant
   d. 6-3-5 Brainwriting

Chapter 14. Retailing and Wholesaling

37. _____ is the area of law concerned with the protection and preservation of the privacy rights of individuals. Increasingly, governments and other public as well as private organizations collect vast amounts of personal information about individuals for a variety of purposes. The law of privacy regulates the type of information which may be collected and how this information may be used.
    a. Collective mark
    b. Madrid system
    c. Trademark attorney
    d. Privacy law

38. _____ is a retail channel for the distribution of goods and services. At a basic level it may be defined as marketing and selling products, direct to consumers away from a fixed retail location. Sales are typically made through party plan, one to one demonstrations, and other personal contact arrangements.
    a. 6-3-5 Brainwriting
    b. Power III
    c. 180SearchAssistant
    d. Direct selling

39. The Oxford University Press defines _____ as 'marketing on a worldwide scale reconciling or taking commercial advantage of global operational differences, similarities and opportunities in order to meet global objectives.' Oxford University Press' Glossary of Marketing Terms.

    Here are three reasons for the shift from domestic to _____ as given by the authors of the textbook, _____ Management--3rd Edition by Masaaki Kotabe and Kristiaan Helsen, 2004.

    One of the product categories in which global competition has been easy to track is in U.S. automotive sales.

    a. Diversity marketing
    b. Digital marketing
    c. Guerrilla Marketing
    d. Global marketing

40. _____ is a retailing concept in which the total range of products sold by a retailer is broken down into discrete groups of similar or related products; these groups are known as product categories. Examples of grocery categories may be: tinned fish, washing detergent, toothpastes, etc.Each category is then run like a 'mini business' (Business Unit) in its own right, with its own set of turnover and/or profitability targets and strategies. An important facet of _____ is the shift in relationship between retailer and supplier : instead of the traditional adversarial relationship, the relationship moves to one of collaboration, exchange of information and data and joint business building.The focus of all negotiations is centered around the effects of the turnover of the total category, not just the sales on the individual products therein.
    a. Category management
    b. Brochure
    c. Market segment
    d. Societal marketing

41. _____ is defined by the American _____ Association as the activity, set of institutions, and processes for creating, communicating, delivering, and exchanging offerings that have value for customers, clients, partners, and society at large. The term developed from the original meaning which referred literally to going to market, as in shopping, or going to a market to sell goods or services.

    _____ practice tends to be seen as a creative industry, which includes advertising, distribution and selling.

    a. Product naming
    b. Marketing myopia
    c. Customer acquisition management
    d. Marketing

Chapter 14. Retailing and Wholesaling

42. _____ is one of the four Ps of the marketing mix. The other three aspects are product, promotion, and place. It is also a key variable in microeconomic price allocation theory.
    a. Price
    b. Relationship based pricing
    c. Competitor indexing
    d. Pricing

43. A _____ is a plan of action designed to achieve a particular goal.

    _____ is different from tactics. In military terms, tactics is concerned with the conduct of an engagement while _____ is concerned with how different engagements are linked.

    a. 180SearchAssistant
    b. Power III
    c. Strategy
    d. 6-3-5 Brainwriting

44. _____, Gross profit margin or Gross Profit Rate can be defined as the amount of contribution to the business enterprise, after paying for direct-fixed and direct-variable unit costs, required to cover overheads (fixed commitments) and provide a buffer for unknown items. It expresses the relationship between gross profit and sales revenue.

    It can be expressed in absolute terms:

    Gross Profit = Revenue − Cost of Goods Sold

    or as the ratio of gross profit to sales revenue, usually in the form of a percentage:

    _____ Percentage = (Revenue-Cost of Goods Sold)/Revenue

    Cost of goods sold includes variable costs and fixed costs directly linked to the product, such as material and labor.

    a. Profit maximization
    b. Power III
    c. 180SearchAssistant
    d. Gross margin

45. _____ is a lightweight markup language, originally created by John Gruber and Aaron Swartz to help maximum readability and 'publishability' of both its input and output forms. The language takes many cues from existing conventions for marking up plain text in email. _____ converts its marked-up text input to valid, well-formed XHTML and replaces left-pointing angle brackets ('<') and ampersands with their corresponding character entity references.
    a. 6-3-5 Brainwriting
    b. Markdown
    c. Power III
    d. 180SearchAssistant

46. In financial accounting the term inventory _____ is the loss of products between point of manufacture or purchase from supplier and point of sale. The total shrink percentage of the retail industry in the United States was 1.7% of sales in 2001 according to the University of Florida's, National Retail Security Survey.

    48.5% of _____ in that time period was due to employee theft and 31.7% due to shoplifting.

Chapter 14. Retailing and Wholesaling

a. M80
b. Shrinkage
c. Better Living Through Chemistry
d. Davie Brown Index

47. In retail an _____, draw tenant, anchor tenant is one of the larger stores in a shopping mall, usually a department store or a major retail chain.

When the planned shopping mall format was developed by Victor Gruen in the mid-1950s, signing larger department stores was necessary for the financial stability of the projects, and to draw retail traffic that would result in visits to the smaller stores in the mall as well. Anchors generally have their rents heavily discounted, and may even receive cash inducements from the mall to remain open.

a. Endcap
b. Outlet store
c. Online ticket brokering
d. Anchor store

48. _____ is a contract between two parties, one being the employer and the other being the employee. An employee may be defined as: 'A person in the service of another under any contract of hire, express or implied, oral or written, where the employer has the power or right to control and direct the employee in the material details of how the work is to be performed.' Black's Law Dictionary page 471 (5th ed. 1979.)

a. ADTECH
b. AMAX
c. Employment
d. ACNielsen

49. A _____ is a company that sells directly to the public via more than one distribution channel. Most _____s sell through mail order catalogs and 'brick ' mortar' retail stores. Some _____s, sell online as well.

a. Gruen transfer
b. Discount store
c. Khodebshchik
d. Multichannel retailer

50. _____ is an organizational lifecycle function within a company dealing with the planning or marketing of a product or products at all stages of the product lifecycle.

_____ and product marketing (outbound focused) are different yet complementary efforts with the objective of maximizing sales revenues, market share, and profit margins. The role of _____ spans many activities from strategic to tactical and varies based on the organizational structure of the company.

a. Product management
b. Service product management
c. Requirement prioritization
d. Product information management

Chapter 14. Retailing and Wholesaling

51. _____ wholesale represents a type of operation within the wholesale sector. Its main features are summarized best by the following definitions:

- _____ is a form of trade in which goods are sold from a wholesale warehouse operated either on a self-service basis, or on the basis of samples (with the customer selecting from specimen articles using a manual or computerized ordering system but not serving himself) or a combination of the two. Customers (retailers, professional users, caterers, institutional buyers, etc.) settle the invoice on the spot and in cash, and carry the goods away themselves.

- Though wholesalers buy primarily from manufacturers and sell mostly to retailers, industrial users and other wholesalers, they also perform many value added functions. The wholesaler, an intermediary, is used based on principles of specialisation and division of labour as well as contractual efficiency. (OECD -Organisation for Economic Cooperation and Development.)

   a. Cash and carry
   b. Containerization
   c. Self branding
   d. Davie Brown Index

52. _____s function as professionals who deal with trade, dealing in commodities that they do not produce themselves, in order to produce profit.

_____s can be of two types:

1. A wholesale _____ operates in the chain between producer and retail _____. Some wholesale _____s only organize the movement of goods rather than move the goods themselves.
2. A retail _____ or retailer, sells commodities to consumers (including businesses.) A shop owner is a retail _____.

A _____ class characterizes many pre-modern societies. Its status can range from high (even achieving titles like that of _____ prince or nabob) to low, such as in Chinese culture, due to the soiling capabilities of profiting from 'mere' trade, rather than from the labor of others reflected in agricultural produce, craftsmanship, and tribute.

In the United States, '_____' is defined (under the Uniform Commercial Code) as any person while engaged in a business or profession or a seller who deals regularly in the type of goods sold.

   a. RFM
   b. Retail loss prevention
   c. Trade credit
   d. Merchant

53. A _____ is a party that mediates between a buyer and a seller. A _____ who also acts as a seller or as a buyer becomes a principal party to the deal. Distinguish agent: one who acts on behalf of a principal.
   a. Spokesperson
   b. Power III
   c. 180SearchAssistant
   d. Broker

54. In artificial intelligence, an _____ is an autonomous entity which observes and acts upon an environment (i.e. it is an agent) and directs its activity towards achieving goals (i.e. it is rational.) _____s may also learn or use knowledge to achieve their goals. They may be very simple or very complex: a reflex machine such as a thermostat is an _____, as is a human being, as is a community of human beings working together towards a goal.
   a. ADTECH
   b. AMAX
   c. ACNielsen
   d. Intelligent agent

Chapter 15. Integrated Marketing Communications and Direct Marketing

1. _____ is a form of communication that typically attempts to persuade potential customers to purchase or to consume more of a particular brand of product or service. 'While now central to the contemporary global economy and the reproduction of global production networks, it is only quite recently that _____ has been more than a marginal influence on patterns of sales and production. The formation of modern _____ was intimately bound up with the emergence of new forms of monopoly capitalism around the end of the 19th and beginning of the 20th century as one element in corporate strategies to create, organize and where possible control markets, especially for mass produced consumer goods.
   a. ADTECH
   b. AMAX
   c. ACNielsen
   d. Advertising

2. _____ , according to The American Marketing Association, is 'a planning process designed to assure that all brand contacts received by a customer or prospect for a product, service, or organization are relevant to that person and consistent over time.' (Marketing Power Dictionary)

   _____ is a term used to describe a holistic approach to marketing. It aims to ensure consistency of message and the complementary use of media. The concept includes online and offline marketing channels.

   a. ADTECH
   b. Integrated marketing communications
   c. AMAX
   d. ACNielsen

3. _____ is defined by the American _____ Association as the activity, set of institutions, and processes for creating, communicating, delivering, and exchanging offerings that have value for customers, clients, partners, and society at large. The term developed from the original meaning which referred literally to going to market, as in shopping, or going to a market to sell goods or services.

   _____ practice tends to be seen as a creative industry, which includes advertising, distribution and selling.

   a. Marketing myopia
   b. Marketing
   c. Product naming
   d. Customer acquisition management

4. _____ refers to messages and related media used to communicate with a market. Those who practice advertising, branding, direct marketing, graphic design, marketing, packaging, promotion, publicity, sponsorship, public relations, sales, sales promotion and online marketing are termed marketing communicators, _____ managers, or more briefly as marcom managers.
   a. Merchandising
   b. Merchandise
   c. Sales promotion
   d. Marketing communication

5. The _____ is generally accepted as the use and specification of the four p's describing the strategic position of a product in the marketplace. One version of the origins of the _____ starts in 1948 when James Culliton said that a marketing decision should be a result of something similar to a recipe. This version continued in 1953 when Neil Borden, in his American Marketing Association presidential address, took the recipe idea one step further and coined the term 'Marketing-Mix'.
   a. 180SearchAssistant
   b. Marketing mix
   c. Power III
   d. 6-3-5 Brainwriting

Chapter 15. Integrated Marketing Communications and Direct Marketing

6. _____ involves disseminating information about a product, product line, brand, or company. It is one of the four key aspects of the marketing mix. (The other three elements are product marketing, pricing, and distribution). P>_____ is generally sub-divided into two parts:

- Above the line _____: Promotion in the media (e.g. TV, radio, newspapers, Internet and Mobile Phones) in which the advertiser pays an advertising agency to place the ad
- Below the line _____: All other _____. Much of this is intended to be subtle enough for the consumer to be unaware that _____ is taking place. E.g. sponsorship, product placement, endorsements, sales _____, merchandising, direct mail, personal selling, public relations, trade shows

a. Promotion
b. Cashmere Agency
c. Davie Brown Index
d. Bottling lines

7. _____ is the reverse of encoding, which is the process of transforming information from one format into another. Information about _____ can be found in the following:

- Digital-to-analog converter, the use of analog circuit for _____ operations
- Code, a rule for converting a piece of information into another form or representation
- Code (cryptography), a method used to transform a message into an obscured form
- _____
- _____ methods, methods in communication theory for _____ codewords sent over a noisy channel
- Digital signal processing, the study of signals in a digital representation and the processing methods of these signals
- Word _____, the use of phonics to decipher print patterns and translate them into the sounds of language
- deCODE genetics

a. Decoding
b. Power III
c. 6-3-5 Brainwriting
d. 180SearchAssistant

8. _____ is the process of transforming information from one format into another. The opposite operation is called decoding.

There are a number of more specific meanings that apply in certain contexts:

- _____ is a basic perceptual process of interpreting incoming stimuli; technically speaking, it is a complex, multi-stage process of converting relatively objective sensory input (e.g., light, sound) into subjectively meaningful experience.
- A content format is a specific _____ format for converting a specific type of data to information.
- Character _____ is a code that pairs a set of natural language characters (such as an alphabet or syllabary) with a set of something else, such as numbers or electrical pulses.
- Text _____ uses a markup language to tag the structure and other features of a text to facilitate processing by computers.
- Semantics _____ of formal language A in formal language B is a method of representing all terms (e.g. programs or descriptions) of language A using language B.
- Electronic _____ transforms a signal into a code optimized for transmission or storage, generally done with a codec.
- Neural _____ is the way in which information is represented in neurons.
- Memory _____ is the process of converting sensations into memories.
- Encryption transforms information for secrecy.

a. ACNielsen
b. ADTECH
c. AMAX
d. Encoding

9. _____ is a sub-discipline and type of marketing. There are two main definitional characteristics which distinguish it from other types of marketing. The first is that it attempts to send its messages directly to consumers, without the use of intervening media.
   a. Direct marketing
   b. Power III
   c. Direct Marketing Associations
   d. Database marketing

10. _____ describes the situation when output from (or information about the result of) an event or phenomenon in the past will influence the same event/phenomenon in the present or future. When an event is part of a chain of cause-and-effect that forms a circuit or loop, then the event is said to 'feed back' into itself.

_____ is also a synonym for:

- _____ Signal; the information about the initial event that is the basis for subsequent modification of the event.
- _____ Loop; the causal path that leads from the initial generation of the _____ signal to the subsequent modification of the event.

_____ is a mechanism, process or signal that is looped back to control a system within itself. Such a loop is called a _____ loop.

a. 180SearchAssistant
b. Feedback
c. 6-3-5 Brainwriting
d. Power III

11. _____ is a market coverage strategy in which a firm decides to ignore market segment differences and go after the whole market with one offer.it is type of marketing (or attempting to sell through persuasion) of a product to a wide audience. The idea is to broadcast a message that will reach the largest number of people possible. Traditionally _____ has focused on radio, television and newspapers as the medium used to reach this broad audience.
   a. Business-to-consumer
   b. Cyberdoc
   c. Marketspace
   d. Mass marketing

12. _____ is the practice of managing the flow of information between an organization and its publics. _____ - often referred to as _____ - gains an organization or individual exposure to their audiences using topics of public interest and news items that do not require direct payment. Because _____ places exposure in credible third-party outlets, it offers a third-party legitimacy that advertising does not have.
   a. Graphic communication
   b. Symbolic analysis
   c. Power III
   d. Public relations

13. _____ is one of the four aspects of promotional mix. (The other three parts of the promotional mix are advertising, personal selling, and publicity/public relations.) Media and non-media marketing communication are employed for a pre-determined, limited time to increase consumer demand, stimulate market demand or improve product availability.
   a. Marketing communication
   b. Merchandise
   c. New Media Strategies
   d. Sales promotion

14. In statistics, an _____ is a term in a statistical model added when the effect of two or more variables is not simply additive. Such a term reflects that the effect of one variable depends on the values of one or more other variables.

Thus, for a response Y and two variables x_1 and x_2 an additive model would be:

$$Y = ax_1 + bx_2 + \text{error}$$

In contrast to this,

$$Y = ax_1 + bx_2 + c(x_1 \times x_2) + \text{error},$$

is an example of a model with an _____ between variables x_1 and x_2 ('error' refers to the random variable whose value by which y differs from the expected value of y.)

   a. AMAX
   b. ADTECH
   c. ACNielsen
   d. Interaction

15. There are four main aspects of a _____. These are:

Chapter 15. Integrated Marketing Communications and Direct Marketing

1 Advertising- Any paid presentation and promotion of ideas, goods, or services by an identified sponsor. Examples: Print ads, radio, television, billboard, direct mail, brochures and catalogs, signs, in-store displays, posters, motion pictures, Web pages, banner ads, and emails.

a. Pick and pack
b. Power III
c. Product manager
d. Promotional mix

16. _____ is the deliberate attempt to manage the public's perception of a subject. The subjects of _____ include people (for example, politicians and performing artists), goods and services, organizations of all kinds, and works of art or entertainment.

From a marketing perspective, _____ is one component of promotion.

a. Little value placed on potential benefits
b. Pearson's chi-square
c. Brando
d. Publicity

17. _____ is a cohort which consists of those people born after the Generation X cohort. Its name is controversial and is synonymous with several alternative names including The Net Generation, Millennials, Echo Boomers, and iGeneration. _____ consists primarily of the offspring of the Generation Jones and Baby Boomers cohorts.

a. AStore
b. Greatest Generation
c. Generation X
d. Generation Y

18. In marketing and advertising, a _____ usually an advertising campaign, is aimed at appealing to. A _____ can be people of a certain age group, gender, marital status, etc. (ex: teenagers, females, single people, etc.)

a. Brand Development Index
b. National brand
c. Target audience
d. Targeted advertising

19. _____ Management is the succession of strategies used by management as a product goes through its _____. The conditions in which a product is sold changes over time and must be managed as it moves through its succession of stages.

The _____ goes through many phases, involves many professional disciplines, and requires many skills, tools and processes.

a. Chain stores
b. Product life cycle
c. Supplier diversity
d. Customer satisfaction

20. _____ is a broad label that refers to any individuals or households that use goods and services generated within the economy. The concept of a _____ is used in different contexts, so that the usage and significance of the term may vary.

A _____ is a person who uses any product or service.

Chapter 15. Integrated Marketing Communications and Direct Marketing

    a. Power III
    c. 6-3-5 Brainwriting
    b. Consumer
    d. 180SearchAssistant

21. _____ usually refers to the marketing of pharmaceutical products but can apply in other areas as well. This form of advertising is directed toward patients, rather than healthcare professionals. Forms of DTC advertising include TV, print, and other mass media.
    a. History of Advertising Trust
    c. Local advertising
    b. Recruitment tool
    d. Direct-to-consumer advertising

22. A _____ is a type of wholesale merchant business that buys goods and bulk products from importers, other wholesalers and then sells to retailers. _____s can deal in any commodity destined for the retail market. Typical categories are food, lumber, hardware, fuel, and textiles.
    a. Tacit collusion
    c. Refusal to deal
    b. Chief privacy officer
    d. Jobbing house

23. The business terms _____ and pull originated in the logistic and supply chain management, but are also widely used in marketing.

A _____-pull-system in business describes the move of a product or information between two subjects. On markets the consumers usually 'pulls' the goods or information they demand for their needs, while the offerers or suppliers '_____es' them toward the consumers.

    a. Push
    c. Gold Key Matching Service
    b. Completely randomized designs
    d. Manufacturers' representatives

24. _____ is one of the four elements of marketing mix. An organization or set of organizations (go-betweens) involved in the process of making a product or service available for use or consumption by a consumer or business user.

The other three parts of the marketing mix are product, pricing, and promotion.

    a. Comparison-Shopping agent
    c. Better Living Through Chemistry
    b. Japan Advertising Photographers' Association
    d. Distribution

25. An _____ is the manufacturing of a good or service within a category. Although _____ is a broad term for any kind of economic production, in economics and urban planning _____ is a synonym for the secondary sector, which is a type of economic activity involved in the manufacturing of raw materials into goods and products.

There are four key industrial economic sectors: the primary sector, largely raw material extraction industries such as mining and farming; the secondary sector, involving refining, construction, and manufacturing; the tertiary sector, which deals with services (such as law and medicine) and distribution of manufactured goods; and the quaternary sector, a relatively new type of knowledge _____ focusing on technological research, design and development such as computer programming, and biochemistry.

    a. Industry
    c. ACNielsen
    b. AMAX
    d. ADTECH

26. A _____ is a plan of action designed to achieve a particular goal.

_____ is different from tactics. In military terms, tactics is concerned with the conduct of an engagement while _____ is concerned with how different engagements are linked.

a. Strategy
c. 180SearchAssistant
b. Power III
d. 6-3-5 Brainwriting

27. _____ is the study of when, why, how, where and what people do or do not buy products. It blends elements from psychology, sociology, social psychology, anthropology and economics. It attempts to understand the buyer decision making process, both individually and in groups. It studies characteristics of individual consumers such as demographics and behavioural variables in an attempt to understand people's wants. It also tries to assess influences on the consumer from groups such as family, friends, reference groups, and society in general.

a. Consumer behavior
c. Communal marketing
b. Consumer confidence
d. Multidimensional scaling

28. _____ is a fee paid on borrowed assets. It is the price paid for the use of borrowed money, or, money earned by deposited funds. Assets that are sometimes lent with _____ include money, shares, consumer goods through hire purchase, major assets such as aircraft, and even entire factories in finance lease arrangements.

a. AMAX
c. ACNielsen
b. ADTECH
d. Interest

29. _____ generally refers to a list of all planned expenses and revenues. It is a plan for saving and spending. A _____ is an important concept in microeconomics, which uses a _____ line to illustrate the trade-offs between two or more goods.

a. 6-3-5 Brainwriting
c. Budget
b. 180SearchAssistant
d. Power III

30. Competitiveness is a comparative concept of the ability and performance of a firm, sub-sector or country to sell and supply goods and/or services in a given market. Although widely used in economics and business management, the usefulness of the concept, particularly in the context of national competitiveness, is vigorously disputed by economists, such as Paul Krugman.

The term may also be applied to markets, where it is used to refer to the extent to which the market structure may be regarded as perfectly _____.

a. Geographical pricing
c. Free trade zone
b. Competitive
d. Customs union

31. _____ is systematic determination of merit, worth, and significance of something or someone using criteria against a set of standards. _____ often is used to characterize and appraise subjects of interest in a wide range of human enterprises, including the arts, criminal justice, foundations and non-profit organizations, government, health care, and other human services.

Depending on the topic of interest, there are professional groups which look to the quality and rigor of the _____ process.

a. ADTECH
b. ACNielsen
c. AMAX
d. Evaluation

32. _____ is a magazine, delivering news, analysis and data on marketing and media. The magazine was started as a broadsheet newspaper in Chicago in 1930. Today, its content appears in a print weekly distributed around the world and on many electronic platforms, including: AdAge.com, daily e-mail newsletters called Ad Age Daily, Ad Age's Mediaworks and Ad Age Digital; weekly newsletters such as Madison ' Vine (about branded entertainment) and Ad Age China; podcasts called Why It Matters and various videos.
   a. Outsert
   b. Ethical Consumer
   c. Adweek
   d. Advertising Age

33. A _____ is a relatively new executive level position at a corporation, company, organization typically reporting directly to the CEO or board of directors. The _____ is responsible for a brand's image, experience, and promise, and propagating it throughout all aspects of the company. The brand officer oversees marketing, advertising, design, public relations and customer service departments.
   a. Financial analyst
   b. Chief executive officer
   c. Chief brand officer
   d. Power III

34. In economics, business, retail, and accounting, a _____ is the value of money that has been used up to produce something, and hence is not available for use anymore. In economics, a _____ is an alternative that is given up as a result of a decision. In business, the _____ may be one of acquisition, in which case the amount of money expended to acquire it is counted as _____.
   a. Variable cost
   b. Fixed costs
   c. Cost
   d. Transaction cost

35. A _____ is a company which help companies to communicate with current and potential consumers and/or the general public.

Media agencies work with their clients to understand the business issues, their markets and their consumers. The _____ then identifies the consumer insights, which can help to devise a channel-neutral communication strategy which really connects with those consumers; using channels ranging from public relations (PR), events and sponsorship to advertising, interactive advertising, word of mouth and direct mail; to build a genuinely integrated campaign.

   a. Heinz pickle pin
   b. Copy testing
   c. Public service advertising
   d. Media Agency

36. The break-even point for a product is the point where total revenue received equals the total costs associated with the sale of the product (TR=TC.) A break-even point is typically calculated in order for businesses to determine if it would be profitable to sell a proposed product, as opposed to attempting to modify an existing product instead so it can be made lucrative. _____ can also be used to analyse the potential profitability of an expenditure in a sales-based business.

In _____, margin of safety is how much output or sales level can fall before a business reaches its break-even point (BEP).

Chapter 15. Integrated Marketing Communications and Direct Marketing

a. Price skimming
c. Pay Per Sale
b. Contribution margin-based pricing
d. Break even analysis

37. _____ is a marketing term that refers to the creation or generation of prospective consumer interest or inquiry into a business' products or services. Leads can be generated for a variety of purposes - list building, e-newsletter list acquisition or for winning customers.

A lead is a sign-up for an advertiser offer that includes contact information and in some cases, demographic information.

a. Sales management
c. Sales process
b. Hit rate
d. Lead generation

38. _____ is a branch of philosophy which seeks to address questions about morality, such as how a moral outcome can be achieved in a specific situation (applied _____), how moral values should be determined (normative _____), what moral values people actually abide by (descriptive _____), what the fundamental semantic, ontological, and epistemic nature of _____ or morality is (meta-_____), and how moral capacity or moral agency develops and what its nature is (moral psychology.)

Socrates was one of the first Greek philosophers to encourage both scholars and the common citizen to turn their attention from the outside world to the condition of man. In this view, Knowledge having a bearing on human life was placed highest, all other knowledge being secondary.

a. ADTECH
c. Ethics
b. ACNielsen
d. AMAX

39. A personal and cultural _____ is a relative ethic _____, an assumption upon which implementation can be extrapolated. A _____ system is a set of consistent _____s and measures that is soo not true. A principle _____ is a foundation upon which other _____s and measures of integrity are based.
a. Package-on-Package
c. Perceptual maps
b. Supreme Court of the United States
d. Value

40. A _____ is a structured collection of records or data that is stored in a computer system. The structure is achieved by organizing the data according to a _____ model. The model in most common use today is the relational model.
a. 6-3-5 Brainwriting
c. Power III
b. 180SearchAssistant
d. Database

41. The Oxford University Press defines _____ as 'marketing on a worldwide scale reconciling or taking commercial advantage of global operational differences, similarities and opportunities in order to meet global objectives.' Oxford University Press' Glossary of Marketing Terms.

Here are three reasons for the shift from domestic to _____ as given by the authors of the textbook, _____ Management--3rd Edition by Masaaki Kotabe and Kristiaan Helsen, 2004.

One of the product categories in which global competition has been easy to track is in U.S. automotive sales.

Chapter 15. Integrated Marketing Communications and Direct Marketing

a. Guerrilla Marketing
c. Diversity marketing
b. Digital marketing
d. Global marketing

42. The term _____ refers to several methods by which individuals can avoid receiving unsolicited product or service information. This ability is usually associated with direct marketing campaigns such as telemarketing, e-mail marketing, or direct mail.

The U.S. Federal Government created the National Do Not Call Registry to reduce the telemarketing calls consumers receive at home.

a. ACNielsen
c. AMAX
b. Opt-out
d. ADTECH

43. _____ refer to a collection of facts usually collected as the result of experience, observation or experiment or a set of premises. This may consist of numbers, words particularly as measurements or observations of a set of variables. _____ are often viewed as a lowest level of abstraction from which information and knowledge are derived.

a. Pearson product-moment correlation coefficient
c. Sample size
b. Mean
d. Data

44. _____ is a term used to describe a process of preparing and collecting data - for example as part of a process improvement or similar project.

_____ usually takes place early on in an improvement project, and is often formalised through a _____ Plan which often contains the following activity.

1. Pre collection activity - Agree goals, target data, definitions, methods
2. Collection - _____
3. Present Findings - usually involves some form of sorting analysis and/or presentation.

A formal _____ process is necessary as it ensures that data gathered is both defined and accurate and that subsequent decisions based on arguments embodied in the findings are valid . The process provides both a baseline from which to measure from and in certain cases a target on what to improve. Types of _____ 1-By mail questionnaires 2-By personal interview

- Six sigma
- Sampling (statistics)

a. 6-3-5 Brainwriting
c. Power III
b. 180SearchAssistant
d. Data collection

144   *Chapter 15. Integrated Marketing Communications and Direct Marketing*

45. _____ laws and regulations seek to protect any individual from loss of privacy due to failures or limitations of corporate customer privacy measures. They recognize that the damage done by privacy loss is typically not measurable, nor can it be undone, and that commercial organizations have little or no interest in taking unprofitable measures to drastically increase privacy of customers - indeed, their motivation is very often quite the opposite, to share data for commercial advantage, and to fail to officially recognize it as sensitive, so as to avoid legal liability for lapses of security that may occur.

_____ concerns date back to the first commercial couriers and bankers, who in every culture took strong measures to protect customer privacy, but also in every culture tended to be subject to very harsh punitive measures for failures to keep a customer's information private.

- a. Personalized marketing
- b. Business-to-government
- c. Consumer privacy
- d. Locator software

46. _____ are national trade organizations that seek to advance all forms of direct marketing.

23 direct marketing trade associations from five continents established an International Federation of _____. Founded in 1989, the IFDirect Marketing Associations was established to develop firm lines of communications between direct marketers around the world, and is dedicated to improving the practice and communicating the value of direct marketing; and to promoting the highest standards for ethical conduct and effective self-regulation of the direct marketing community.

- a. Database marketing
- b. Direct marketing
- c. Power III
- d. Direct Marketing Associations

47. The _____ is an independent agency of the United States government, established in 1914 by the _____ Act. Its principal mission is the promotion of 'consumer protection' and the elimination and prevention of what regulators perceive to be harmfully 'anti-competitive' business practices, such as coercive monopoly.

The _____ Act was one of President Wilson's major acts against trusts.

- a. 180SearchAssistant
- b. Federal Trade Commission
- c. 6-3-5 Brainwriting
- d. Power III

48. _____ is the ability of an individual or group to seclude themselves or information about themselves and thereby reveal themselves selectively. The boundaries and content of what is considered private differ among cultures and individuals, but share basic common themes. _____ is sometimes related to anonymity, the wish to remain unnoticed or unidentified in the public realm.
- a. Power III
- b. Privacy
- c. 6-3-5 Brainwriting
- d. 180SearchAssistant

49. _____ is an advertisement in which a particular product specifically mentions a competitor by name for the express purpose of showing why the competitor is inferior to the product naming it.

Chapter 15. Integrated Marketing Communications and Direct Marketing

This should not be confused with parody advertisements, where a fictional product is being advertised for the purpose of poking fun at the particular advertisement, nor should it be confused with the use of a coined brand name for the purpose of comparing the product without actually naming an actual competitor. ('Wikipedia tastes better and is less filling than the Encyclopedia Galactica.')

In the 1980s, during what has been referred to as the cola wars, soft-drink manufacturer Pepsi ran a series of advertisements where people, caught on hidden camera, in a blind taste test, chose Pepsi over rival Coca-Cola.

a. Cost per conversion
b. Heavy-up
c. Comparative advertising
d. GL-70

50. The _____ is a professional association for marketers. As of 2008 it had approximately 40,000 members. There are collegiate chapters on 250 campuses.
a. ACNielsen
b. American Marketing Association
c. AMAX
d. ADTECH

51. _____ is the management of the flow of goods, information and other resources, including energy and people, between the point of origin and the point of consumption in order to meet the requirements of consumers (frequently, and originally, military organizations.) _____ involves the integration of information, transportation, inventory, warehousing, material-handling, and packaging. _____ is a channel of the supply chain which adds the value of time and place utility.
a. Power III
b. Logistics
c. 6-3-5 Brainwriting
d. 180SearchAssistant

52. the term _____ is that part of Supply Chain Management that plans, implements, and controls the efficient, effective, forward, and reverse flow and storage of goods, services, and related information between the point of origin and the point of consumption in order to meet customers' requirements.

Software is used for logistics automation which helps the supply chain industry in automating the work flow as well as management of the system. There are very few generalized software available in the new market in the said topology.

a. Logistics management
b. Corporate transparency
c. Digital strategy
d. Crisis management

53. A _____ is a process that can allow an organization to concentrate its limited resources on the greatest opportunities to increase sales and achieve a sustainable competitive advantage. A _____ should be centered around the key concept that customer satisfaction is the main goal.

A _____ is most effective when it is an integral component of corporate strategy, defining how the organization will successfully engage customers, prospects, and competitors in the market arena.

a. Cyberdoc
b. Psychographic
c. Marketing strategy
d. Societal marketing

Chapter 16. Advertising, Sales Promotion, and Public Relations

1. _____ is the practice of using video games to advertise a product, organization or viewpoint. The term 'advergames' was coined in January 2000 by Anthony Giallourakis, and later mentioned by Wired's 'Jargon Watch' column in 2001. It has been applied to various free online games commissioned by major companies.
   - a. Advergaming
   - b. ADTECH
   - c. AMAX
   - d. ACNielsen

2. _____ is a form of communication that typically attempts to persuade potential customers to purchase or to consume more of a particular brand of product or service. 'While now central to the contemporary global economy and the reproduction of global production networks, it is only quite recently that _____ has been more than a marginal influence on patterns of sales and production. The formation of modern _____ was intimately bound up with the emergence of new forms of monopoly capitalism around the end of the 19th and beginning of the 20th century as one element in corporate strategies to create, organize and where possible control markets, especially for mass produced consumer goods.
   - a. Advertising
   - b. ACNielsen
   - c. AMAX
   - d. ADTECH

3. _____ or personalisation is tailoring a consumer product, electronic or written medium to a user based on personal details or characteristics they provide. More recently, it has especially been applied in the context of the World Wide Web.

   Web pages are personalized based on the interests of an individual.
   - a. Sexism,
   - b. Flighting
   - c. Complex sale
   - d. Personalization

4. _____ and converging technologies are terms used to cover various cutting-edge developments in the emergence and convergence of technology.

   _____ are those which represent new and significant developments within a field; converging techologies represent previously distinct fields which are in some way moving towards stronger inter-connection and similar goals.

   Over time, new methods and topics are developed and opened up.
   - a. Arcis Communications
   - b. International organization
   - c. Interstate Bakeries
   - d. Emerging technologies

5. A _____ is a collection of symbols, experiences and associations connected with a product, a service, a person or any other artifact or entity.

   _____s have become increasingly important components of culture and the economy, now being described as 'cultural accessories and personal philosophies'.

   Some people distinguish the psychological aspect of a _____ from the experiential aspect.
   - a. Brand equity
   - b. Brandable software
   - c. Store brand
   - d. Brand

Chapter 16. Advertising, Sales Promotion, and Public Relations

6. In grammar, the _____ is the form of an adjective or adverb which denotes the degree or grade by which a person, thing and is used in this context with a subordinating conjunction, such as than, as...as, etc.

The structure of a _____ in English consists normally of the positive form of the adjective or adverb, plus the suffix -er e.g. 'he is taller than his father is', or 'the village is less picturesque than the town nearby'.

a. 180SearchAssistant
b. Power III
c. Comparative
d. 6-3-5 Brainwriting

7. Competitiveness is a comparative concept of the ability and performance of a firm, sub-sector or country to sell and supply goods and/or services in a given market. Although widely used in economics and business management, the usefulness of the concept, particularly in the context of national competitiveness, is vigorously disputed by economists, such as Paul Krugman.

The term may also be applied to markets, where it is used to refer to the extent to which the market structure may be regarded as perfectly _____.

a. Free trade zone
b. Competitive
c. Geographical pricing
d. Customs union

8. _____ is an advertisement in which a particular product specifically mentions a competitor by name for the express purpose of showing why the competitor is inferior to the product naming it.

This should not be confused with parody advertisements, where a fictional product is being advertised for the purpose of poking fun at the particular advertisement, nor should it be confused with the use of a coined brand name for the purpose of comparing the product without actually naming an actual competitor. ('Wikipedia tastes better and is less filling than the Encyclopedia Galactica.')

In the 1980s, during what has been referred to as the cola wars, soft-drink manufacturer Pepsi ran a series of advertisements where people, caught on hidden camera, in a blind taste test, chose Pepsi over rival Coca-Cola.

a. GL-70
b. Cost per conversion
c. Heavy-up
d. Comparative Advertising

9. _____ is the pursuit of influencing outcomes -- including public-policy and resource allocation decisions within political, economic, and social systems and institutions -- that directly affect people's current lives. (Cohen, 2001)

Therefore, _____ can be seen as a deliberate process of speaking out on issues of concern in order to exert some influence on behalf of ideas or persons. Based on this definition, Cohen (2001) states that 'ideologues of all persuasions advocate' to bring a change in people's lives.

a. ACNielsen
b. Advocacy
c. AMAX
d. ADTECH

Chapter 16. Advertising, Sales Promotion, and Public Relations

10. In operant conditioning, _____ occurs when an event following a response causes an increase in the probability of that response occurring in the future. Response strength can be assessed by measures such as the frequency with which the response is made (for example, a pigeon may peck a key more times in the session), or the speed with which it is made (for example, a rat may run a maze faster.) The environment change contingent upon the response is called a reinforcer.
    a. Completely randomized designs
    b. Reinforcement
    c. Generic brands
    d. Relationship Management Application

11. _____ is a specialized form of marketing research conducted to improve the efficiency of advertising. According to MarketConscious.com, 'It may focus on a specific ad or campaign, or may be directed at a more general understanding of how advertising works or how consumers use the information in advertising. It can entail a variety of research approaches, including psychological, sociological, economic, and other perspectives.'

1879 - N.W. Ayer conducts custom research in an attempt to win the advertising business of Nichols-Shepard Co., a manufacturer of agricultural machinery.
    a. INVISTA
    b. Electrolux
    c. Advertising Research
    d. American Medical Association

12. The _____ is a nonprofit industry association for creating, aggregating, synthesizing and sharing the knowledge in the fields of advertising and media. It was founded in 1936 by the Association of National Advertisers and the American Association of Advertising Agencies. Its stated mission is to improve the practice of advertising, marketing and media research in pursuit of more effective marketing and advertising communications.
    a. ACNielsen
    b. IDDEA
    c. Intent scale translation
    d. Advertising Research Foundation

13. _____ generally refers to a list of all planned expenses and revenues. It is a plan for saving and spending. A _____ is an important concept in microeconomics, which uses a _____ line to illustrate the trade-offs between two or more goods.
    a. 180SearchAssistant
    b. Power III
    c. 6-3-5 Brainwriting
    d. Budget

14. In economics, business, retail, and accounting, a _____ is the value of money that has been used up to produce something, and hence is not available for use anymore. In economics, a _____ is an alternative that is given up as a result of a decision. In business, the _____ may be one of acquisition, in which case the amount of money expended to acquire it is counted as _____.
    a. Variable cost
    b. Transaction cost
    c. Fixed costs
    d. Cost

15. The _____ is an independent agency of the United States government, created, directed, and empowered by Congressional statute , and with the majority of its commissioners appointed by the current President.
    a. 180SearchAssistant
    b. 6-3-5 Brainwriting
    c. Power III
    d. Federal Communications Commission

16. In marketing and advertising, a _____ usually an advertising campaign, is aimed at appealing to. A _____ can be people of a certain age group, gender, marital status, etc. (ex: teenagers, females, single people, etc.)

a. Targeted advertising
b. National brand
c. Brand Development Index
d. Target audience

17. The break-even point for a product is the point where total revenue received equals the total costs associated with the sale of the product (TR=TC.) A break-even point is typically calculated in order for businesses to determine if it would be profitable to sell a proposed product, as opposed to attempting to modify an existing product instead so it can be made lucrative. _____ can also be used to analyse the potential profitability of an expenditure in a sales-based business.

In _____, margin of safety is how much output or sales level can fall before a business reaches its break-even point (BEP).

a. Contribution margin-based pricing
b. Pay Per Sale
c. Price skimming
d. Break even analysis

18. _____ are uniquely different from the rhetorical appeal to fear. There has been nearly 50 years of research on _____ in various disciplines and these studies have collectively garnered mixed results However, _____ are commonly used in persuasive health campaigns designed to modify behavior.
a. Power III
b. 6-3-5 Brainwriting
c. Fear appeals
d. 180SearchAssistant

19. _____ is the use of sexual or erotic imagery in advertising to draw interest to a particular product, for purpose of sale. A feature of _____ is that the imagery used, such as that of a pretty woman, typically has no connection to the product being advertised. The purpose of the imagery is to attract attention of the potential customer or user.
a. Sex in advertising
b. Power III
c. 6-3-5 Brainwriting
d. 180SearchAssistant

20. _____ is a magazine, delivering news, analysis and data on marketing and media. The magazine was started as a broadsheet newspaper in Chicago in 1930. Today, its content appears in a print weekly distributed around the world and on many electronic platforms, including: AdAge.com, daily e-mail newsletters called Ad Age Daily, Ad Age's Mediaworks and Ad Age Digital; weekly newsletters such as Madison ' Vine (about branded entertainment) and Ad Age China; podcasts called Why It Matters and various videos.
a. Ethical Consumer
b. Adweek
c. Outsert
d. Advertising Age

21. A _____ is a relatively new executive level position at a corporation, company, organization typically reporting directly to the CEO or board of directors. The _____ is responsible for a brand's image, experience, and promise, and propagating it throughout all aspects of the company. The brand officer oversees marketing, advertising, design, public relations and customer service departments.
a. Chief executive officer
b. Chief brand officer
c. Power III
d. Financial analyst

22. A _____ is a large outdoor advertising structure (a billing board), typically found in high traffic areas such as alongside busy roads. _____s present large advertisements to passing pedestrians and drivers. Typically showing large, ostensibly witty slogans, and distinctive visuals, _____s are highly visible in the top designated market areas.

a. 180SearchAssistant
c. Power III
b. 6-3-5 Brainwriting
d. Billboard

23. _____ are long-format television commercials, typically five minutes or longer.. _____ are also known as paid programming (or teleshopping in Europe.) Originally, they were a phenomenon that started in the United States where they were typically shown overnight (usually 2:00 a.m. to 6:00 a.m.)

a. ADTECH
c. Infomercials
b. ACNielsen
d. AMAX

24. Advertising mail junk mail is the delivery of advertising material to recipients of postal mail. The delivery of advertising mail forms a large and growing service for many postal services, and _____ marketing forms a significant portion of the direct marketing industry. Some organizations attempt to help people opt-out of receiving advertising mail, in many cases motivated by a concern over its negative environmental impact.

a. Direct mail
c. Telemarketing
b. Phishing
d. Directory Harvest Attack

25. _____ - an information and communication based electronic exchange environment - is a relatively new concept in marketing. Since physical boundaries no longer interfere with buy/sell decisions, the world has grown into several industry specific _____s which are integration of marketplaces through sophisticated computer and telecommunication technologies. The term _____ was introduced by Rayport and Sviokla in 1994 (see Rayport, Jeffrey F.

a. Marketspace
c. Market segment
b. Value chain
d. Kano model

26. A _____ or subscription radio is a digital radio signal that is broadcast by a communications satellite, which covers a much wider geographical range than terrestrial radio signals.

For now, _____ offers a meaningful alternative to ground-based radio services in some countries, notably the United States. Mobile services, such as Sirius, XM, and Worldspace, allow listeners to roam across an entire continent, listening to the same audio programming anywhere they go.

a. 6-3-5 Brainwriting
c. 180SearchAssistant
b. Satellite radio
d. Power III

27. _____ is a form of promotion that uses the Internet and World Wide Web for the expressed purpose of delivering marketing messages to attract customers. Examples of _____ include contextual ads on search engine results pages, banner ads, Rich Media Ads, Social network advertising, online classified advertising, advertising networks and e-mail marketing, including e-mail spam.

Online video directories for brands are a good example of interactive advertising.

a. ACNielsen
c. AMAX
b. Online advertising
d. ADTECH

28. _____ uses online or offline interactive media to communicate with consumers and to promote products, brands, services, and public service announcements, corporate or political groups.

Chapter 16. Advertising, Sales Promotion, and Public Relations

In the inaugural issue of the Journal of _____ , editors Li and Leckenby (2000) defined _____ as the 'paid and unpaid presentation and promotion of products, services and ideas by an identified sponsor through mediated means involving mutual action between consumers and producers.' This is most commonly performed through the Internet as a medium.

It is these mutual actions or interactions that enhance what _____ is trying to achieve.

- a. Enterprise Search Marketing
- b. Internet currency
- c. Interactive advertising
- d. Audience Screening

29. _____, sometimes referred to as information richness theory, is a framework that can be used to describe a communications medium by describing its ability to reproduce the information sent over it. It was developed by Richard L. Daft and Robert H. Lengel. For example, a phone call will not be able to reproduce visual social cues such as gestures.
- a. Power III
- b. 180SearchAssistant
- c. 6-3-5 Brainwriting
- d. Media richness theory

30. Foreign _____ in its classic form is defined as a company from one country making a physical investment into building a factory in another country. It is the establishment of an enterprise by a foreigner. Its definition can be extended to include investments made to acquire lasting interest in enterprises operating outside of the economy of the investor.
- a. Fountain Fresh International
- b. Brash Brands
- c. VideoJug
- d. Direct investment

31. _____ is an advertising term for a timing pattern in which commercials are scheduled to run during intervals that are separated by periods in which no advertising messages appear for the advertised item. Any period of time during which the messages are appearing is called a flight, and a period of message inactivity is usually called a hiatus.

The advantage of the _____ technique is that it allows an advertiser who does not have funds for running spots continuously to conserve money and maximize the impact of the commercials by airing them at key strategic times.

- a. Consumocracy
- b. Flighting
- c. Strict liability
- d. Concession

32. The _____ illustrates the decline of memory retention in time. A related concept is the strength of memory that refers to the durability that memory traces in the brain. The stronger the memory, the longer period of time that a person is able to recall it.
- a. 180SearchAssistant
- b. 6-3-5 Brainwriting
- c. Power III
- d. Forgetting curve

33. _____ , according to The American Marketing Association, is 'a planning process designed to assure that all brand contacts received by a customer or prospect for a product, service, or organization are relevant to that person and consistent over time.' (Marketing Power Dictionary)

_____ is a term used to describe a holistic approach to marketing. It aims to ensure consistency of message and the complementary use of media. The concept includes online and offline marketing channels.

a. ADTECH
b. ACNielsen
c. AMAX
d. Integrated marketing communications

34. _____ is defined by the American _____ Association as the activity, set of institutions, and processes for creating, communicating, delivering, and exchanging offerings that have value for customers, clients, partners, and society at large. The term developed from the original meaning which referred literally to going to market, as in shopping, or going to a market to sell goods or services.

_____ practice tends to be seen as a creative industry, which includes advertising, distribution and selling.

a. Product naming
b. Marketing myopia
c. Customer acquisition management
d. Marketing

35. _____ refers to messages and related media used to communicate with a market. Those who practice advertising, branding, direct marketing, graphic design, marketing, packaging, promotion, publicity, sponsorship, public relations, sales, sales promotion and online marketing are termed marketing communicators, _____ managers, or more briefly as marcom managers.

a. Sales promotion
b. Merchandising
c. Merchandise
d. Marketing communication

36. _____ is a broad label that refers to any individuals or households that use goods and services generated within the economy. The concept of a _____ is used in different contexts, so that the usage and significance of the term may vary.

A _____ is a person who uses any product or service.

a. 6-3-5 Brainwriting
b. Power III
c. 180SearchAssistant
d. Consumer

37. In marketing a _____ is a ticket or document that can be exchanged for a financial discount or rebate when purchasing a product. Customarily, _____s are issued by manufacturers of consumer packaged goods or by retailers, to be used in retail stores as a part of sales promotions. They are often widely distributed through mail, magazines, newspapers, the Internet, and mobile devices such as cell phones.

a. Marketing communication
b. Merchandising
c. Merchandise
d. Coupon

38. _____ in economics and business is the result of an exchange and from that trade we assign a numerical monetary value to a good, service or asset. If I trade 4 apples for an orange, the _____ of an orange is 4 - apples. Inversely, the _____ of an apple is 1/4 oranges.

a. Pricing
b. Contribution margin-based pricing
c. Discounts and allowances
d. Price

39. _____ involves disseminating information about a product, product line, brand, or company. It is one of the four key aspects of the marketing mix. (The other three elements are product marketing, pricing, and distribution). P>_____ is generally sub-divided into two parts:

- Above the line _____: Promotion in the media (e.g. TV, radio, newspapers, Internet and Mobile Phones) in which the advertiser pays an advertising agency to place the ad
- Below the line _____: All other _____. Much of this is intended to be subtle enough for the consumer to be unaware that _____ is taking place. E.g. sponsorship, product placement, endorsements, sales _____, merchandising, direct mail, personal selling, public relations, trade shows

   a. Bottling lines
   b. Cashmere Agency
   c. Davie Brown Index
   d. Promotion

40. _____ is one of the four aspects of promotional mix. (The other three parts of the promotional mix are advertising, personal selling, and publicity/public relations.) Media and non-media marketing communication are employed for a pre-determined, limited time to increase consumer demand, stimulate market demand or improve product availability.

   a. Merchandise
   b. Marketing communication
   c. New Media Strategies
   d. Sales promotion

41. The _____ is an independent agency of the United States government, established in 1914 by the _____ Act. Its principal mission is the promotion of 'consumer protection' and the elimination and prevention of what regulators perceive to be harmfully 'anti-competitive' business practices, such as coercive monopoly.

The _____ Act was one of President Wilson's major acts against trusts.

   a. Power III
   b. 180SearchAssistant
   c. 6-3-5 Brainwriting
   d. Federal Trade Commission

42. In the United States consumer sales promotions known as _____ or simply sweeps (both single and plural) have become associated with marketing promotions targeted toward both generating enthusiasm and providing incentive reactions among customers by enticing consumers to submit free entries into drawings of chance (and not skill) that are tied to product or service awareness wherein the featured prizes are given away by sponsoring companies. Prizes can vary in value from less than one dollar to more than one million U.S. dollars and can be in the form of cash, cars, homes, electronics, etc.

_____ frequently have eligibility limited by international, national, state, local, or other geographical factors.

   a. Claritas Prizm
   b. Commercial planning
   c. Sweepstakes
   d. Market segment

43. _____s are structured marketing efforts that reward, and therefore encourage, loyal buying behaviour -- behaviour which is potentially of benefit to the firm.

In marketing generally and in retailing more specifically, a loyalty card, rewards card, points card, advantage card, or club card is a plastic or paper card, visually similar to a credit card or debit card, that identifies the card holder as a member in a _____. Loyalty cards are a system of the loyalty business model.

Chapter 16. Advertising, Sales Promotion, and Public Relations

a. Power III
b. 180SearchAssistant
c. 6-3-5 Brainwriting
d. Loyalty program

44. A _____ is a type of wholesale merchant business that buys goods and bulk products from importers, other wholesalers and then sells to retailers. _____s can deal in any commodity destined for the retail market. Typical categories are food, lumber, hardware, fuel, and textiles.
   a. Chief privacy officer
   b. Refusal to deal
   c. Tacit collusion
   d. Jobbing house

45. _____ is a form of advertisement, where branded goods or services are placed in a context usually devoid of ads, such as movies, the story line of television shows Broadcasting ' Cable reported, 'Two thirds of advertisers employ 'branded entertainment'--_____--with the vast majority of that (80%) in commercial TV programming.' The story, based on a survey by the Association of National Advertisers, added, 'Reasons for using in-show plugs varied from 'stronger emotional connection' to better dovetailing with relevant content, to targetting a specific group.'

   _____ became common in the 1980s, but can be traced back to the nineteenth century in publishing.

   a. 6-3-5 Brainwriting
   b. Power III
   c. 180SearchAssistant
   d. Product placement

46. A _____ is an amount paid by way of reduction, return, or refund on what has already been paid or contributed. It is a type of sales promotion marketers use primarily as incentives or supplements to product sales. The mail-in _____ is the most common.
   a. Personalization
   b. Lifestyle city
   c. Strand
   d. Rebate

47. An _____ is the manufacturing of a good or service within a category. Although _____ is a broad term for any kind of economic production, in economics and urban planning _____ is a synonym for the secondary sector, which is a type of economic activity involved in the manufacturing of raw materials into goods and products.

   There are four key industrial economic sectors: the primary sector, largely raw material extraction industries such as mining and farming; the secondary sector, involving refining, construction, and manufacturing; the tertiary sector, which deals with services (such as law and medicine) and distribution of manufactured goods; and the quaternary sector, a relatively new type of knowledge _____ focusing on technological research, design and development such as computer programming, and biochemistry.

   a. Industry
   b. AMAX
   c. ACNielsen
   d. ADTECH

48. A _____ is defined by the International Co-operative Alliance's Statement on the Co-operative Identity as an autonomous association of persons united voluntarily to meet their common economic, social, and cultural needs and aspirations through a jointly-owned and democratically-controlled enterprise. It is a business organization owned and operated by a group of individuals for their mutual benefit. A _____ may also be defined as a business owned and controlled equally by the people who use its services or who work at it.

a. 6-3-5 Brainwriting
b. Power III
c. Cooperative
d. 180SearchAssistant

49. Merchandising refers to the methods, practices and operations conducted to promote and sustain certain categories of commercial activity. The term is understood to have different specific meanings depending on the context. _____ is a sale goods at a store

In marketing, one of the definitions of merchandising is the practice in which the brand or image from one product or service is used to sell another.

a. Sales promotion
b. Merchandising
c. New Media Strategies
d. Merchandise

50. _____ is the practice of managing the flow of information between an organization and its publics. _____ - often referred to as _____ - gains an organization or individual exposure to their audiences using topics of public interest and news items that do not require direct payment. Because _____ places exposure in credible third-party outlets, it offers a third-party legitimacy that advertising does not have.

a. Graphic communication
b. Symbolic analysis
c. Power III
d. Public relations

51. A _____ or community service announcement (CSA) is a non-commercial advertisement broadcast on radio or television, ostensibly for the public interest. _____s are intended to modify public attitudes by raising awareness about specific issues.

The most common topics of _____s are health and safety.

a. 180SearchAssistant
b. Power III
c. 6-3-5 Brainwriting
d. Public service announcement

52. _____ is the deliberate attempt to manage the public's perception of a subject. The subjects of _____ include people (for example, politicians and performing artists), goods and services, organizations of all kinds, and works of art or entertainment.

From a marketing perspective, _____ is one component of promotion.

a. Brando
b. Pearson's chi-square
c. Little value placed on potential benefits
d. Publicity

Chapter 17. Personal Selling and Sales Management

1. Importance of _____ is critical for any commercial organization. Expanding business is not possible without increasing sales volumes, and effective _____ goal is to organize sales team work in such a manner that ensures a growing flow of regular customers and increasing amount of sales.

The four phase-model of Management Process

1. Conception
2. Planning
3. Execution
4. Control

This model is cyclical, so it is a constant/continuous process.

=== _____ is attainment of sales force goals in a effective ' efficient manner through planning, staffing, training, leading ' controlling organizational resources.

a. Sales process
c. Hit rate
b. Request for proposal
d. Sales management

2. The _____, a unit of the United States Department of Labor, is the principal fact-finding agency for the U.S. government in the broad field of labor economics and statistics. The BLS is an independent national statistical agency that collects, processes, analyzes, and disseminates essential statistical data to the American public, the U.S. Congress, other Federal agencies, State and local governments, business, and labor representatives. The BLS also serves as a statistical resource to the Department of Labor.

a. Consumer Expenditure Survey
c. Power III
b. Gross national product
d. Bureau of Labor Statistics

3. _____ is a mathematical science pertaining to the collection, analysis, interpretation or explanation, and presentation of data. It also provides tools for prediction and forecasting based on data. It is applicable to a wide variety of academic disciplines, from the natural and social sciences to the humanities, government and business.

a. Median
c. Type I error
b. Null hypothesis
d. Statistics

4. _____ consists of the processes a company uses to track and organize its contacts with its current and prospective customers. _____ software is used to support these processes; information about customers and customer interactions can be entered, stored and accessed by employees in different company departments. Typical _____ goals are to improve services provided to customers, and to use customer contact information for targeted marketing.

a. Product bundling
c. Commercialization
b. Demand generation
d. Customer relationship management

5. _____ - an information and communication based electronic exchange environment - is a relatively new concept in marketing. Since physical boundaries no longer interfere with buy/sell decisions, the world has grown into several industry specific _____ s which are integration of marketplaces through sophisticated computer and telecommunication technologies. The term _____ was introduced by Rayport and Sviokla in 1994 (see Rayport, Jeffrey F.

a. Market segment
b. Kano model
c. Marketspace
d. Value chain

6. _____ is defined by the American _____ Association as the activity, set of institutions, and processes for creating, communicating, delivering, and exchanging offerings that have value for customers, clients, partners, and society at large. The term developed from the original meaning which referred literally to going to market, as in shopping, or going to a market to sell goods or services.

_____ practice tends to be seen as a creative industry, which includes advertising, distribution and selling.

a. Product naming
b. Marketing myopia
c. Customer acquisition management
d. Marketing

7. Customer _____ consists of the processes a company uses to track and organize its contacts with its current and prospective customers. CRelationship management software is used to support these processes; information about customers and customer interactions can be entered, stored and accessed by employees in different company departments. Typical CRelationship management goals are to improve services provided to customers, and to use customer contact information for targeted marketing.

a. Marketing
b. Relationship management
c. Green marketing
d. Product bundling

8. A personal and cultural _____ is a relative ethic _____, an assumption upon which implementation can be extrapolated. A _____ system is a set of consistent _____s and measures that is soo not true. A principle _____ is a foundation upon which other _____s and measures of integrity are based.

a. Package-on-Package
b. Perceptual maps
c. Supreme Court of the United States
d. Value

9. _____ is a method of direct marketing in which a salesperson solicits to prospective customers to buy products or services, either over the phone or through a subsequent face to face or Web conferencing appointment scheduled during the call.

_____ can also include recorded sales pitches programmed to be played over the phone via automatic dialing. _____ has come under fire in recent years, being viewed as an annoyance by many.

a. Joe job
b. Telemarketing
c. Phishing
d. Directory Harvest Attack

10. _____ is an advertisement in which a particular product specifically mentions a competitor by name for the express purpose of showing why the competitor is inferior to the product naming it.

This should not be confused with parody advertisements, where a fictional product is being advertised for the purpose of poking fun at the particular advertisement, nor should it be confused with the use of a coined brand name for the purpose of comparing the product without actually naming an actual competitor. ('Wikipedia tastes better and is less filling than the Encyclopedia Galactica.')

In the 1980s, during what has been referred to as the cola wars, soft-drink manufacturer Pepsi ran a series of advertisements where people, caught on hidden camera, in a blind taste test, chose Pepsi over rival Coca-Cola.

a. Cost per conversion
b. GL-70
c. Heavy-up
d. Comparative advertising

11. _____ is the physical search for minerals, fossils, precious metals or mineral specimens, and is also known as fossicking.

_____ is synonymous in some ways with mineral exploration which is an organised, large scale and at least semi-scientific effort undertaken by mineral resource companies to find commercially viable ore deposits. To actually be considered a prospector you must become registered as a professional prospector.

a. 180SearchAssistant
b. 6-3-5 Brainwriting
c. Power III
d. Prospecting

12. _____ is a broad label that refers to any individuals or households that use goods and services generated within the economy. The concept of a _____ is used in different contexts, so that the usage and significance of the term may vary.

A _____ is a person who uses any product or service.

a. 6-3-5 Brainwriting
b. Consumer
c. Power III
d. 180SearchAssistant

13. _____ is a form of government regulation which protects the interests of consumers. For example, a government may require businesses to disclose detailed information about products--particularly in areas where safety or public health is an issue, such as food. _____ is linked to the idea of consumer rights (that consumers have various rights as consumers), and to the formation of consumer organizations which help consumers make better choices in the marketplace.

a. Sound trademark
b. Federal Bureau of Investigation
c. Trademark dilution
d. Consumer Protection

14. Regulation refers to 'controlling human or societal behaviour by rules or restrictions.' Regulation can take many forms: legal restrictions promulgated by a government authority, self-regulation, social regulation (e.g. norms), co-regulation and market regulation. One can consider regulation as actions of conduct imposing sanctions (such as a fine.) This action of administrative law, or implementing _____ law, may be contrasted with statutory or case law.

a. Robinson-Patman Act
b. Regulatory
c. Right to Financial Privacy Act
d. Privacy law

15. _____ is the variety of human societies or cultures in a specific region, or in the world as a whole. (The term is also sometimes used to refer to multiculturalism within an organisation)

a. 180SearchAssistant
b. 6-3-5 Brainwriting
c. Power III
d. Cultural diversity

Chapter 17. Personal Selling and Sales Management

16. The term _____ was first coined by New York Times best selling author, Linda Richardson. _____ emphasizes customer needs and meeting those needs with solutions combining products and/or services. A consultative salesperson typically provides detailed instruction or advice on which solution best meets these needs.
   a. Request for proposal
   b. Sales management
   c. Lead generation
   d. Consultative selling

17. _____ is the study of the Earth and its lands, features, inhabitants, and phenomena. A literal translation would be 'to describe or write about the Earth'. The first person to use the word '_____' was Eratosthenes .
   a. Geography
   b. Power III
   c. 180SearchAssistant
   d. 6-3-5 Brainwriting

18. Competitiveness is a comparative concept of the ability and performance of a firm, sub-sector or country to sell and supply goods and/or services in a given market. Although widely used in economics and business management, the usefulness of the concept, particularly in the context of national competitiveness, is vigorously disputed by economists, such as Paul Krugman .

The term may also be applied to markets, where it is used to refer to the extent to which the market structure may be regarded as perfectly _____.

   a. Customs union
   b. Geographical pricing
   c. Competitive
   d. Free trade zone

19. A _____ is a list of the general tasks and responsibilities of a position. Typically, it also includes to whom the position reports, specifications such as the qualifications needed by the person in the job, salary range for the position, etc. A _____ is usually developed by conducting a job analysis, which includes examining the tasks and sequences of tasks necessary to perform the job.
   a. Power III
   b. 180SearchAssistant
   c. Job description
   d. 6-3-5 Brainwriting

20. A _____ is a group of employees from various functional areas of the organization - research, engineering, marketing, finance. human resources, and operations, for example - who are all focused on a specific objective and are responsible to work as a team to improve coordination and innovation across divisions and resolve mutual problems.
   a. Cross-functional team
   b. 180SearchAssistant
   c. Power III
   d. Job analysis

21. _____ is the realization of an application idea, model, design, specification, standard, algorithm an _____ is a realization of a technical specification or algorithm as a program, software component, or other computer system. Many _____s may exist for a given specification or standard.
   a. ACNielsen
   b. AMAX
   c. ADTECH
   d. Implementation

22. _____ refers to various methodologies for analyzing the requirements of a job.

Chapter 17. Personal Selling and Sales Management

The general purpose of _____ is to document the requirements of a job and the work performed. Job and task analysis is performed as a basis for later improvements, including: definition of a job domain; describing a job; developing performance appraisals, selection systems, promotion criteria, training needs assessment, and compensation plans.

a. Cross-functional team
b. Job analysis
c. 180SearchAssistant
d. Power III

23. _____ is the set of reasons that determines one to engage in a particular behavior. The term is generally used for human _____ but, theoretically, it can be used to describe the causes for animal behavior as well
a. Role playing
b. Power III
c. 180SearchAssistant
d. Motivation

24. _____ is a form of communication that typically attempts to persuade potential customers to purchase or to consume more of a particular brand of product or service. 'While now central to the contemporary global economy and the reproduction of global production networks, it is only quite recently that _____ has been more than a marginal influence on patterns of sales and production. The formation of modern _____ was intimately bound up with the emergence of new forms of monopoly capitalism around the end of the 19th and beginning of the 20th century as one element in corporate strategies to create, organize and where possible control markets, especially for mass produced consumer goods.
a. ADTECH
b. AMAX
c. ACNielsen
d. Advertising

25. In environmental modeling and especially in hydrology, a _____ model means a model that is acceptably consistent with observed natural processes, i.e. that simulates well, for example, observed river discharge. It is a key concept of the so-called Generalized Likelihood Uncertainty Estimation (GLUE) methodology to quantify how uncertain environmental predictions are.
a. 180SearchAssistant
b. Power III
c. 6-3-5 Brainwriting
d. Behavioral

26. A _____ attribute is one that exists in a range of magnitudes, and can therefore be measured. Measurements of any particular _____ property are expressed as a specific quantity, referred to as a unit, multiplied by a number. Examples of physical quantities are distance, mass, and time.
a. BeyondROI
b. Dolly Dimples
c. Lifestyle city
d. Quantitative

27. _____ is systematic determination of merit, worth, and significance of something or someone using criteria against a set of standards. _____ often is used to characterize and appraise subjects of interest in a wide range of human enterprises, including the arts, criminal justice, foundations and non-profit organizations, government, health care, and other human services.

Depending on the topic of interest, there are professional groups which look to the quality and rigor of the _____ process.

a. ADTECH
b. AMAX
c. ACNielsen
d. Evaluation

28. An _____ is a special-purpose computer system designed to perform one or a few dedicated functions, often with real-time computing constraints. It is usually embedded as part of a complete device including hardware and mechanical parts. In contrast, a general-purpose computer, such as a personal computer, can do many different tasks depending on programming.

a. AMAX
b. Embedded system
c. ACNielsen
d. ADTECH

29. Sales force management systems are information systems used in marketing and management that help automate some sales and sales force management functions. They are frequently combined with a marketing information system, in which case they are often called Customer Relationship Management (CRM) systems.

_____ Systems , typically a part of a company's customer relationship management system, is a system that automatically records all the stages in a sales process.

a. Sales force automation
b. Power III
c. 6-3-5 Brainwriting
d. 180SearchAssistant

Chapter 18. Implementing Interactive and Multichannel Marketing

1. _____ is the management of the flow of goods, information and other resources, including energy and people, between the point of origin and the point of consumption in order to meet the requirements of consumers (frequently, and originally, military organizations.) _____ involves the integration of information, transportation, inventory, warehousing, material-handling, and packaging. _____ is a channel of the supply chain which adds the value of time and place utility.

   a. 180SearchAssistant
   b. Power III
   c. Logistics
   d. 6-3-5 Brainwriting

2. the term _____ is that part of Supply Chain Management that plans, implements, and controls the efficient, effective, forward, and reverse flow and storage of goods, services, and related information between the point of origin and the point of consumption in order to meet customers' requirements.

   Software is used for logistics automation which helps the supply chain industry in automating the work flow as well as management of the system. There are very few generalized software available in the new market in the said topology.

   a. Crisis management
   b. Digital strategy
   c. Corporate transparency
   d. Logistics management

3. _____ - an information and communication based electronic exchange environment - is a relatively new concept in marketing. Since physical boundaries no longer interfere with buy/sell decisions, the world has grown into several industry specific _____s which are integration of marketplaces through sophisticated computer and telecommunication technologies. The term _____ was introduced by Rayport and Sviokla in 1994 (see Rayport, Jeffrey F.

   a. Market segment
   b. Marketspace
   c. Kano model
   d. Value chain

4. _____ is a cohort which consists of those people born after the Generation X cohort. Its name is controversial and is synonymous with several alternative names including The Net Generation, Millennials, Echo Boomers, and iGeneration. _____ consists primarily of the offspring of the Generation Jones and Baby Boomers cohorts.

   a. Greatest Generation
   b. Generation X
   c. AStore
   d. Generation Y

5. _____ is the practice of individuals including commercial businesses, governments and institutions, facilitating the sale of their products or services to other companies or organizations that in turn resell them, use them as components in products or services they offer _____ is also called business-to-_____ for short. (Note that while marketing to government entities shares some of the same dynamics of organizational marketing, B2G Marketing is meaningfully different.)

   a. Disruptive technology
   b. Business marketing
   c. Law of disruption
   d. Mass marketing

6. _____ is the sum of all experiences a customer has with a supplier of goods or services, over the duration of their relationship with that supplier. It can also be used to mean an individual experience over one transaction; the distinction is usually clear in context.

   Analysts and commentators who write about _____ and CRM have increasingly recognized the importance of managing the customer's experience.

Chapter 18. Implementing Interactive and Multichannel Marketing

a. COPC Inc.
b. Customer experience
c. Customer service
d. Customer Integrated System

7. _____ is defined by the American _____ Association as the activity, set of institutions, and processes for creating, communicating, delivering, and exchanging offerings that have value for customers, clients, partners, and society at large. The term developed from the original meaning which referred literally to going to market, as in shopping, or going to a market to sell goods or services.

_____ practice tends to be seen as a creative industry, which includes advertising, distribution and selling.

a. Marketing
b. Product naming
c. Marketing myopia
d. Customer acquisition management

8. The _____ is a marketing term and refers to all of the forces outside of marketing that affect marketing management's ability to build and maintain successful relationships with target customers. The _____ consists of both the macroenvironment and the microenvironment.

The microenvironment refers to the forces that are close to the company and affect its ability to serve its customers.

a. Psychographic
b. Market environment
c. Customer franchise
d. Business-to-consumer

9. A _____ is a written document that details the necessary actions to achieve one or more marketing objectives. It can be for a product or service, a brand, or a product line. _____s cover between one and five years.
a. Disruptive technology
b. Prosumer
c. Marketing strategy
d. Marketing plan

10. _____ is the examining of goods or services from retailers with the intent to purchase at that time. _____ is an activity of selection and/or purchase. In some contexts it is considered a leisure activity as well as an economic one.
a. Discount store
b. Hawkers
c. Khodebshchik
d. Shopping

11. In economics, _____ is a measure of the relative satisfaction from consumption of various goods and services. Given this measure, one may speak meaningfully of increasing or decreasing _____, and thereby explain economic behavior in terms of attempts to increase one's _____. For illustrative purposes, changes in _____ are sometimes expressed in units called utils.
a. ACNielsen
b. AMAX
c. ADTECH
d. Utility

12. A personal and cultural _____ is a relative ethic _____, an assumption upon which implementation can be extrapolated. A _____ system is a set of consistent _____s and measures that is soo not true. A principle _____ is a foundation upon which other _____s and measures of integrity are based.
a. Package-on-Package
b. Perceptual maps
c. Value
d. Supreme Court of the United States

Chapter 18. Implementing Interactive and Multichannel Marketing

13. _____ consists of the processes a company uses to track and organize its contacts with its current and prospective customers. _____ software is used to support these processes; information about customers and customer interactions can be entered, stored and accessed by employees in different company departments. Typical _____ goals are to improve services provided to customers, and to use customer contact information for targeted marketing.
    a. Commercialization
    b. Demand generation
    c. Product bundling
    d. Customer relationship management

14. _____ refers to the evolving trend in marketing whereby marketing has moved from a transaction-based effort to a conversation. The definition of _____ comes from John Deighton at Harvard, who says _____ is the ability to address the customer, remember what the customer says and address the customer again in a way that illustrates that we remember what the customer has told us (Deighton 1996.) _____ is not synonymous with online marketing, although _____ processes are facilitated by internet technology.
    a. Interactive marketing
    b. European Information Technology Observatory
    c. Outsourcing relationship management
    d. InfoNU

15. Customer _____ consists of the processes a company uses to track and organize its contacts with its current and prospective customers. CRelationship management software is used to support these processes; information about customers and customer interactions can be entered, stored and accessed by employees in different company departments. Typical CRelationship management goals are to improve services provided to customers, and to use customer contact information for targeted marketing.
    a. Green marketing
    b. Product bundling
    c. Marketing
    d. Relationship management

16. _____ is a recursive process where two or more people or organizations work together toward an intersection of common goals -- for example, an intellectual endeavor that is creative in nature--by sharing knowledge, learning and building consensus. _____ does not require leadership and can sometimes bring better results through decentralization and egalitarianism. In particular, teams that work collaboratively can obtain greater resources, recognition and reward when facing competition for finite resources. _____ is also present in opposing goals exhibiting the notion of adversarial _____, though this notion is atypical of the annotation that people have given towards their understanding of _____.
    a. 180SearchAssistant
    b. 6-3-5 Brainwriting
    c. Power III
    d. Collaboration

17. _____ is the process of filtering for information or patterns using techniques involving collaboration among multiple agents, viewpoints, data sources, etc. Applications of _____ typically involve very large data sets. _____ methods have been applied to many different kinds of data including sensing and monitoring data - such as in mineral exploration, environmental sensing over large areas or multiple sensors; financial data - such as financial service institutions that integrate many financial sources; or in electronic commerce and web 2.0 applications where the focus is on user data, etc.
    a. Power III
    b. 180SearchAssistant
    c. Collaborative filtering
    d. 6-3-5 Brainwriting

18. _____ or personalisation is tailoring a consumer product, electronic or written medium to a user based on personal details or characteristics they provide. More recently, it has especially been applied in the context of the World Wide Web.

Web pages are personalized based on the interests of an individual.

a. Flighting
b. Complex sale
c. Sexism,
d. Personalization

19. _____ is a term used in marketing in general and e-marketing specifically. Marketers will ask permission before advancing to the next step in the purchasing process. For example, they ask permission to send advertisements to prospective customers.

a. Spam Lit
b. Personalized marketing
c. Live banner
d. Permission marketing

20. _____ refers to messages and related media used to communicate with a market. Those who practice advertising, branding, direct marketing, graphic design, marketing, packaging, promotion, publicity, sponsorship, public relations, sales, sales promotion and online marketing are termed marketing communicators, _____ managers, or more briefly as marcom managers.

a. Sales promotion
b. Merchandise
c. Merchandising
d. Marketing Communication

21. On an intranet or B2E Enterprise Web portals, personalization is often based on user attributes such as department, functional area, or role. The term _____ in this context refers to the ability of users to modify the page layout or specify what content should be displayed.

There are two categories of personalizations:

1. Rule-based
2. Content-based

Web personalization models include rules-based filtering, based on 'if this, then that' rules processing, and collaborative filtering, which serves relevant material to customers by combining their own personal preferences with the preferences of like-minded others. Collaborative filtering works well for books, music, video, etc.

a. Movin'
b. Self branding
c. Cashmere Agency
d. Customization

22. _____ is a broad label that refers to any individuals or households that use goods and services generated within the economy. The concept of a _____ is used in different contexts, so that the usage and significance of the term may vary.

A _____ is a person who uses any product or service.

a. 6-3-5 Brainwriting
b. 180SearchAssistant
c. Power III
d. Consumer

Chapter 18. Implementing Interactive and Multichannel Marketing

23. _____ is the study of when, why, how, where and what people do or do not buy products. It blends elements from psychology, sociology, social psychology, anthropology and economics. It attempts to understand the buyer decision making process, both individually and in groups. It studies characteristics of individual consumers such as demographics and behavioural variables in an attempt to understand people's wants. It also tries to assess influences on the consumer from groups such as family, friends, reference groups, and society in general.

   a. Communal marketing
   b. Consumer behavior
   c. Multidimensional scaling
   d. Consumer confidence

24. _____ is an advertisement in which a particular product specifically mentions a competitor by name for the express purpose of showing why the competitor is inferior to the product naming it.

   This should not be confused with parody advertisements, where a fictional product is being advertised for the purpose of poking fun at the particular advertisement, nor should it be confused with the use of a coined brand name for the purpose of comparing the product without actually naming an actual competitor. ('Wikipedia tastes better and is less filling than the Encyclopedia Galactica.')

   In the 1980s, during what has been referred to as the cola wars, soft-drink manufacturer Pepsi ran a series of advertisements where people, caught on hidden camera, in a blind taste test, chose Pepsi over rival Coca-Cola.

   a. GL-70
   b. Cost per conversion
   c. Comparative advertising
   d. Heavy-up

25. _____ is anything that is intended to save time, energy or frustration. A _____ store at a petrol station, for example, sells items that have nothing to do with gasoline/petrol, but it saves the consumer from having to go to a grocery store. '_____' is a very relative term and its meaning tends to change over time.

   a. Demographic profile
   b. MaxDiff
   c. Marketing buzz
   d. Convenience

26. _____, in strategic management and marketing, is the percentage or proportion of the total available market or market segment that is being serviced by a company. It can be expressed as a company's sales revenue (from that market) divided by the total sales revenue available in that market. It can also be expressed as a company's unit sales volume (in a market) divided by the total volume of units sold in that market.

   a. Demand generation
   b. Cyberdoc
   c. Customer relationship management
   d. Market share

27. _____ is a neologism, defined as the combination of operational customization and marketing customization.

   _____ is considered one of the key drivers underpinning the new economy. Most companies today are changing their marketing model from a seller-centric to a buyer-centric one.

   a. Market intelligence
   b. Product planning
   c. Targeted advertising
   d. Customerization

Chapter 18. Implementing Interactive and Multichannel Marketing

28. _____ is a form of communication that typically attempts to persuade potential customers to purchase or to consume more of a particular brand of product or service. 'While now central to the contemporary global economy and the reproduction of global production networks, it is only quite recently that _____ has been more than a marginal influence on patterns of sales and production. The formation of modern _____ was intimately bound up with the emergence of new forms of monopoly capitalism around the end of the 19th and beginning of the 20th century as one element in corporate strategies to create, organize and where possible control markets, especially for mass produced consumer goods.
   a. ADTECH
   b. ACNielsen
   c. AMAX
   d. Advertising

29. A _____ is a type of website, usually maintained by an individual with regular entries of commentary, descriptions of events, or other material such as graphics or video. Entries are commonly displayed in reverse-chronological order. '_____' can also be used as a verb, meaning to maintain or add content to a _____.
   a. Blog
   b. 6-3-5 Brainwriting
   c. 180SearchAssistant
   d. Power III

30. _____ and viral advertising refer to marketing techniques that use pre-existing social networks to produce increases in brand awareness or to achieve other marketing objectives (such as product sales) through self-replicating viral processes, analogous to the spread of pathological and computer viruses. It can be word-of-mouth delivered or enhanced by the network effects of the Internet. Viral promotions may take the form of video clips, interactive Flash games, advergames, ebooks, brandable software, images, or even text messages.
   a. 180SearchAssistant
   b. New Media Marketing
   c. Power III
   d. Viral marketing

31. _____ refers to 'controlling human or societal behaviour by rules or restrictions.' _____ can take many forms: legal restrictions promulgated by a government authority, self-_____, social _____, co-_____ and market _____. One can consider _____ as actions of conduct imposing sanctions (such as a fine.) This action of administrative law, or implementing regulatory law, may be contrasted with statutory or case law.
   a. Regulation
   b. Non-conventional trademark
   c. CAN-SPAM
   d. Rule of four

32. In economics, business, retail, and accounting, a _____ is the value of money that has been used up to produce something, and hence is not available for use anymore. In economics, a _____ is an alternative that is given up as a result of a decision. In business, the _____ may be one of acquisition, in which case the amount of money expended to acquire it is counted as _____.
   a. Fixed costs
   b. Transaction cost
   c. Cost
   d. Variable cost

33. Why do retail stores need _____? With respect to the key objectives of growth and profit for any retail entity, _____ should significantly improve sales margins and increase sales by enabling the vendor to price variably and hence suitably and to control its product range based on profit margins. The retail stores will be able to compete more effectively with rivals in the form of mixed multiples, mail order and online retailers, who are often able to undercut but who do not generally have the same understanding of the retail market. In particular _____ is recognised as encouraging impulse buys, cross-selling of products and repeat sales.
   a. 180SearchAssistant
   b. Power III
   c. 6-3-5 Brainwriting
   d. Dynamic pricing

Chapter 18. Implementing Interactive and Multichannel Marketing

34. _____ in economics and business is the result of an exchange and from that trade we assign a numerical monetary value to a good, service or asset. If I trade 4 apples for an orange, the _____ of an orange is 4 - apples. Inversely, the _____ of an apple is 1/4 oranges.

   a. Pricing
   b. Contribution margin-based pricing
   c. Discounts and allowances
   d. Price

35. The break-even point for a product is the point where total revenue received equals the total costs associated with the sale of the product (TR=TC.) A break-even point is typically calculated in order for businesses to determine if it would be profitable to sell a proposed product, as opposed to attempting to modify an existing product instead so it can be made lucrative. _____ can also be used to analyse the potential profitability of an expenditure in a sales-based business.

   In _____, margin of safety is how much output or sales level can fall before a business reaches its break-even point (BEP).

   a. Pay Per Sale
   b. Break even analysis
   c. Contribution margin-based pricing
   d. Price skimming

36. _____ is one of the four Ps of the marketing mix. The other three aspects are product, promotion, and place. It is also a key variable in microeconomic price allocation theory.

   a. Relationship based pricing
   b. Price
   c. Competitor indexing
   d. Pricing

37. _____ is the ability of an individual or group to seclude themselves or information about themselves and thereby reveal themselves selectively. The boundaries and content of what is considered private differ among cultures and individuals, but share basic common themes. _____ is sometimes related to anonymity, the wish to remain unnoticed or unidentified in the public realm.

   a. Power III
   b. 6-3-5 Brainwriting
   c. 180SearchAssistant
   d. Privacy

38. _____ is a branch of philosophy which seeks to address questions about morality, such as how a moral outcome can be achieved in a specific situation (applied _____), how moral values should be determined (normative _____), what moral values people actually abide by (descriptive _____), what the fundamental semantic, ontological, and epistemic nature of _____ or morality is (meta-_____), and how moral capacity or moral agency develops and what its nature is (moral psychology.)

   Socrates was one of the first Greek philosophers to encourage both scholars and the common citizen to turn their attention from the outside world to the condition of man. In this view, Knowledge having a bearing on human life was placed highest, all other knowledge being secondary.

   a. ACNielsen
   b. Ethics
   c. AMAX
   d. ADTECH

39. _____ is marketing using many different marketing channels to reach a customer. In this sense, a channel might be a retail store, a web site, a mail order catalogue, or direct personal communications by letter, email or text message. The objective of the company doing the marketing is to make it easy for a consumer to buy from them in whatever way is most appropriate.

Chapter 18. Implementing Interactive and Multichannel Marketing

a. Blitz QFD
b. Multichannel marketing
c. Macromarketing
d. Buy one, get one free

40. _____ is one of the four elements of marketing mix. An organization or set of organizations (go-betweens) involved in the process of making a product or service available for use or consumption by a consumer or business user.

The other three parts of the marketing mix are product, pricing, and promotion.

a. Japan Advertising Photographers' Association
b. Better Living Through Chemistry
c. Comparison-Shopping agent
d. Distribution

41. _____ consists of the sale of goods or merchandise from a fixed location, such as a department store or kiosk in small or individual lots for direct consumption by the purchaser. _____ may include subordinated services, such as delivery. Purchasers may be individuals or businesses.

a. Warehouse store
b. Charity shop
c. Thrifting
d. Retailing

42. _____ occurs when manufacturers (brands) disintermediate their channel partners, such as distributors, retailers, dealers, and sales representatives, by selling their products direct to consumers through general marketing methods and/or over the internet through eCommerce.

Some manufacturers want their brands to capture the power of the internet but do not want to create conflict with their other distribution channels, as these partners are necessary and viable for any manufacturer to maintain and gain success. The Census Bureau of the U.S. Department of Commerce reported that online sales in 2005 grew 24.6 percent over 2004 to reach 86.3 billion dollars.

a. Trade Symbols
b. Retail design
c. Store brand
d. Channel conflict

43. _____ is a retail channel for the distribution of goods and services. At a basic level it may be defined as marketing and selling products, direct to consumers away from a fixed retail location. Sales are typically made through party plan, one to one demonstrations, and other personal contact arrangements.

a. Power III
b. 180SearchAssistant
c. 6-3-5 Brainwriting
d. Direct selling

44. A _____ is a type of wholesale merchant business that buys goods and bulk products from importers, other wholesalers and then sells to retailers. _____s can deal in any commodity destined for the retail market. Typical categories are food, lumber, hardware, fuel, and textiles.

a. Tacit collusion
b. Chief privacy officer
c. Refusal to deal
d. Jobbing house

45. _____ is an organizational lifecycle function within a company dealing with the planning or marketing of a product or products at all stages of the product lifecycle.

Chapter 18. Implementing Interactive and Multichannel Marketing

_____ and product marketing (outbound focused) are different yet complementary efforts with the objective of maximizing sales revenues, market share, and profit margins. The role of _____ spans many activities from strategic to tactical and varies based on the organizational structure of the company.

a. Product management
b. Service product management
c. Product information management
d. Requirement prioritization

46. Competitiveness is a comparative concept of the ability and performance of a firm, sub-sector or country to sell and supply goods and/or services in a given market. Although widely used in economics and business management, the usefulness of the concept, particularly in the context of national competitiveness, is vigorously disputed by economists, such as Paul Krugman .

The term may also be applied to markets, where it is used to refer to the extent to which the market structure may be regarded as perfectly _____.

a. Geographical pricing
b. Customs union
c. Free trade zone
d. Competitive

47. _____ is the provision of service to customers before, during and after a purchase.

According to Turban et al., '_____ is a series of activities designed to enhance the level of customer satisfaction - that is, the feeling that a product or service has met the customer expectation.'

Its importance varies by product, industry and customer.

a. Customer experience
b. COPC Inc.
c. Facing
d. Customer service

48. _____ refer to a collection of facts usually collected as the result of experience, observation or experiment or a set of premises. This may consist of numbers, words particularly as measurements or observations of a set of variables. _____ are often viewed as a lowest level of abstraction from which information and knowledge are derived.

a. Mean
b. Pearson product-moment correlation coefficient
c. Sample size
d. Data

49. _____, also referred to as i-marketing, web marketing, online marketing is the marketing of products or services over the Internet.

The Internet has brought many unique benefits to marketing, one of which being lower costs for the distribution of information and media to a global audience. The interactive nature of _____, both in terms of providing instant response and eliciting responses, is a unique quality of the medium.

a. ACNielsen
b. ADTECH
c. AMAX
d. Internet marketing

Chapter 18. Implementing Interactive and Multichannel Marketing

50. _____ is a list for goods and materials held available in stock by a business. It is also used for a list of the contents of a household and for a list for testamentary purposes of the possessions of someone who has died. In accounting _____ is considered an asset.

   a. Ending Inventory
   b. ACNielsen
   c. Inventory
   d. ADTECH

51. _____ is the area of applied ethics which deals with the moral principles behind the operation and regulation of marketing. Some areas of _____ overlap with media ethics.

Possible frameworks:

- Value-oriented framework, analyzing ethical problems on the basis of the values which they infringe (e.g. honesty, autonomy, privacy, transparency.) An example of such an approach is the AMA Statement of Ethics.
- Stakeholder-oriented framework, analysing ethical problems on the basis of whom they affect (e.g. consumers, competitors, society as a whole.)
- Process-oriented framework, analysing ethical problems in terms of the categories used by marketing specialists (e.g. research, price, promotion, placement.)

None of these frameworks allows, by itself, a convenient and complete categorization of the great variety of issues in _____.

Contrary to popular impressions, not all marketing is adversarial, and not all marketing is stacked in favour of the marketer.

   a. 6-3-5 Brainwriting
   b. 180SearchAssistant
   c. Power III
   d. Marketing ethics

52. Consumer market research is a form of applied sociology that concentrates on understanding the behaviours, whims and preferences, of consumers in a market-based economy, and aims to understand the effects and comparative success of marketing campaigns. The field of consumer _____ as a statistical science was pioneered by Arthur Nielsen with the founding of the ACNielsen Company in 1923.

Thus _____ is the systematic and objective identification, collection, analysis, and dissemination of information for the purpose of assisting management in decision making related to the identification and solution of problems and opportunities in marketing.

   a. Marketing research process
   b. Marketing research
   c. Focus group
   d. Logit analysis

53. In business and engineering, new _____ is the term used to describe the complete process of bringing a new product or service to market. There are two parallel paths involved in the Nproduct development process: one involves the idea generation, product design, and detail engineering; the other involves market research and marketing analysis. Companies typically see new _____ as the first stage in generating and commercializing new products within the overall strategic process of product life cycle management used to maintain or grow their market share.

Chapter 18. Implementing Interactive and Multichannel Marketing

a. New product development
c. New product screening
b. Product development
d. Specification tree

54. A _____ researches, selects, develops, and places a company's products.

A _____ considers numerous factors such as target demographic, the products offered by the competition, and how well the product fits in with the company's business model. Generally, a _____ manages one or more tangible products.

a. Product manager
c. Power III
b. Pick and pack
d. Promotional mix

55. _____ involves disseminating information about a product, product line, brand, or company. It is one of the four key aspects of the marketing mix. (The other three elements are product marketing, pricing, and distribution). P>_____ is generally sub-divided into two parts:

- Above the line _____: Promotion in the media (e.g. TV, radio, newspapers, Internet and Mobile Phones) in which the advertiser pays an advertising agency to place the ad
- Below the line _____: All other _____. Much of this is intended to be subtle enough for the consumer to be unaware that _____ is taking place. E.g. sponsorship, product placement, endorsements, sales _____, merchandising, direct mail, personal selling, public relations, trade shows

a. Cashmere Agency
c. Davie Brown Index
b. Promotion
d. Bottling lines

56. _____ is the practice of managing the flow of information between an organization and its publics. _____ - often referred to as _____ - gains an organization or individual exposure to their audiences using topics of public interest and news items that do not require direct payment. Because _____ places exposure in credible third-party outlets, it offers a third-party legitimacy that advertising does not have.

a. Power III
c. Symbolic analysis
b. Graphic communication
d. Public relations

57. _____ is one of the four aspects of promotional mix. (The other three parts of the promotional mix are advertising, personal selling, and publicity/public relations.) Media and non-media marketing communication are employed for a pre-determined, limited time to increase consumer demand, stimulate market demand or improve product availability.

a. Marketing communication
c. New Media Strategies
b. Merchandise
d. Sales promotion

58. A _____ or logistics network is the system of organizations, people, technology, activities, information and resources involved in moving a product or service from supplier to customer. _____ activities transform natural resources, raw materials and components into a finished product that is delivered to the end customer. In sophisticated _____ systems, used products may re-enter the _____ at any point where residual value is recyclable.

a. Supply chain network
c. Demand chain management
b. Purchasing
d. Supply chain

Chapter 18. Implementing Interactive and Multichannel Marketing 173

59. _____ is a business discipline which is focused on the practical application of marketing techniques and the management of a firm's marketing resources and activities. Marketing managers are often responsible for influencing the level, timing, and composition of customer demand accepted definition of the term. In part, this is because the role of a marketing manager can vary significantly based on a business' size, corporate culture, and industry context.
   a. Marketing management
   b. Performance-based advertising
   c. Business structure
   d. Door-to-door

60. _____ in an organizational setting, according to the EFQM definition, refers to a comprehensive, systematic and regular review of an organization's activities and results referenced against the EFQM Excellence Model. The _____ process allows the organization to discern clearly its strengths and areas in which improvements can be made and culminates in planned improvement actions which are then monitored for progress.

   _____ in an educational setting involves students making judgments about their own work.

   a. 6-3-5 Brainwriting
   b. Power III
   c. 180SearchAssistant
   d. Self-assessment

61. _____ is a measure of the strength of a brand, product, service relative to competitive offerings. There is often a geographic element to the competitive landscape. In defining _____, you must see to what extent a product, brand, or firm controls a product category in a given geographic area.
   a. Discretionary spending
   b. Productivity
   c. Market system
   d. Market dominance

62. A _____ is a structured collection of records or data that is stored in a computer system. The structure is achieved by organizing the data according to a _____ model. The model in most common use today is the relational model.
   a. Power III
   b. Database
   c. 6-3-5 Brainwriting
   d. 180SearchAssistant

63. _____ is a fee paid on borrowed assets. It is the price paid for the use of borrowed money, or, money earned by deposited funds. Assets that are sometimes lent with _____ include money, shares, consumer goods through hire purchase, major assets such as aircraft, and even entire factories in finance lease arrangements.
   a. Interest
   b. ADTECH
   c. ACNielsen
   d. AMAX

64. The _____ assessment is a psychometric questionnaire designed to measure psychological preferences in how people perceive the world and make decisions.[1] These preferences were extrapolated from the typological theories originated by Carl Gustav Jung, as published in his 1921 book Psychological Types. The original developers of the personality inventory were Katharine Cook Briggs and her daughter, Isabel Briggs Myers. They began creating the indicator during World War II, believing that a knowledge of personality preferences would help women who were entering the industrial workforce for the first time identify the sort of war-time jobs where they would be 'most comfortable and effective'.[xiii] The initial questionnaire grew into the _____, which was first published in 1962.
   a. Power III
   b. 180SearchAssistant
   c. Myers-Briggs Type Indicator
   d. 6-3-5 Brainwriting

Chapter 18. Implementing Interactive and Multichannel Marketing

65. A _____ aims to describe aspects of a person's character that remain stable throughout that person's lifetime, the individual's character pattern of behavior, thoughts, and feelings. An early model of personality was posited by Greek philosopher/physician Hippocrates. The 20th century heralded a new interest in defining and identifying separate personality types, in close correlation with the emergence of the field of psychology.

a. Personality test
b. 6-3-5 Brainwriting
c. Power III
d. 180SearchAssistant

66. _____ is a term used to describe a process of preparing and collecting data - for example as part of a process improvement or similar project.

_____ usually takes place early on in an improvement project, and is often formalised through a _____ Plan which often contains the following activity.

1. Pre collection activity - Agree goals, target data, definitions, methods
2. Collection - _____
3. Present Findings - usually involves some form of sorting analysis and/or presentation.

A formal _____ process is necessary as it ensures that data gathered is both defined and accurate and that subsequent decisions based on arguments embodied in the findings are valid . The process provides both a baseline from which to measure from and in certain cases a target on what to improve. Types of _____ 1-By mail questionnaires 2-By personal interview

- Six sigma
- Sampling (statistics)

a. Data collection
b. 6-3-5 Brainwriting
c. Power III
d. 180SearchAssistant

67. _____ is a contract between two parties, one being the employer and the other being the employee. An employee may be defined as: 'A person in the service of another under any contract of hire, express or implied, oral or written, where the employer has the power or right to control and direct the employee in the material details of how the work is to be performed.' Black's Law Dictionary page 471 (5th ed. 1979).

a. ACNielsen
b. Employment
c. AMAX
d. ADTECH

68. _____ is a magazine, delivering news, analysis and data on marketing and media. The magazine was started as a broadsheet newspaper in Chicago in 1930. Today, its content appears in a print weekly distributed around the world and on many electronic platforms, including: AdAge.com, daily e-mail newsletters called Ad Age Daily, Ad Age's Mediaworks and Ad Age Digital; weekly newsletters such as Madison ' Vine (about branded entertainment) and Ad Age China; podcasts called Why It Matters and various videos.

a. Adweek
b. Outsert
c. Advertising Age
d. Ethical Consumer

Chapter 18. Implementing Interactive and Multichannel Marketing

69. An _____ is a company that matches workers to open jobs. The first _____ in the United States was opened by Fred Winslow who opened Engineering Agency in 1893. It later became part of General Employment Enterprises who also owned Businessmen's Clearing House (est.

    a. ADTECH   b. ACNielsen
    c. AMAX   d. Employment agency

70. Many institutions make a distinction between circulating _____ and collecting _____ Many modern _____ are a mixture of both, as they contain a general collection for circulation, and a reference collection which is often more specialized, as well as restricted to the library premises.

Also, the governments of most major countries support national _____.

    a. 180SearchAssistant   b. 6-3-5 Brainwriting
    c. Libraries   d. Power III

71. The _____ is an English-language international daily newspaper published by Dow Jones ' Company in New York City with Asian and European editions. As of 2007, It has a worldwide daily circulation of more than 2 million, with approximately 931,000 paying online subscribers. It was the largest-circulation newspaper in the United States until November 2003, when it was surpassed by USA Today.

    a. Power III   b. 6-3-5 Brainwriting
    c. Wall Street Journal   d. 180SearchAssistant

72. _____ in organizations and public policy is both the organizational process of creating and maintaining a plan; and the psychological process of thinking about the activities required to create a desired goal on some scale. As such, it is a fundamental property of intelligent behavior. This thought process is essential to the creation and refinement of a plan, or integration of it with other plans, that is, it combines forecasting of developments with the preparation of scenarios of how to react to them.

    a. Power III   b. 6-3-5 Brainwriting
    c. 180SearchAssistant   d. Planning

Chapter 1

1. a	2. a	3. c	4. a	5. b	6. a	7. d	8. a	9. d	10. c
11. c	12. d	13. a	14. b	15. b	16. d	17. d	18. a	19. c	20. d
21. d	22. a	23. d	24. a	25. c	26. c	27. b			

Chapter 2

1. d	2. a	3. d	4. b	5. c	6. c	7. d	8. d	9. d	10. d
11. d	12. a	13. d	14. d	15. a	16. d	17. a	18. b	19. b	20. d
21. a	22. d	23. a	24. d	25. d	26. d	27. b	28. d	29. d	30. d
31. a	32. d	33. d							

Chapter 3

1. b	2. d	3. a	4. d	5. d	6. b	7. c	8. b	9. a	10. d
11. d	12. a	13. b	14. d	15. d	16. d	17. a	18. b	19. c	20. d
21. c	22. d	23. d	24. d	25. a	26. c	27. d	28. d	29. d	30. d
31. d	32. c	33. d	34. b	35. d	36. d	37. d	38. d	39. d	40. c
41. d	42. d	43. d	44. d	45. a	46. a	47. c	48. b	49. b	50. d
51. d	52. d	53. d	54. d	55. b	56. c	57. d	58. d	59. a	60. d
61. d	62. d	63. d	64. b	65. c	66. b	67. d	68. b	69. d	70. c
71. d	72. a	73. b	74. b	75. d	76. d	77. a	78. c	79. d	80. b
81. d									

Chapter 4

1. d	2. d	3. a	4. d	5. d	6. d	7. d	8. c	9. a	10. b
11. d	12. c	13. c	14. d	15. d	16. b	17. c	18. b	19. a	20. b
21. a	22. d	23. d	24. a	25. d	26. a	27. d	28. d	29. a	30. a
31. b	32. a	33. c	34. a	35. d	36. b	37. d	38. b	39. d	40. b
41. d	42. a	43. a	44. d	45. c	46. c				

Chapter 5

1. d	2. d	3. d	4. a	5. d	6. d	7. d	8. c	9. a	10. d
11. d	12. b	13. a	14. d	15. a	16. d	17. d	18. d	19. d	20. b
21. d	22. c	23. d	24. c	25. a	26. d	27. d	28. d	29. d	30. d
31. d	32. b	33. d	34. d	35. d	36. a	37. b	38. d	39. b	40. d
41. d	42. d	43. d	44. a	45. c					

Chapter 6

1. d	2. d	3. d	4. d	5. d	6. a	7. d	8. d	9. b	10. d
11. d	12. d	13. a	14. d	15. d	16. d	17. c	18. c	19. b	20. d
21. a	22. d	23. a	24. d	25. b	26. a				

ANSWER KEY

Chapter 7

1. b	2. a	3. d	4. d	5. c	6. a	7. a	8. a	9. d	10. d
11. d	12. d	13. c	14. b	15. b	16. a	17. d	18. b	19. d	20. d
21. d	22. b	23. b	24. c	25. d	26. a	27. d	28. d	29. d	30. d
31. a	32. d	33. d	34. d	35. d	36. b	37. c	38. c	39. b	40. b
41. d	42. d	43. a	44. d	45. a	46. c	47. a	48. a	49. d	50. d
51. d	52. d								

Chapter 8

1. b	2. c	3. d	4. d	5. d	6. d	7. a	8. b	9. a	10. a
11. d	12. c	13. d	14. c	15. a	16. c	17. a	18. c	19. b	20. d
21. d	22. d	23. b	24. d	25. d	26. c	27. d	28. d	29. d	30. a
31. c	32. c	33. a	34. b	35. a					

Chapter 9

1. d	2. c	3. d	4. d	5. d	6. d	7. c	8. d	9. d	10. b
11. d	12. d	13. b	14. d	15. d	16. d	17. d	18. c	19. b	20. d
21. d	22. c	23. d	24. b	25. d	26. c	27. d	28. b	29. d	30. d
31. d	32. a	33. d	34. d	35. d					

Chapter 10

1. d	2. c	3. b	4. a	5. a	6. d	7. d	8. a	9. a	10. c
11. a	12. d	13. c	14. a	15. d	16. d	17. d	18. d	19. c	20. d
21. d	22. a	23. d	24. d	25. c	26. d	27. c	28. c	29. a	30. d
31. d	32. d	33. a	34. d	35. a	36. c	37. d	38. c	39. d	40. b
41. d	42. d								

Chapter 11

1. d	2. b	3. b	4. c	5. a	6. c	7. d	8. a	9. c	10. c
11. d	12. d	13. d	14. b	15. a	16. d	17. b	18. d	19. d	20. c
21. c	22. c	23. b	24. a	25. a	26. d	27. d	28. d	29. d	30. d
31. d	32. b	33. d	34. d	35. d	36. d	37. d	38. b	39. d	40. a
41. a	42. d	43. d	44. a	45. d	46. d	47. c	48. d	49. d	50. d
51. b	52. b	53. d	54. c	55. d	56. d				

Chapter 12

1. d	2. c	3. b	4. c	5. d	6. d	7. c	8. d	9. d	10. a
11. b	12. c	13. a	14. b	15. d	16. a	17. d	18. c	19. d	20. c
21. d	22. d	23. a	24. b	25. b	26. c	27. c	28. a	29. b	30. c
31. d	32. d	33. d	34. b	35. d	36. b	37. c	38. d	39. b	40. c
41. c	42. d	43. b	44. d	45. d	46. d	47. d	48. a	49. c	50. d
51. b	52. d	53. d	54. d	55. a	56. d	57. d	58. b	59. d	60. d
61. d	62. a	63. d							

Chapter 13

1. d	2. d	3. d	4. b	5. a	6. d	7. d	8. d	9. c	10. a
11. d	12. a	13. c	14. d	15. d	16. d	17. d	18. d	19. d	20. a
21. a	22. a	23. b	24. d	25. d	26. d	27. d	28. b	29. a	30. a
31. c	32. b	33. c	34. b	35. d	36. d				

Chapter 14

1. d	2. c	3. d	4. b	5. d	6. d	7. a	8. b	9. a	10. b
11. d	12. a	13. c	14. c	15. d	16. d	17. d	18. d	19. c	20. a
21. d	22. d	23. a	24. a	25. d	26. c	27. d	28. c	29. a	30. d
31. c	32. d	33. a	34. c	35. a	36. a	37. d	38. d	39. d	40. a
41. d	42. d	43. c	44. d	45. b	46. b	47. d	48. c	49. d	50. a
51. a	52. d	53. d	54. d						

Chapter 15

1. d	2. b	3. b	4. d	5. b	6. a	7. a	8. d	9. a	10. b
11. d	12. d	13. d	14. d	15. d	16. d	17. d	18. c	19. b	20. b
21. d	22. d	23. a	24. d	25. a	26. a	27. a	28. d	29. c	30. b
31. d	32. d	33. c	34. c	35. d	36. d	37. d	38. c	39. d	40. d
41. d	42. b	43. d	44. d	45. c	46. d	47. b	48. b	49. c	50. b
51. b	52. a	53. c							

Chapter 16

1. a	2. a	3. d	4. d	5. d	6. c	7. b	8. d	9. b	10. b
11. c	12. d	13. d	14. d	15. d	16. d	17. d	18. c	19. a	20. d
21. b	22. d	23. c	24. a	25. a	26. b	27. b	28. c	29. d	30. d
31. b	32. d	33. d	34. d	35. d	36. d	37. d	38. d	39. d	40. d
41. d	42. c	43. d	44. d	45. d	46. d	47. a	48. c	49. d	50. d
51. d	52. d								

Chapter 17

1. d	2. d	3. d	4. d	5. c	6. d	7. b	8. d	9. b	10. d
11. d	12. b	13. d	14. b	15. d	16. d	17. a	18. c	19. c	20. a
21. d	22. b	23. d	24. d	25. d	26. d	27. d	28. b	29. a	

Chapter 18

1. c	2. d	3. b	4. d	5. b	6. b	7. a	8. b	9. d	10. d
11. d	12. c	13. d	14. a	15. d	16. d	17. c	18. d	19. d	20. d
21. d	22. d	23. b	24. c	25. d	26. d	27. d	28. d	29. a	30. d
31. a	32. c	33. d	34. d	35. b	36. d	37. d	38. b	39. b	40. d
41. d	42. d	43. d	44. d	45. a	46. d	47. d	48. d	49. d	50. c
51. d	52. b	53. b	54. a	55. b	56. d	57. d	58. d	59. a	60. d
61. d	62. b	63. a	64. c	65. a	66. a	67. b	68. c	69. d	70. c
71. c	72. d								

www.ingramcontent.com/pod-product-compliance
Lightning Source LLC
Chambersburg PA
CBHW082203230426
43672CB00015B/2875